MICHIGAN BREWERIES

MICHIGAN BREWERIES

PAUL RUSCHMANN & MARYANNE NASIATKA

STACKPOLE
BOOKS

STACKPOLE BOOKS
5067 Ritter Road
Mechanicsburg, PA 17055
www.stackpolebooks.com

The authors and publisher encourage all readers to visit the breweries and sample their beers, but recommend that those who consume alcoholic beverages travel with a nondrinking driver.

Printed in the United States of America

10 9 8 7 6 5 4 3 2 1

FIRST EDITION

Cover design by Caroline Stover

Labels and logos used with permission of the breweries.

Library of Congress Cataloging-in-Publication Data

Ruschmann, Paul.
    Michigan breweries / Paul Ruschmann and Maryanne Nasiatka.
       p.   cm.
    Includes index.
    ISBN-13: 978-0-8117-3299-4 (pbk.)
    ISBN-10: 0-8117-3299-1 (pbk.)
    1. Bars (Drinking establishments)–Michigan–Guidebooks. 2. Microbreweries–Michigan–Guidebooks. 3. Breweries–Michigan–Guidebooks. I. Nasiatka, Maryanne. II. Title.
TX950.57.M55R87   2006
647.9509774–dc22

                                                           2006010318

CONTENTS

FOREWORD

Thirty-five years ago, the United States didn't have a single microbrewery. By the mid-1980s, the Midwest had only a handful. Today Michigan's brewing scene has become integral to the state's traveling culture. Michigan is ranked sixth in the nation in terms of breweries per state. In the Midwest, only Wisconsin has more breweries than Michigan, and that state includes Milwaukee, the onetime brewery capital of the nation.

The beer and breweries of Michigan are some of the cultural treasures to be discovered while traveling. No matter where you start from in our state, I'd venture to guess that you're never more than an hour and a half from a local brewery. Michigan's breweries make for a diverse and interesting beerscape. Our brewing signature is one of depth, choice, and personality. There are countless influences on our breweries—international, regional, and a strong dose of good old-fashioned ingenuity. The American craft-brewing revolution is alive and well in Michigan, and it shows up in the flavor and diversity of every beer we brew.

When I first began to visit Michigan from my native Chicago, I was struck by how much everyone traveled. It seemed that more often than not, the person on the barstool next to me had personal experiences from all over the state. Over the years, I've met hikers, bikers, boaters, photographers, skiers, snowboarders, beer drinkers, and surfers throughout Michigan. Whether they were telling me about Ann Arbor, Grand Rapids, Lansing, Kalamazoo, Saugatuck, Detroit, Traverse City, or the Upper Peninsula, they traveled extensively to experience Michigan. They also offered plenty of "have to dos" and "gotta sees" that have shown me how special this state is.

Michigan's diverse landscape is rich with seasonal treasures and regional treats. Our lush green summers, colorful falls, snowy winters, and uplifting springs are all distinctively different. You can venture north, south, east, or west and uncover unique pleasures both geographically and culturally. The dunes of the western shore have a completely different feel in the crisp winter air than during the busy and sunny afternoons of summer. The shore of Lake Superior is majestic in any season but like a completely different world at different times of year.

In Michigan, I've grown to expect all kinds of treats throughout the seasons. I love it when roadside stands offering fresh flowers, asparagus, snap peas, apples, cherries, and blueberries begin to dot the shoulders of Michigan's country roads. However, the regionalism of food and drink is not wholly agricultural. The fudge stands in northern Michigan and the pasties of the Upper Peninsula are prime examples. They are the signatures of people, of community. Take pasties, for example, a simple yet delectable meal of meat and vegetables baked into a crust. I can't help but revisit my fond memories of the Upper Peninsula any time I think of one. I'm also not likely to make a trip over the bridge without indulging in at least one pasty.

The opportunities for discovering treasures among Michigan's beers are endless. You may find a cask-conditioned pale ale in one of our brewpubs that inspires you to return simply to enjoy it once again. You might discover an IPA or amber ale from one of our packaging breweries that you learn is available elsewhere in the Midwest and beyond. Perhaps you'll find a barrel-aged beer at a festival or pub that may never be brewed again, living on only in the memory you created while taking in the experience. Or maybe you'll visit a brew-on-premises that invites you to contribute to the state's brewing signature by helping you brew your own beer.

The beauty of beer and beer culture lives in its people. Beer culture is about people and their art. The brewer's art is about creating not only interesting beers, but also interesting breweries and memorable experiences. The artful results call us to visit, inspiring travel and adventure. Michigan's innovative craft brewers continue to contribute artistically to the breadth of choice available to today's beer drinker. There has never been a better time to reach out for adventure and variety in beer and brewing, especially in Michigan.

I have countless beer memories from my fifteen years of "Bringing Beer to the People." My favorites go beyond the initial pleasure of the beer to include the people and experiences that were paired with those deliciously memorable lagers and ales. My time with the beer people of Michigan and the Michigan Brewers Guild has enriched my life more than I can express. My hope is that this book will act as more than a travel guide for you. I hope it also inspires you to look inside our industry through our pubs and breweries to see the vibrant, intriguing people that make our state like nowhere else in the world.

I welcome and invite you to explore our Great Lake State. I'm confident that the personality, effort, and character of the people in our breweries will provide for an interesting journey and a rewarding experience. I offer my sincere thanks to Paul and Maryanne for their help in showing you the way. Whether your memories of Michigan's beers are paired with the perfect meal, the company you kept, or the brewery you visited, I hope you enjoy the rich culture Michigan has to offer.

Fred Bueltmann

President, Michigan Brewers Guild
www.michiganbrewersguild.org

Vice President, New Holland Brewing Company
www.newhollandbrew.com

ACKNOWLEDGMENTS

People who have written guidebooks told us that the travel itself is the fun part, but that doing the research is where you spend the most time. That was certainly true in the case of *Michigan Breweries*. That's one of many reasons why we're grateful to Fred Bueltmann of the New Holland Brewing Company and the Michigan Brewers Guild for his insights into our state's brewing industry and his words of encouragement. We'd also like to tip our hats to Rick Perkins, Director of the Enforcement Division of the Michigan Liquor Control Commission, for keeping us posted on the comings and goings of Michigan breweries.

Of course, this book would not have been possible without the help of Michigan's brewing community. Many thanks to those who welcomed us into their breweries and shared their stories—and their beer—with us. Some went above and beyond the call of duty: Jon Svoboda at Grand Rapids Brewing Company, Tim Suprise at Arcadia Brewing Company, Matt and Rene Greff of Arbor Brewing Company, Kim Schneider of Bastone, and Brett VanderKamp and John Haggerty of New Holland Brewing, to mention just a few.

We'd like to extend special recognition to the elder statesmen of the state's craft-brewing movement: Bill Wamby at Redwood Lodge, Curt Hecht at Frankenmuth Brewing, and Hazen Schumacher at Atwater Block Brewing Company. They reminded us that although our state's breweries are young, its brewers are the inheritors of a rich brewing tradition.

A nod to Lew Bryson for his winning books in Stackpole's state-by-state series on breweries. We based our format on his three existing guides: *New York Breweries*, *Pennsylvania Breweries*, and *Virginia, Maryland, and Delaware Breweries*.

And finally, a big thank-you to those who support Michigan breweries by "drinking locally." Cheers, everyone!

INTRODUCTION

Welcome to Michigan, the Great Lake State. Or as the Michigan Brewers Guild prefers to say, the "Great Beer State." Our state's brewing industry has grown from a handful of breweries just two decades ago to more than seventy. They brew everything from the malty Helles like that served in Bavarian beer gardens to Flemish-style witbier to audacious imperial stouts that pack a bigger alcoholic punch than most wines. Not to mention English bitters, pale ales and India pale ales, porters flavored with Michigan cherries, and unique styles you'll never see described in a beer-judging manual.

Michigan beer is underappreciated, and because much of it is consumed at the brewery, you'll have to come here to enjoy it for yourself. That's where this book, *Michigan Breweries*, comes in. It's the result of our having traveled the length and breadth of Michigan to visit its breweries. In our travels, we found plenty of interesting stories to share with you.

The beer you'll find in Michigan breweries is the result of nearly four hundred years of evolution. Beer was a part of our culture long before Michigan was a state, or for that matter, even before there was a United States. So before exploring our state, let's take a trip back in time and look at how we got here.

The Early Days of American Beer

The story of American beer goes back at least as far as the Pilgrims, who ended up at Plymouth Rock, not their intended destination of Virginia, because they were running low on beer. Homebrewing was an essential skill even before the first Thanksgiving and remained so for centuries.

Beer also helped the move toward independence. Taxes were high on the list of colonists' grievances against the king, and some of the most-hated levies were on ale. Colonists got even by organizing a "buy American" campaign, which meant "brew American."

Delegates to the Constitutional Convention met in Philadelphia, then the nation's brewing capital. They debated by day and continued their discussions—and found common ground—in taverns at night. Perhaps modern-day politicians can learn something from the Framers' experience.

And what did the Framers drink? According to beer historian Gregg Smith, it was something that, if it were served to you, you'd probably send back. It was an ale, considerably stronger than today's mainstream lagers, dark and cloudy, and probably made with improvised substitutes for barley and hops.

From colonial times onward, lawmakers struggled with the regulation of alcohol. They knew that beer was good for the economy, but its side effects—public drunkenness, accidents, and lost productivity—had a price tag. Morality also entered the debate. By the early 1800s, some clergymen saw alcohol as an instrument of Satan. The temperance movement was born.

Lager and Prohibition

A pivotal date in American history was 1840. That was when the first glass of lager was served. It was a cleaner, crisper beverage than the ale we described, and it soon became a national fad—especially among trend-setting young men. Some things never change.

With lager came waves of immigrants from Germany who settled large swaths of the Midwest, including Michigan, during the late nineteenth century. The Germans brought with them their beloved beer gardens. There, people of all ages and walks of life got together over beer, and drunkenness and violence were strictly verboten. Beer's defenders pointed to the German model of drinking and touted the beverage as one of moderation. For a while, the prohibitionist tide was stemmed.

But not for long. Religious leaders, women's groups, and reformers continued to push for the abolition of liquor and the saloons that served it. They were joined by businessmen who wanted more sober, productive workers. Even so, prohibitionists were divided over whether to ban beer. Then came World War I, which unleashed public sentiment against things German—including the nation's beer barons.

Michigan got a head start on the nation, banning alcohol nearly two years before the Eighteenth Amendment took effect. In fact, Detroit was the first major American city to go dry. One consequence of Prohibition was the resurgence of homebrewing. The other was large-scale smuggling. By one estimate, three-quarters of all liquor smuggled into the United States came from Ontario, especially the thirty-mile stretch between Lake Erie and the St. Clair River.

Mass-Market Beer and the Rise of the Craft Brewers

The "Great Experiment" devastated the brewing industry. Only a fraction of those breweries that existed before Prohibition reopened after the Twenty-first Amendment repealed it in 1933. Another effect of

Prohibition was a change in beer drinkers' tastes. People had gotten used to a lighter version of lager, a trend that continued after beer was once again legal.

Even more breweries disappeared in the years that followed, as economies of scale favored the big breweries and forced smaller ones to either merge or close. Advertising further encouraged the trend toward consolidation: National brands arose at the expense of regionals, and Americans associated "beer" with light lager. By the seventies, there were fewer than a hundred breweries in the United States, and some predicted that the industry would end up controlled by a handful of megabrewers.

Then something happened. Many Americans who traveled overseas fell in love with the classic beers of the British Isles and the Continent. When they couldn't find them back home, they took matters into their own hands: They started brewing their own. Homebrewing officially became legal in 1978, but before then, more than a few Americans were surreptitiously making their own.

A new generation of brewers arose from the ranks of homebrewers. One was Jack McAuliffe. He and his friends started the New Albion Brewing Company in Sonoma, California, building a brewing system out of old pipes, army surplus, and used dairy equipment. New Albion was hardly a threat to the big brewers. At its peak, its production was only a few hundred barrels a year, and it operated on a shoestring before a lack of capital forced it to close in 1982. But it had an enormous impact on American brewing. In a sense, New Albion lives on: Its brewing equipment was bought by the Mendocino Brewing Company, which still uses the original strain of New Albion yeast.

Most early craft brewers concentrated on ales, for several reasons. Most were homebrewers who couldn't afford the equipment required to cool and store lager beers. Many were influenced by Britain's Campaign for Real Ale, a grass-roots movement aimed at preserving that country's traditional beer, and aimed to brew traditional English-style ales. And they associated lager with the big national breweries. That has changed: Most breweries today offer at least one lager, and some specialize in classic Continental pilsners.

Beginning in the eighties, state legislators amended the liquor laws, creating an exception to decades-old laws banning "tied houses," or retail outlets owned by breweries. The result was the next phase of the craft-brewing movement—namely, brewpubs. For the record, the first modern brewpub opened in Yakima, Washington, in 1982 after Bert

Grant, the owner of Yakima Brewing and Malting Company, discovered that his state had never gotten around to banning them.

Michigan lawmakers were rather late in making the changes needed to support craft brewing; they didn't get around to passing the needed legislation until the nineties. But as you'll see, our state's brewers have more than made up for lost time.

How We Got Interested in Beer

What got us interested in beer? Ethnicity certainly plays a part. One of us is Polish, the other German and Irish. No doubt our ancestors enjoyed a few tall cold ones, both here and in the Old Country. Both of our fathers were World War II veterans, proud members of a generation that relished its beer. Where we grew up had an influence, too. Bars were thick on the ground in New Jersey, and the corner tavern was very much a neighborhood institution. And then there's the Notre Dame factor. Beer was definitely on the list of extracurriculars in South Bend, especially on game days. Both of us went there at different times—and met afterward, at a beer bash the night before a football game.

The first beers we drank were national-brand lagers, but our horizons widened as we saw more of the world. Trips to California meant a chance to scavenge through delis. Places that looked from the outside like holes in the wall carried several hundred brands of imported beer, some of which we lugged home to the amusement of airline security personnel. Travel to the West also exposed us to brewpubs, an innovation we wished would come to our part of the world. Trans-Atlantic trips opened up more of the world of beer. We not only drank the classic styles of Europe, but did so in historic surroundings, like the Löwenbräukeller, the Lamb and Flag, and a la Mort Subite. In our travels, we filled notebooks with scribbled beer notes, collected a lifetime of memories, and developed an appreciation for better beer.

In writing *Michigan Breweries*, we approached it as beer travelers. That's who we are. In fact, we write the "Beer Travelers" column in *All About Beer* magazine. We love good beer, but we're also interested in stories that beer can tell us. Is some larger-than-life figure linked to the beer? Does the brewery have a history? Did some noteworthy event happen where we drank it? That's our focus. You won't find detailed technical descriptions of the beer we sampled or one- to five-star ratings for the breweries; there are plenty of other people who do that and do it well. What you will find is a book that, we hope, will encourage you to explore Michigan and find out for yourself about our beer. We look forward to seeing you!

How to Use This Book

Michigan Breweries is a guidebook about our state's breweries. It's also about beer sites other than microbreweries and brewpubs, as well as interesting attractions you might want to visit while in the area. We've included history and lore about beer that we've acquired through years of traveling in Michigan and elsewhere.

In our travels around the state, we found that just about every brewery had a story to tell. Some, such as Larry Bell's rise to fame, have been told many times. But others were waiting to be told, and we found many of the stories both surprising and fascinating. We also made a number of discoveries about Michigan's brewing community. First, it's homegrown; most of the brewers and brewery owners were born and raised here. In fact, some of our brewers discovered microbrewed beer out West but still came back home to follow their dream of making great beer of their own. Second, our brewers have an inventive streak. Many followed the example of the first craft brewers, scrounging for equipment, using their technical know-how to cobble together brewing systems, and running a business on a shoestring. Third, they do it for the love of beer. One successful brewery owner, who shall remain nameless, told us that "brewing beer isn't a fast track to riches" and proudly added, "I still drive a pickup truck."

For the most part, *Michigan Breweries* follows the organization of Lew Bryson's excellent titles in this series. We've presented the information about the breweries themselves in seven sections: Detroit and the Downriver Area; Suburban Detroit; Big Ten Country (the Ann Arbor–Lansing area); the Western Heartland, which encompasses the areas of Battle Creek, Kalamazoo, and Grand Rapids; the West Coast; the Northeast, which includes the busy I-75 freeway; and the Upper Peninsula. The "A word about . . ." sections in between are aimed at broadening your knowledge about Michigan and its breweries.

Part of the charm of visiting brewpubs and microbrewery taprooms is tasting their continually changing lineup of beers. Many brewpubs are proud that they never have to brew the same beer twice, unless they want to. Frequently, the brewer makes what he or she likes to drink and what the customers request.

Michigan's microbreweries, in addition to a regular lineup of beers, make experimental batches that are served only in their on-premises taprooms, where locals and beer travelers give them feedback on their latest recipes. Although many "experiments" never make it onto the store shelves, they are among the most interesting and fun-to-drink beers we found during our travels.

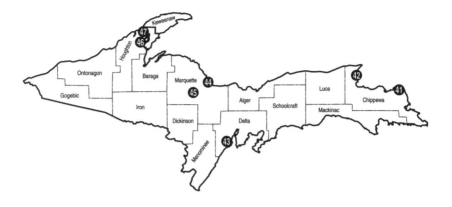

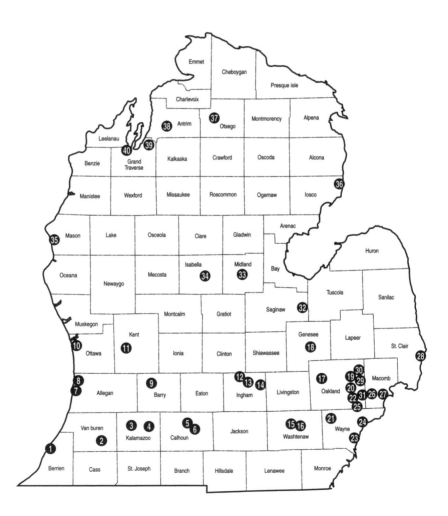

16 Arbor Brewing Company, Ann Arbor
5 Arcadia Brewing Company, Battle Creek
24 Atwater Block Brewery, Detroit
31 Bastone Belgian Brewery and Restaurant, Royal Oak
4 Bell's Brewery, Galesburg
29 Big Buck Brewery and Steakhouse, Auburn Hills
37 Big Buck Brewery and Steakhouse, Gaylord
20 Big Rock Chop House, Birmingham
19 Bo's Brewery and Bistro, Pontiac
21 Bonfire Bistro and Brewery, Northville
17 CJ's Brewing Company, Commerce Township
22 Copper Canyon Brewery and Restaurant, Southfield
6 Dark Horse Brewing Company, Marshall
24 Detroit Beer Company, Detroit
26 Dragonmead Microbrewery, Warren
22 Etoufee, Southfield
23 Fort Street Brewery, Lincoln Park
11 Founders Brewing Company, Grand Rapids
32 Frankenmuth Brewery, Frankenmuth
11 Grand Rapids Brewing Company, Grand Rapids
27 Great Baraboo Brewing Company, Clinton Township
16 Grizzly Peak Brewing Company, Ann Arbor
12 Harper's Restaurant and Brewpub, East Lansing
11 Hideout Brewing Company, Grand Rapids
35 Jamesport Brewing Company, Ludington
15 Jolly Pumpkin Artisan Ales, Dexter
19 King Brewing Company, Pontiac
3 Kraftbräu Brewery, Kalamazoo
26 Kuhnhenn Brewing Company, Warren
16 Leopold Brothers of Ann Arbor Brewery and Distilling, Ann Arbor
31 Lily's Seafood Grill and Brewery, Royal Oak
40 Mackinaw Brewing Company, Traverse City
14 Michigan Brewing Company, Webberville
9 Middle Villa Inn, Middleville
24 Motor City Brewing Works and Winery, Detroit

34 Mountain Town Station, Mount Pleasant
8 New Holland Brewing Company, Holland
40 North Peak Brewing Company, Traverse City
10 Old Boys' Brewhouse, Spring Lake
3 Olde Peninsula Brewpub and Restaurant, Kalamazoo
28 Quay Street Brewing Company, Port Huron
18 Redwood Lodge Mesquite Grill and Brewpub, Flint
30 Rochester Mills Beer Company, Rochester
31 Royal Oak Brewery, Royal Oak
33 Sanford Lake Bar and Grill, Sanford
7 Saugatuck Brewing Company, Douglas
11 Schmoz Brewing Company, Grand Rapids
38 Short's Brewing Company, Bellaire
32 Sullivan's Black Forest Brew Keller, Frankenmuth
1 The Livery, Benton Harbor
2 The Old Hat Brewery, Lawton
29 Thunder Bay Brewing Company, Auburn Hills
24 Traffic Jam and Snug, Detroit
13 Travelers Club International Restaurant and Tuba Charlie's Brewery, Okemos
39 Traverse Brewing Company, Williamsburg
8 Via Maria Trattoria, Holland
36 Wiltse's Brew Pub and Family Restaurant, Oscoda
25 Woodward Avenue Brewers, Ferndale

Upper peninsula map

43 Hereford and Hops Restaurant and Brewpub, Escanaba
45 Jasper Ridge Brewery and Restaurant, Ishpeming
46 Keweenaw Brewing Company, Houghton
46 Library Bar and Restaurant, Houghton
47 Red Jacket Brewing Company, Calumet
41 Superior Coast Winery and Brewery, Sault Sainte Marie
42 Tahquamenon Falls Brewery and Pub, Paradise
44 Vierling Restaurant/Marquette Harbor Brewery, Marquette

So as you begin your own beer travels in Michigan, keep in mind that you may find a slightly different beer list when you arrive at an establishment. Don't worry. Pull up a chair and enjoy whatever's available. If we've told you good things about the brewery, or the brewer, you'll still find good things there.

In this volume, we've included other area attractions and beer sites in the introduction to each section. Southeast Michigan is densely populated, and many attractions are, relatively speaking, a short distance away from one another. As for beer sites, we've discovered that in Michigan, you're more likely to find craft beer in microbreweries and brewpubs than in beer bars.

For each brewery, we start by telling its story, with an emphasis on what makes it special. This is followed by specific information, beginning with the class of license—brewery, microbrewery, or brewpub. We then give the month and year the brewery opened. For breweries whose ownership has changed hands, this is the date the current owners took over. For restaurants that later added a brewery, this is when they started brewing. We provide other information, including the size, manufacturer, and brewing capacity in barrels per year of the brewery's system, when available. Homemade systems are identified by the owner's or brewer's name. Distribution is listed when you can find a microbrewery's products at retail. Brewpub beer cannot be sold at other locations. Hours may vary, as some Michigan breweries are small or have a highly seasonal business, so it's best to call before visiting. Only a handful of breweries have scheduled tours, but most brewers are willing to show visitors around. Always call ahead to make sure the brewer is available.

Detroit and Downriver

Detroit is Michigan's oldest and largest city, dating back to 1701, when the French established a trading post on the Detroit River. The city's primary to claim to fame is its auto industry, which is why locals and out-of-towners alike call it the "Motor City." Detroit is also famous for the Motown sound of Stevie Wonder, Diana Ross and the Supremes, and the Jackson Five, just to name a few.

During the 1950s, Detroit was a prosperous city built around its neighborhoods, a place where a young man could go straight from high school to a good-paying job on the assembly line. But in the years that followed, Detroit lost residents to the suburbs, and those who stayed divided along racial lines. Some believe that the city has never recovered from deadly riots of 1967 and the lingering bad feelings that followed.

Detroit isn't the only American city that has suffered from poverty, urban blight, and violence. Nevertheless, it has been singled out by late-night comedians as a butt of jokes. The city's detractors rarely miss a chance to mention the riot after the 1984 World Series, in which a police cruiser was set on fire; or Devil's Night, the night before Halloween, which Detroiters celebrated by burning abandoned homes.

But that's old news. Fans of the Detroit Red Wings celebrated three National Hockey League championships with few incidents, and a concerted effort by authorities and residents has all but put a stop to Devil's Night arson. Crime is also down sharply from the seventies, when Detroit was called the "Murder City."

Public officials and business leaders are teaming up to help bring Detroit back to life. The best-known effort is that started by Mike Ilitch, who made a fortune with Little Caesar's Pizza, to revive the "Foxtown" area, the neighborhood surrounding the now beautifully restored Fox Theater. It has evolved into a theater district, which also includes the State and Gem Theatres and the Detroit Opera House. Other neighborhoods, such as Corktown, the area around old Tiger Stadium, are being revived, as is the industrial area along the riverfront.

That said, the city faces serious financial problems. In January 2006, as Kwame Kilpatrick took the oath of office for his second term as mayor, the prospect of municipal bankruptcy hung over his city. The mayor has convened a team of business and civic leaders to find a way to cut the cost of government, attract businesses, and stop the flight of residents to the suburbs.

Detroit's unofficial symbol is the seventy-story Renaissance Center, the tallest building on the city's skyline. It's a retail and convention center that was once the world's tallest hotel. Nowadays, it's the headquarters building of General Motors Corporation, which is also trying to figure a way to turn itself around. Close by is Hart Plaza, which hosts the Detroit International Jazz Festival and ethnic and music festivals during the summer.

The city's cultural district is the area near Wayne State University. The top cultural attraction there is the Detroit Institute of Arts (5200 Woodward Avenue, 313-833-7900, www.dia.org), which has more than a hundred galleries. Its signature attraction is Diego Rivera's epic 1932 mural, *Detroit Industry*. Nearby is the Charles H. Wright Museum of African American History (315 East Warren Street, 313-484-5800, www.maah-detroit.org), the world's largest African American museum, whose best-known exhibit is a sculpture of a slave ship. Thousands of mourners came to the museum to say good-bye to civil rights figure Rosa Parks before she was laid to rest.

Few cities have more passionate sports fans than Detroit. Where else would fans organize a pregame protest march to demand a regime change in the Lions' front office? Three of the area's four professional sports teams play their home games inside the city. The Lions' den is Ford Field (2000 Brush Street, 313-262-2000, www.fordfield.com), which hosted Super Bowl XL. Next door is Comerica Park (2100 Woodward Avenue, 313-471-2255, detroit.tigers.mlb.com), the home of the Tigers. Home ice for the Detroit Red Wings is the Joe Louis Arena (600 Civic Center Drive, 313-567-6000, www.olympiaentertainment.com). The Pistons used to play at Cobo Arena but have long since moved to Oakland County—still a sore point with some Detroiters.

Detroit has become America's biggest casino gambling city between Atlantic City and Las Vegas, with three casinos: Greektown Casino (555 East Lafayette Boulevard, 888-771-4386, www.greektowncasino.com); MGM Grand Detroit Casino (1300 John C. Lodge Freeway, 877-888-

2121, detroit.mgmgrand.com); and Motor City Casino (2901 Grand River Avenue, 877-777-0711, www.motorcitycasino.com). Speaking of Greektown, this area of ethnic restaurants and bars still attracts visitors, even those who don't gamble. The signature dish is saganaki, cheese that's fried in a batter, then taken to the table and set on fire. Custom requires that you yell, "Opa!"

Last but not least, there's the Motown Museum (2648 West Grand Boulevard, 313-875-2264, www.motownmuseum.com), also known as "Hitsville U.S.A." It was once both the home of music impresario Berry Gordy Jr. and the nation's largest independent record label. Inside, you'll find Studio A, where Motown's greatest hits were recorded.

Windsor, Ontario, on the other side of the Detroit River, is still a popular destination, even though border security has been tightened and the U.S. dollar isn't as strong as it used to be. Attractions include ethnic restaurants, shopping, and Casino Windsor. City officials would rather it not be, but it's also known as "Sin City." Visitors flock to strip clubs, known as the "Windsor Ballet"; massage parlors; and stores selling Cuban cigars, which are contraband in the United States. You're also likely to run into nineteen- and twenty-year-old Michiganders, who can drink legally in Ontario. In Windsor, you find national brands Labatt and Molson, but also beer by microbrewers such as Brick Brewing Company, Creemore Springs Brewery, and Muskoka Brewing.

Dearborn, to the west of Detroit, was the hometown of Henry Ford I, who built the auto company that bears his name and still has a family member as CEO. Once notoriously lily white, Dearborn is now home to the nation's largest Arab American community.

Henry Ford was also the driving force behind The Henry Ford (20900 Oakwood Boulevard, 313-982-6001, www.thehenryford.org), a world-class museum and one of Michigan's leading tourist attractions. The enormous museum features the Automobile in American Life exhibit and consumer products ranging from baseball cards to washing machines. Items on display also include the limousine President Kennedy was riding in when he was assassinated and the bus on which Rosa Parks refused to give up her seat. Also part of The Henry Ford museum complex is Greenfield Village, an American town from a century ago. Its many buildings include Ford's own birthplace, the Wright Brothers' cycle shop, and Thomas Edison's laboratory. Costumed hosts demonstrate everything from weaving to how to repair punctured tires. The Henry Ford's newest attraction is inside the company's sprawling Rouge Plant, where you can take a walking tour and see assembly line workers building the popular F-150 pickup truck.

Back to downtown Detroit for a moment. At the intersection of Jefferson Boulevard and Woodward Avenue, you'll find a huge bronze fist. It's a memorial to boxer Joe Louis, who grew up in the city. Some see the fist as a reminder of Detroit's sometimes violent past. But locals disagree; they consider it a tribute to the grit and toughness of Detroiters.

Convention and Visitors Bureaus
Detroit: www.visitdetroit.com
Windsor: www.visitwindsor.com

Recommended Beer Bars
Detroit
Cadieux Café, 4300 Cadieux, 313-882-8560, www.cadieuxcafe.com. Bills itself as the home of America's only two feather bowling lanes. Offers a wide selection of bottled Belgians as well as local micros on tap.
Dakota Inn Rathskeller, 17342 John R. Street, 313-867-9722, www.dakota-inn.com. A German beer hall that opened in 1933 and has stayed much the same ever since.
Jacoby's, 624 Brush Street, 313-962-7067. A two-story German-style bar that has been in business for more than a hundred years.
Ye Olde Taproom, 14915 Charlevoix, 313-824-1030. Opened as a brewery before Prohibition and now a beer bar offering ten taps, some of which rotate, and more than two hundred bottles.

Wyandotte
Oak Café, 1167 Oak Street, 734-283-8380. Offers twenty taps and more than two hundred bottled beers.

Traffic Jam and Snug

511 West Canfield Avenue, Detroit, MI 48201
313-831-9470
www.traffic-jam.com

No, you're not seeing things. That is a urinal high up on the front wall. For twenty years or so, that outsize bathroom fixture, which in the summer doubles as a planter, was Traffic Jam and Snug's only signage. That's just one of many stories that can be told about this venerable watering hole.

Some parts of the building date back to the 1880s, others to the 1920s. Even today, exposed brick walls and old wooden tables are part of the charm. Traffic Jam and Snug, or "TJ's" as regulars refer to it, opened its doors in 1965. It acquired that name because someone told the man who opened it, "if you ever do any business there, it will be a real traffic jam."

Even after its regulars left Detroit and fled for the suburbs, TJ's remained one of the friendly establishments they frequented when they came back to see a play or spend the afternoon at a museum. And its proximity to the Wayne State University campus and medical center has always fed it a steady clientele of students and faculty.

Part of the reason for TJ's popularity was its owners' willingness to make and promote artisanal food. Fast food was overtaking the country, but TJ's took a stand against it. Its owners decided to make as much as possible from scratch. It set up a full-scale bakery operation, serving loaves of freshly baked bread with meals. It also branched out into cheesemaking, becoming the first restaurant to be licensed by the Department of Agriculture as a dairy. TJ's also collected art for its customers to enjoy, along with an interesting mix of Detroit memorabilia including—what else?—a traffic light.

Another logical extension of the artisan movement was craft-brewed beer, and TJ's owners had long been interested in brewing. Unfortunately, Michigan law did not allow either microbreweries

Beers brewed: There are five beers on tap. The menu beers are Pale Ale; Pilsner, the best-seller and the only filtered menu beer; Steam; and Stout. The rotating seasonals include a witbier, a high-gravity beer, a winter warmer, and a hefeweizen.

Our Picks: Paul went with Canfield Pale Ale, an American pale ale. Maryanne's first choice was a seasonal, Belgian White.

or brewpubs. But it turned out that TJ's attorney cared very much about this issue. He'd been a homebrewer since the seventies and had worked at microbreweries in Oregon and Colorado. He waged a ten-year-long legal battle, in which he unsuccessfully challenged Michigan's liquor laws in court but did manage to persuade state lawmakers to allow restaurants to brew a small amount of beer and sell it to customers. That was 1992.

But the new law didn't allow the owner of a brewery to hold a retail liquor license as well. So TJ's problem still wasn't solved. Ultimately, TJ's attorney swapped his briefcase for brewer's boots and opened his own brewery across the street, the Detroit and Mackinac Brewing Company. It still exists, though it's under different ownership and is now known as the Motor City Brewing Works. After another tweak of the Michigan liquor laws, TJ's obtained a brewpub license in 1993, the first issued by the state. (Actually, two brewpub licenses were issued that day; the other went to the Grand Rapids Brewing Company.)

Then, just as it finally appeared that TJ's would realize its dream, a sad thing happened: Tom Burns was diagnosed with terminal cancer. To make a long story short, TJ's brewing operation was confined for years to buying wort elsewhere and pitching the yeast on-site. Thus, though TJ's claims to be Michigan's first brewpub—literally true if you look at its license number—it's drawn its share of raised eyebrows from the brewing community.

Over the years, TJ's continued to be a popular spot even though the surrounding area fell into decline. In 1999, current owners Carolyn Howard and Scott Lowell took over. They've continued to offer artisanal products—including craft-brewed beer—to customers. And speaking of customers, Carolyn and Scott hope to see more now that the neighborhood has begun to come back, as buildings around TJ's are being converted to lofts.

In 2004, Carolyn—who, by the way, worked at TJ's while she was a student and watched the saga unfold—and Scott hired Chris Reilly as brewmaster and cheesemaker. The original dream had finally come true.

TJ's is still a restaurant that makes outstanding cheese and baked goods. But now its beer is attracting a following, too. Ninety percent of its beer sales are the house brews. Chris's lineup includes four year-round beers and a rotating seasonal. He brews true to style and told us that you won't find any off-the-wall beers while he's around. Recently, Chris honeymooned in Belgium and came back excited about getting a few wooden casks and trying his hand at barleywine and gueuze. When you stop in, make sure you climb up to the "observation deck," from

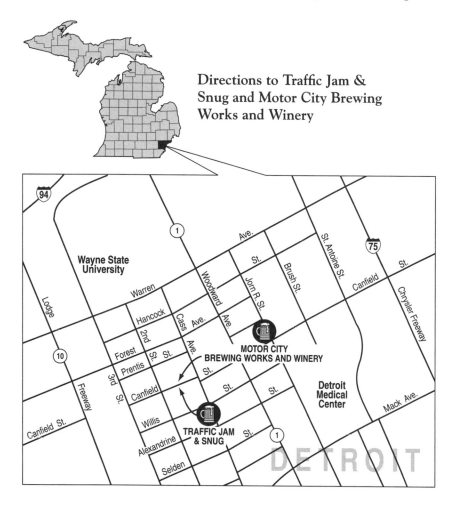

Directions to Traffic Jam & Snug and Motor City Brewing Works and Winery

which you can look down and see the brewery—where, depending on the day, you might see Chris making either beer or cheese. The equipment, just like everything else at TJ's, is eclectic.

By the way, according to local legend, that urinal was nailed to the outside because Ben Johnson, the man who opened TJ's, didn't want to pay the junk man $25 to haul it away. So he just kept it until he found something to do with it.

Class of license: Brewpub.
Opened: Licensed as a brewpub in November 1993. Full-scale brewing operation since 2004.
Owners: Carolyn Howard and Scott Lowell.
Brewer: Chris Reilly.

System: 7ish-barrel TJ's: Capacity is 350 barrels per year.
Production: 150 barrels in 2004.
Hours: Monday through Thursday, 11 A.M. to 10:30 P.M.; Friday, 11 A.M. to midnight; Saturday, noon to midnight; Sunday, noon to 8 P.M.
Tours: Yes, by appointment. You can also climb onto an "observation deck" overlooking the brewery.
Take-out beer: Kegs and quart-size Mason jars.
Food: Carolyn describes the menu as "American eclectic, with accents from around the world." Vegetarian-friendly, with meatless dishes accounting for half the items. Menu changes monthly.
Extras: TJ's is a regular stop on Detroit pub crawls. Monthly "pint nights" with either a DJ or an art exhibition. Artisanal breads, cheeses, and cookies for sale. Minimal electronic distractions. Smoke-free.
Happy hour: Monday through Friday, 3 to 7 P.M., with discounts on beer.
Parking: Fenced-in, guarded private parking lot across the street.
Directions: Third Street goes one way, southbound, and Second Street goes north. From the Lodge (M-10), go east on Forest, which becomes a divided cobblestone street. TJ's is on the south side of the street.

Motor City Brewing Works and Winery

470 West Canfield Avenue, Detroit, MI 48201
313-832-2700
www.motorcitybeer.com

We discovered an interesting split within Michigan's brewing community. One faction has a scientific background and tends to brew by the book. The other has an artistic bent, and these brewers brew what they like.

John Linardos, the owner of Motor City Brewing Works and Winery, falls into the latter category. He's an urban pioneer in the truest sense. John has lived and worked in the Cass Corridor since the early eighties, when he began his art studies at Wayne State University. He had no idea that he'd someday own one of Michigan's oldest microbreweries. "It just kind of evolved," he told us. "I never set out to do it."

But that's what he did. John's story dovetails with that of two other brewing institutions. One is the Detroit and Mackinac Brewery, which once stood at this location. After Tom Burns, the founder, passed away, the brewery closed and the building eventually stood empty. In 1994, John rented the building and resumed brewing operations. The other institution is Traffic Jam and Snug. Until TJ's started brewing its own, Motor City hauled batches of wort across the street to be fermented there.

Before sitting down to beers, John showed us around the brewery. In back of the taproom were the fermentation tanks and the bottling machine that saw service at a Budweiser brewery half a century ago. Motor City started bottling in 2000 in hopes of distributing well beyond Detroit. Upstairs was the 20-barrel brewing system, which John assembled from old dairy vessels.

Beers brewed: Ghettoblaster, Motor City Amber Wheat, Motor City Honey Porter, Motor City Lager, Motor City Nut Brown Ale, Motor City Pale Ale, and Motor City Strong Ale.

Our Picks: Ghettoblaster is a strange name for an English mild ale, but it's been Paul's favorite Motor City beer for a long time. It's smooth, nutty, and malty. Maryanne was partial to the Motor City Lager, which delivered just what she expected in craft-brewed lager—malty, clean, and refreshing.

Also upstairs was what sets Motor City apart from other Michigan breweries. It's John's other passion, a sound studio. He's produced two CDs in the "Ghettoblaster" series and is working on a third. "Motor City," it turns out, is recognized as a distinctive genre of music and has a far-flung audience. The CDs have grabbed the attention of *Playboy* magazine's music critic and have been played on radio stations as far away as Europe.

Our final stop was Motor City's taproom. It's one of the smallest in the state, yet one of the most intriguing. John, a sculptor by trade, put it together with the help of some very artistic friends. One put in the tile floors—even the ladies' room floor is tiled—using material left over from other jobs. Another built the metal staircase that leads to the upstairs deck. And yet another helped John fashion the bar out of cast concrete.

We had a question for John. For years we've enjoyed Motor City beer at home, but lately we hadn't seen very much of it in stores. John explained why. All of Motor City's beers are unpasteurized and unfiltered, which means they need extra TLC after they leave the brewery. Once again, beer distribution raised its ugly head. It's a sore point with many Michigan brewers, and they can't do much about it: Michigan law forbids brewers to self-distribute.

Turning to a more pleasant topic—namely, the beer itself—John told us that he tries to keep his beers accessible to the consumer. His styles are fairly mainstream, at least by Michigan standards, and despite being a member of the artistic faction, he considers it important to stay close to traditional style guidelines.

With sunlight streaming through the skylight and a radio playing softly in the background, the taproom was an oasis in the middle of Detroit. Now that it's open seven days a week, John told us, it's become a gathering place for workers at the nearby hospital, students from Wayne State, and members of the arts community. With lofts being built in the neighborhood, he expects even more visitors. His plans include expanding the taproom, opening a "sculpture beer garden" outside, and perhaps adding a tapas menu.

Motor City invites you to do a little urban pioneering of your own. Detroit isn't as scary as you've been led to believe. And once you get here, there's a reward waiting for you: a glimpse at Michigan brewing history and a taste of the brewer's art.

Class of license: Microbrewery.
Opened: Motor City distributed its first batch in January 1995.
Owner: John Linardos.
Brewer: George Murphy handles most of the brewing these days.
System: 20-barrel Linardos. Capacity is about 1,200 barrels a year.
Production: 800 barrels in 2004; 1,000 barrels estimated for 2005.
Distribution: Tap accounts only for the time being, primarily in Detroit and select suburban establishments.
Hours: Daily, 4 P.M. to midnight.
Tours: Groups only, call in advance.
Take-out beer: Six-packs and cases, quarter and half barrels.
Food: None when we visited. Motor City is planning to add a tapas menu as part of the taproom's expansion.
Extras: Open-air patio upstairs. Frequent stop on organized pub crawls. Wine and mead are available.
Parking: Lot in front of the taproom. (See map on page 7.)

Atwater Block Brewery

237 Joseph Campau Street, Detroit, MI 48027
313-877-9205
www.atwaterbeer.com

The Renaissance Center on the Detroit River is a symbol of Detroit. It's also a symbol of the city's long struggle to turn things around. One focal point of that effort is the industrial district east of the RenCen. That's where you'll find the Atwater Block Brewery.

The building was originally constructed in 1916 as a warehouse. It's located on a city block between Atwater and Wight Streets, hence the brewery's name. Across the street from the brewery is Stroh River Place, a building that once housed the Stroh brewery's laboratory. Actually, there have been two Atwater Block Breweries. Let's hit the rewind button and go back a decade.

In 1996, a group of investors turned the building, which had been vacant for ten years, into the Atwater Block Brewery. They bought a top-of-the-line brewery from Germany's Kaspar Schultz, the world's oldest manufacturer of brewing equipment. They hired a German brewer as a consultant. And they hired a German-trained brewing team.

The original Atwater Block's lineup consisted of four classic German-style lagers: Hell, Dunkel, Rost, and Pilsner. The beers won medals at the 1999 Great American Beer Festival and gained a following back home. Even though the brewery did well, its owners squabbled among themselves and ultimately decided to close. The next owner was the Stoney Creek Brewing Company, which up to then was a "virtual brewery" that contracted out its production. After a few years, Stoney Creek also shut down the brewery.

That is where the current owners, Mark Rieth and Howard Hampton, come in. We talked with Mark, along with Hazen Schumacher, the brewer, inside Atwater Block's spacious dining area. It has a distinctly industrial look and feel, with brick

Beers brewed: There will be eight beers on tap. Four are the original Atwater Block beers, all lagers: Dunkel; Hell, the flagship beer; Pilsner; and Rost, a rust-colored beer. They've been joined by Hefeweizen, Salvation IPA, and Shaman's Porter, along with a seasonal rotation that includes Blocktoberfest, Winter Bock, Spring Bock, and Kölsch.

Awards won: 1999 GABF—Silver, German-Style Marzen/Oktoberfest; 1999 GABF—Gold, European-Style Marzen/Dunkel.

walls and stone floors. At one end of the room is a long wooden bar with blond maple chairs. If you take a seat at the bar, you can look through windows and watch the brewer at work.

Opposite the bar is a row of wooden tables and a stone fireplace at the end. The walls are lined with display cases containing bottles and labels from old Detroit breweries. By day, Atwater Block draws a business clientele. At night, the crowd is dominated by sports fans who watch games on strategically placed television sets.

Our Picks: Paul got to know Atwater Hell when it debuted under the original owners and was overjoyed to learn that it's back. It reminded him of the crisp, flavorful Helles that's served in Munich beer gardens. Maryanne's choice was a newcomer, Shaman's Porter. She found it smooth with a generous malty flavor.

Mark told us that he frequently stopped at the original Atwater Block, and that he'd also homebrewed for years and wanted to own a brewery for some time. That chance came when Stoney Creek threw in the towel. He and Howard bought the building and equipment and, once they did, went back to the formula that made the brewery successful in the first place. Starting with the beer: They gave Hazen the green light to bring back the original lagers.

Hazen's professional brewing career began when he offered a batch of his homebrewed beer to Larry Bell, who gave him a job. He worked his way up to a place on Bell's brew team, then became the assistant brewer at the original Atwater Block. For the new owners, he's added an India pale ale and a range of seasonals, including several bock beers and a Kölsch. He assured us, though, that the emphasis will remain on German-style lagers.

Atwater Block plans to expand operations—there's plenty of capacity at its disposal—and introduce its beer into neighboring states. The brewery is also thinking of adding wine and brandy and holding beer-tasting events. Longer-term, the owners hope that redevelopment efforts along the riverfront, which faces Windsor, Ontario, will attract bigger crowds.

One more thing about this brewery: It's haunted. The spirit is believed to be a Native American who passed away centuries ago. Rieth and Schumacher think they might have to call in a shaman to put his troubled soul to rest. Until they find one, they've done the next best thing: They've put Shaman's Porter on the menu.

Class of license: Microbrewery.
Opened: May 2005 under current ownership.
Owners: Howard Hampton and Mike Rieth.
Brewer: Hazen Schumacher.

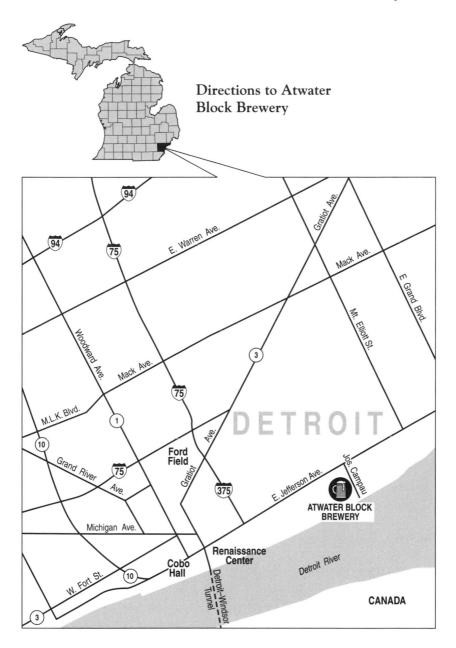

Directions to Atwater
Block Brewery

System: 20-barrel Kasper Schulz. Capacity is 30,000 barrels per year.
Production: 3,000 barrels estimated for 2005 and 5,000 barrels for 2006,
its first full year of operation.
Distribution: In 2006, Atwater Block plans to distribute throughout
Michigan, and to select retailers in Illinois, Indiana, Ohio, and

Pennsylvania. Atwater Block Hell is served at Comerica Park and Ford Field.

Hours: Monday through Friday, 11 A.M. to midnight; Saturday, noon to midnight. Closed Sunday.

Tours: Yes, call ahead. Atwater Block may add scheduled tours.

Take-out beer: Six-packs, kegs, growlers, and quarter and half barrels.

Food: American and German specialties prevail, with appetizers, hamburgers, salads, and German-style sausages on the menu. The Brewer's Platter, which consists of three German-style sausages, is similar to what you'll find in German beer halls.

Extras: Annual Blocktoberfest and Detroit Rivertown Beer Fest. Themed tastings. Shuttle bus to sporting events.

Happy hour: 4 P.M. to 7 P.M. with reduced-price beer.

Mug club: Atwater Block is starting one.

Parking: Fenced-in lot across the street, corner of Guoin and Joseph Campau. Parking can be hard to find on weekend nights.

Detroit Beer Company

1529 East Broadway, Detroit, MI 48226
313-962-1529
www.detroitbeerco.com

Welcome to Foxtown, a district that pizza baron Mike Ilitch has breathed back to life. Its focal point is the Fox Theatre, which Ilitch restored to its former glory. From there it's a short walk to the Hockeytown Café, a gathering place for fans of Ilitch's Detroit Red Wings. Across the street is Comerica Park, where Ilitch's Detroit Tigers now play. And though Ilitch hasn't bought the Detroit Lions, they've also moved into the neighborhood.

One of Foxtown's newer neighbors is the Detroit Beer Company. The third and newest member of the Beer Companies, it occupies the bottom floors of a six-story, late-Victorian-era building that was originally home to a pharmaceutical supply store.

The Detroit Beer Company is a magnet for sports fans, so it was no coincidence that when we poked our heads in, the hosts of a sports talk show had set up a makeshift studio and were engaged in a lively debate about the Lions' chances this year. Next to the studio were clouds of condensing steam and the aroma of malt. Both were rising from the brewhouse, which we could see and smell through an opening cut into the floor. Nearby was the bar and, above it, the stainless steel serving tanks—a Beer Companies signature. Beyond the bar was a metal staircase leading to a second-floor dining area.

Finally we entered a small room with brick walls, tin ceilings, and walls decorated with breweriana and black-and-white photos of the Detroit of yesteryear. It was there that we sat down with Ed Granchi, the managing partner, and Travis Fritts, the brewer. Congratulations to Travis were in order: He'd just been named a partner. A homebrewer from an early age, he joined for love of beer and worked his way up the ranks.

Travis came to Detroit from the small mid-Michigan town of Dimondale, with a detour through Germany. He homebrewed while he was a student at Michigan State University, then parlayed his MSU credits and love of brewing into the equivalent of a bachelor's in microbiology, earning credentials as both a brewer and a maltster from the Research Institute of Brewing in Berlin. Back in the States, he brewed professionally at Arcadia Brewing Company and the Michigan Brewing Company before joining the Beer Companies.

It goes without saying that German beers heavily influence what Travis brews. One of the beers we tasted was a dunkel weizenbock brewed with a special German yeast strain. Travis keeps at least one wheat on tap at all times; in the summer, he sometimes offers three or four. And then there's the Detroit Dwarf, a beer rarely found in the States. It's a Zwickel beer, which in Germany means a beer drawn from a small tap while it matures in the tank. Zwickel is a young beer, cloudy and hoppy. The Dwarf has proved so popular that it's been worked into the year-round lineup. Travis also brews a variety of non-German beers, including a light beer that's the largest seller here, and offers at least one dark beer at all times.

Ed described the Detroit Beer Company as an "event-driven" establishment, whether it's a marquee event like the Super Bowl or baseball's

Beers brewed: You'll usually find seven beers on tap. The menu beers are Broadway Light, Detroit Red, Local 1529 IPA, Schizoweizen. The Detroit Dwarf (GABF Bronze, 2004) has been added to the lineup by popular demand. Seasonals and specialties include Baseball Beer, an English mild; Dimondale Dunkelweizen; Hot Town Wit; Nut Brown Ale; People Mover Porter; St. Brigid's Stout; and Spiced Ale, a 90-shilling ale with autumn spices. One dark beer and one wheat beer available at all times.

Our Pick: If you're into rare beer styles, and we suspect you are, the obvious pick is the Detroit Dwarf, their GABF winner.

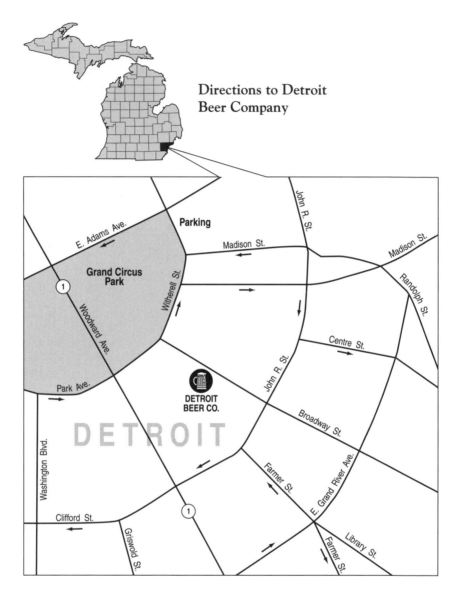

Directions to Detroit Beer Company

All-Star Game or one of Detroit's pro teams' home games. We found television screens placed all over the first floor, and Ed assured us that there's not a bad seat in the house when the game starts.

The menu borrows heavily from the two other Beer Companies. The specialties include fried-chicken dinners made from scratch, jambalaya, shepherd's pie, fish and chips, and chicken pizza. Travis's beers go into a number of menu items—ice cream with oatmeal stout is a popular dessert—and the bread bowls and pizzas are made using spent grain.

Detroit sports fans are passionate. They celebrate victories and commiserate after defeats over what a popular hockey announcer calls "a few pops." Which is why the Beer Companies built a brewpub in Detroit. And why they come.

Class of license: Brewpub.
Opened: September 2003.
Owners: Drew Ciora and Michael Plesz.
Brewer: Travis Fritts.
System: 10-hectoliter Specific Mechanical.
Production: 550 barrels estimated for 2005.
Hours: Monday through Thursday, 11 A.M. to midnight; Friday and Saturday, 11 A.M. to 2 A.M.; Sunday, noon to midnight.
Tours: Yes, just ask.
Take-out beer: Bottles and growlers.
Food: Many popular items at the other Beer Companies appear on the menu here.
Extras: Beer 101, a yearlong course in beer basics Travis teaches in monthly installments. Guest taps include Michigan microbrewed beers. Anniversary party in October. After-work That's My Jam party on Friday. Shuttle bus to Red Wings games. Ford Field and Comerica Park are within walking distance.
Happy hour: Monday through Friday, 4 to 6 P.M., with discounted pints and appetizers. Also discounted pints during Monday Night Football and college football Saturdays.
Mug club: Annual membership is $35. For $15 a year more, your membership is good at all three Beer Companies.
Parking: Grand Circus and Premier Underground parking garages; Detroit Beer Company will validate your ticket, half off for the first two hours. Detroit Opera House parking garage across the street. Comerica Park lot at Madison and Witherell Streets.

Fort Street Brewery

1660 Fort Street, Lincoln Park, MI 48146
313-369-9620
www.fortstreetbrewery.com
and www.fortstreetbeer.com

The Downriver communities south of Detroit suffer from image problems, but many believe that this once bustling industrial avenue has hit bottom and is on its way back. The believers include Pete Romain and Dave Atchison, two cousins who wanted to be their own bosses. They've made a $1.3 million bet that the city of Lincoln Park can turn things around.

Their contribution to the local economy is Fort Street Brewery, which opened on Valentine's Day 2005. It took the owners a while to find a location they liked. It's easy to see why they chose this spot, convenient to three major freeways.

Pete and Dave found a corner lot on the city's busy main drag where a burned-down drugstore once stood. Starting from scratch, they erected a brand new, immaculate brick building trimmed with green awnings. It has the same classic look as the new ballparks inspired by Oriole Park at Camden Yards.

Except for the brewhouse, which is behind three-quarters-high glass, the brewpub is a large, open room: no alcoves, no sectioned-off areas. It is industrial modern, with exposed ductwork softened by burgundy and green walls and blond wooden tables and chairs. Huge picture windows look out on Fort Street. A long, L-shaped oaken bar runs much of the length of the building, and six serving tanks are lined up behind the bar along with liquor bottles and growlers. The brewhouse is in the back.

If you're lucky, you might find brewmaster Doug Beedy at work inside the brewhouse. Beedy is a walking oral history of Michigan craft brewing and a veteran brewer in more ways than one. His résumé includes a hitch in the army, and he's worked at a dozen or so breweries, some of which didn't survive the shakeout of the nineties. He's also a graduate of the Siebel Institute's brewing school.

Beers brewed: Lincoln Lager, the biggest seller; 4x4, a pale wheat ale; Brown Bomber; Downriver Red; Piston Pale; Third Shift Breakfast Stout; and the Big Three, an American IPA. Cask ale is poured every other Thursday.

Our Picks: Paul chose the Port o' Porter, which, as the name implies, is flavored with port wine. Maryanne's pick was Summer Sunsation, the 2005 version of which was a rye beer made with honey malt and fermented with a special yeast strain from Germany that gave it a banana, apple, and clove flavor. Both choices are seasonals.

When Fort Street first opened, Beedy trod gently, assuming that locals were loyal to national-brand lagers and needed to be eased into craft beers. So he offered Lincoln Lager as a transition, and it became Fort Street's best-seller. His initial rotation also included an ESB; an India pale ale; a barrel-aged porter; and 4x4, a beer made with four different grains.

But as the summer gave way to fall, Beedy saw an opportunity to bring some industrial-strength beers into the mix. His Summer Sunsation was a rye beer brewed with honey malt. He's followed up with a biere de garde and a stout made with three different coffees. It's called Third Shift Draft Stout in honor of those who work nights and knock off when the rest of us are waking up. Once in a while, Fort Street throws a Third Shift Party, complete with a breakfast menu and reduced pints.

Expect to find more adventurous beer at Fort Street, which is doing a lot to educate customers about beer. It even holds a monthly Beer Fantasy Camp, where "campers" get an up-close-and-personal look at the brewing process, enjoy fresh beer and good food, and receive a pint glass to take home. Beedy also brings out a cask-conditioned beer on Thursdays.

Sports fans will feel at home here. There are plenty of television screens, and when local teams are playing, you can get reduced-price pitchers. Most of the wooden tables seat four, and they're conducive to game-day conversation.

To make the brewpub a reality, Romain and Atchison knew they had to watch expenses like hawks. They assume that their guests are as frugal as they are, so they've kept beer prices reasonable and stocked the food menu with affordable items: appetizers, sandwiches, and Tex-Mex favorites. Count on big portions, especially if you order the already legendary 22-inch cheese steak.

In its first year, Fort Street has earned good reviews. A few visitors found the ambience a little bit stark, but that isn't likely to last. The owners plan to decorate the brewpub with vintage Detroit breweriana. And a down-to-earth establishment like this, like a classic ballpark, will soon develop a personality of its own.

Class of license: Brewpub.
Opened: February 2005, on Valentine's Day.
Owners: Pete Romain and Dave Atchison.
Brewer: Doug Beedy.
System: 14-barrel CDC. Capacity is 850 barrels.
Production: 500–600 barrels estimated for 2005.
Hours: Monday through Saturday, 11 A.M. to 2 A.M. (kitchen closes 11 P.M. Monday through Thursday, midnight Friday and Saturday); Sunday, 3 to 10 P.M. (kitchen closes 9 P.M.).

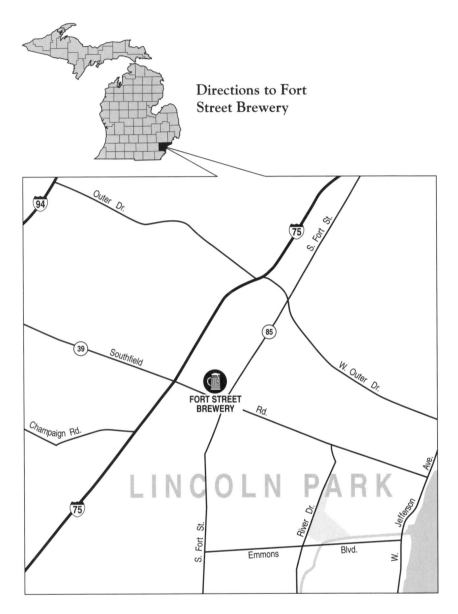

Directions to Fort Street Brewery

Tours: Yes, call ahead.

Take-out beer: Growlers, 5-gallon Cornelius kegs, and half barrels.

Food: Pub menu. Deli sandwiches and wraps are the most popular items.

Extras: Kids' menu, including house-brewed sodas. Live blues jam on Wednesdays. Entertainment every other Saturday night. Pitcher specials during many sporting events. Outdoor seating.

Happy hour: Daily, 3 to 6 P.M., with discounted pints.

Parking: Free street parking in the area. Parking lot behind the brewery.

Brewed in Detroit

In our conversations with members of the brewing community, a number of our hosts recommended a book called *Brewed in Detroit: Breweries and Beers since 1830* (Detroit: Wayne State University Press, 1999). Fortunately, we'd gotten our hands on a copy and read it before going out on the road. It gave us a good perspective on Michigan brewing history and the economics of the industry.

The author, Peter Blum, worked for the Stroh Brewing Company—for years Michigan's flagship brewery—and also served as archivist to the Stroh family. Much of his book focuses on the Stroh story, but he also tells the story of Detroit's brewing from its modest beginnings. Blum divides that story into six eras:

• *The early British ale brewers, beginning about 1830.* Expatriate New Englanders were first to arrive in Michigan. They were of English stock, and those who indulged in beer preferred ale; lager had yet to make its appearance. These early breweries were about the size of a homebrew operation, and the beer truly was handcrafted.

• *The arrival of the Germans.* Although some Germans had moved into the Ann Arbor area and the Saginaw River valley town of Frankenmuth, they didn't arrive in numbers until after the European upheavals of the 1840s. One of them was Bernhard Stroh, the father of the brewery that eventually bore his name. At first ale and lager breweries coexisted, but by 1880, lager became the dominant style. Still, some breweries kept an ale or two in their product line almost to the century's end.

• *Brewing's Golden Age, from 1890 until 1910.* By this point, many breweries had grown to the size of a modern brewpub. Some sold directly to homes within a radius of half a mile or so, and their entire production was draft beer. But things started to change as the nineteenth century ended. Breweries that could get their hands on enough capital bought the latest technology, including bottling equipment that enabled them to expand their distribution. They also could buy saloons, known as "tied houses," that sold only their brand. Breweries that couldn't afford to mechanize, and those that couldn't produce enough to turn a profit, fell by the wayside. Blum relates an interesting story about tied houses:

21

Some saloon owners tried to fight back by pooling their money and buying a small brewery to supply them. At one point, Detroit had four "mutually owned" breweries.

• *Prohibition.* For years, "dry" sentiment ran high in Michigan, and the state prohibited alcohol in 1917, almost three years before the Eighteenth Amendment took effect nationwide. Prohibition was widely flouted in Detroit. The river between Detroit and Windsor was called "the Detroit/Windsor funnel," a pun on the newly opened tunnel to Canada, and speakeasies flourished in the Michigan city. Breweries were allowed to sell "near beer," which entailed brewing beer in the usual manner but removing its alcohol before shipping it. Some breweries were less than diligent about doing so, at least for trusted customers. Predictably, the liquor trade fell into the hands of organized criminals. In Detroit, as elsewhere, the "Great Experiment" devastated the brewing industry: Cash-flow problems and the loss of key family members caused breweries to shut down or left them unable to compete after Repeal.

• *Post-Repeal competition.* According to Blum, the end of Prohibition in 1933 was followed by a "bubble" in which entrepreneurs hoped to cash in by opening breweries. But they overestimated the demand for beer and underestimated the ferocity of the competition. Small breweries worked under an added disadvantage: Under the new "three-tier" system, they could no longer sell directly to consumers. Making matters worse were ex-bootleggers who found another line of work, drifting into labor unions and extorting money from breweries. Not only did many newcomers fail during the thirties, but some that had survived Prohibition were forced to close.

• *The post–World War II industry shakeout.* The first blow to Detroit's brewers was a drop in beer consumption to mid-1930s levels, creating a buyers' market for the product. Then came competition from bigger brewers from outside the region. Finally, there was a rise of national advertising and distribution along with increasing demands that a brewery "grow or go." After the war, the economically desirable size for a brewery doubled every ten to fifteen years, and by the seventies, it stood at 8 million barrels per year. One by one, Michigan's old-guard breweries merged, were bought out, or simply closed their doors. The last of them was G. Heileman, which closed its plant in Frankenmuth in 1991.

Understandably, Blum devotes a substantial part of his book to the Stroh Brewery Company, which not only was the state's largest for much of the twentieth century, but also was very much part of the

Detroit area's culture. For years, the brewery sponsored Detroit Tigers broadcasts—it was instrumental in bringing Hall of Fame announcer Ernie Harwell to Detroit—and its Strohaus at the Gratiot Avenue brewery was one of metro Detroiters' favorite ways to misspend an afternoon. Stroh was a rarity in that it survived both Prohibition and postwar consolidation. In the end, it couldn't compete with the Big Three—Anheuser-Busch, Miller, and Coors—but it went down fighting.

The story began with Bernhard Stroh's arrival in Detroit in 1850. He originally called his business Brewery of B. Stroh but changed the name to Lion Brewery in 1875. Bernhard died in 1882, and his widow and sons put aside their differences long enough to reincorporate the brewery as B. Stroh. In the 1890s, Stroh shipped its beer regionally, even as far east as New England. It established a "branch," the forerunner of a distributorship, only owned by the brewery, across the lake in Cleveland. By century's end, annual production was approaching half a million barrels a year, number one in the city.

In 1911, Stroh sent its brewmaster to Europe to find out about the newest brewing trends. At a municipal brewery, he saw copper kettles heated by direct fire. That was the inspiration for Stroh's "fire brewed" beer, a slogan that appeared on its bottles and cans for years afterward.

When Prohibition came, Stroh survived by selling near beer, soft drinks, hopped syrup (its most popular item), and ice cream. The ice cream stayed in the Stroh product line after Repeal, and you could find Stroh's ice cream parlors in metro Detroit as late as the seventies. Stroh quickly got up and running after Repeal. Like many breweries, it had a cellar full of beer waiting for dealcoholization, a process that was no longer necessary.

In much the same way as Coors, Stroh was a conservative company run by stubborn German Americans. For decades, it continued to use the same recipe for its lager that had won it a Gold Medal at the Chicago World's Fair in 1893. During World War II, it chose to cut back production rather than water down its beer. (That proved a mistake; the wartime product got Americans used to drinking lighter beer.) Stroh also refused to use cans long after the state of the art had improved.

During the fifties, aggressive breweries challenged Stroh and briefly knocked it out of the number-one spot in Detroit. Goebel gave Stroh a run for its money before running into an economic wall; it wound up in the hands of Stroh, which for a while brought back Goebel beer using the original yeast. Another competitor was Tivoli, the maker of Altes beer. It was taken over during the mid-fifties and eventually wound up in the hands of G. Heileman, but Altes was brewed for years afterward.

Another rival was Pfeiffer, which tried to survive by acquiring other regional breweries—a strategy also tried unsuccessfully by Heileman.

Stroh sales peaked in 1977 at around 8 million barrels per year. As Blum put it, its management "bet the farm" in order to survive the long-running industry shakeout. It made the beer lighter and spent more on advertising. It also acquired other breweries. At one point during the eighties, Stroh rose to the number-three spot nationally. But then came the final blow: competition from national breweries, which began taking market share from the remaining regionals.

In 1985, Stroh management closed the Gratiot Avenue brewery for the same reason Schlitz closed its brewery in Milwaukee: It was obsolete. The brewery was designed for the days when beer was delivered by horses and, later, by truck. The company soldiered on for another ten years, but facing a price war in the late nineties, the Stroh family threw in the towel. It sold the brewery's assets to other brewing companies.

The Stroh name lives on. The Stroh family bought a historic building that once housed a pharmaceutical company and converted it into a hotel and office complex called the Stroh River Place. And Stroh's beer is still on the market. According to Ken Wells, the author of *Travels with Barley*, the Pabst Brewing Company owns Stroh's and a number of other brands from now-defunct breweries. Pabst found its niche by becoming a "virtual brewer" that contract-brews these brands. It also spends little on advertising, relying on nostalgia to sell these beers.

In 1992, brewing resumed in Detroit after a seven-year hiatus. But the new face of Detroit brewing—the Detroit and Mackinac Brewery Company—was far different: Stroh's Gratiot Avenue plant probably brewed more during an eight-hour shift than the tiny D&M did in an entire year. Today there are three brewpubs and a microbrewery within the city limits, and some two dozen breweries in the metropolitan area. Blum, who died in 2002, predicted in his book that the trend toward brewpubs would someday lead to the revival of large breweries in Detroit. That hasn't happened yet—small breweries face formidable distribution problems—but perhaps it will in the years to come.

Suburbia

T he same automobile that fueled Detroit's growth and prosperity proved the city's undoing. With cars came suburbs, complete with subdivisions, shopping malls, and commutes. And everyone who could afford it bought into the American dream of a house with a back-yard and lawn. By the hundreds of thousands, they left the city behind.

Today the children of those who left Detroit for places like Warren and Redford are making their homes in communities even farther from downtown Detroit. Their houses are bigger, their commutes are longer, and free time has become a scarce commodity. But the dream is the same. And even those who live an hour's drive from the Renaissance Center and can count on the fingers of one hand how many times they've been downtown in the past year still say they're from Detroit. They still root for the local teams, drink Faygo and Vernor's, and drive American cars.

Detroit's suburbs account for most of the state's population, and dividing them up for this book proved much tougher than we expected. That's because their breweries didn't pay much heed to the traditional dividing lines. Take Woodward Avenue, for instance. It has been the line of demarcation between the West Side and the East Side. That's a big distinction around here. If you listen to old-timers who've lived their entire lives on one side of Woodward or the other, you come away with the impression that people are as divided as East and West Germans. The division isn't quite that stark—especially now that I-696 allows for easier east-west travel—but there are still distinct differences between West and East Siders in culture, ethnicity, and even politics.

Another dividing line in this region is Eight Mile Road, made famous by Eminem's movie of the same name. It runs for miles in a straight line, separating the city of Detroit from what used to be white-bread suburbs on the other side. The suburbs to the north have slowly integrated, but Eight Mile remains a divide, and the region has to do quite a bit more to overcome years of misunderstanding.

Let's take a quick tour around suburbia, starting with Macomb County. Politics is a contact sport here, and its voters have fascinated political scientists for years. Nowhere in Macomb County is local politics more raucous than in Warren, Detroit's largest suburb and the state's third-largest city. Warren is also the home of the Army Tank Command, the General Motors Tech Center, and the world headquarters of Big Boy Restaurants.

Macomb County is itself divided between the south, where you'll find mature communities such as Warren and Sterling Heights, and the newer communities to the north, which have seen explosive growth in recent years, igniting debates over land use and provoking warnings about sprawl. Mount Clemens, the county seat, has the opposite problem: aging infrastructure and making financial ends meet. A century ago, people flocked to its hot springs in hopes of finding a cure for what ailed them. Medical science has changed a lot since then.

To the west is Oakland County, which is becoming more urbanized and more diverse. Southfield is the broadcast media center for the Detroit area and the home of Northland Center, one of America's oldest shopping malls, as well as numerous corporate office towers and office parks. Royal Oak and Ferndale are a couple of once-stagnant blue-collar towns that were rejuvenated by an influx of young people, gays, and artists. Royal Oak is the home of the Shrine of the Little Flower (2123 Roseland Avenue, 248-541-4122, www.shrinechurch.com), where right-wing "radio priest" Father Charles Coughlin once preached, and the Detroit Zoo (8450 West 10 Mile Road, 248-398-0900, www.detroitzoo.org), whose main attraction is a new polar bear exhibit. Woodward Avenue is the site of the annual Detroit Dream Cruise, one night in August on which thousands of enthusiasts bring their classic cars out of the garage and relive the happy days of their youth.

In addition to middle-class suburbs, Oakland has a number of communities populated by the wealthy, who built golf courses and exclusive subdivisions, as well as fancy homes on the shores of the area's many lakes. In Bloomfield Hills, newspaper baron George Gough Booth and his wife, Ellen Scripps Booth, built themselves Cranbook House, the area's oldest manor. It's now part of an educational community (39221 Woodward Avenue, 877-462-7262, www.cranbrook.edu) that includes schools, a science institute and planetarium, and an art museum.

By contrast, Pontiac, the county's largest city, is trying to make the transition to a postindustrial era. Its downtown bars and clubs have become an attraction for young people, especially on weekend nights.

For years, the Detroit Lions brought thousands of football fans to the Silverdome, which offered a roof over fans' heads and little more. It's still used for occasional concerts and monster truck shows while local officials decide what to do with the land underneath it.

The Detroit Pistons also used to play at the Silverdome, but they've moved to the Palace of Auburn Hills, where they've hung three National Basketball Association championship banners. Auburn Hills is the home of Great Lakes Crossing, one of the state's largest shopping malls, and the American headquarters of DaimlerChrysler Corporation. And speaking of shopping, Troy is also another destination: It's where you'll find the tony Somerset Collection shopping center.

Wayne County is one of the country's most populous, and strangely, its suburbs have just three breweries—one fewer than the city of Detroit. Only one can be found in the western part of the county, where we live. There are plenty of people who enjoy better beer and plenty of brewers who've made a go of it under tougher conditions, so the lack of breweries has us scratching our heads. Maybe there's a homebrewer or two out there with big dreams who see what we see: a big and untapped market.

Recommended Beer Bars
Berkley
Berkley Front, 3087 West Twelve Mile Road, 248-547-3331. About fifty beers, with some rotating seasonals. Entertainment upstairs.

Clarkston
Clarkston Union, 54 South Main Street, 248-620-6100. Former 1840s church turned upscale beer bar, with thirty-five beers on taps.

Plymouth
Box Bar & Grill, 777 West Ann Arbor Trail, 734-459-7390. A town hangout for more than half a century. Has fifty taps and one of the area's biggest selection of bottled beers.

Royal Oak
Gusoline Alley, 309 Center Street, 248-545-2235. A wide selection of bottled beers, but not for the faint of heart—it's tiny, funky, and often packed.

St. Clair Shores
Shores Inn Food & Spirits, 23410 Greater Mack Avenue, 586-773-8940. A local hangout with more than 150 domestic and imported beers.

Dragonmead Microbrewery

14600 East Eleven Mile Road, Warren, MI 48089
586-776-9428
dragonmead.com

Perhaps the makers of Dungeons and Dragons should put a disclaimer on the box: "Playing this game may cause you to brew strange beer." That's what happened to Larry Channell, Earl Scherbarth, and Bill Wrobel, the owners of Dragonmead. They got into D&D while they were students at Michigan State University.

Their interest in the Middle Ages led them into the world of wassail feasts, which are holiday celebrations with food, music, costumed performers—and ale. The next step was homebrewing, which was the only way they could enjoy European styles that weren't available at home. One more thing: This being Michigan, it shouldn't surprise you that all three gentlemen have auto industry backgrounds. As Larry told us, "There's the Big Three in the auto world, and there's the Big Three in the brewing world."

We've learned not to judge a book by its cover or a brewery by its exterior. From the outside, Dragonmead is a nondescript building on a freeway service drive. But the interior decor is best described as classic King Arthur, with heraldic flags, a suit of armor, and even gargoyles in the windows. There are modern necessities as well, including televisions and audio equipment for the bands that perform here. The owners want their brewery to become a "place to be," and they're reaching out to music lovers, sports fans, and homebrewers.

Not satisfied with brewing their own beer, the friends made the leap into professional brewing. As Larry said, "We've been described as homebrewers on steroids." The brewery's name, Dragonmead, is a salute to their D&D

Beers brewed: Forty to fifty are on tap at any given time; check the website for what's available. The flagship beers are Final Absolution Belgian Trippel and Wee Heavy Scotch Ale, but you'll find almost every style imaginable.

Awards won: 2004 WBC Bronze, Strong Scotch Ale.

Our Picks: Paul chose Final Absolution, which he fell in love with at a beer festival a few years ago. He wishes the owners had followed through on their threat to call it Extreme Unction. Maryanne chose Under the Kilt, an award-winning Scottish export ale. You can't go wrong with a beer that won a medal in the World Beer Cup.

days at State. But the brewing side of their business is strictly twenty-first century. Larry used his process-engineering background to squeeze the last possible drop of production out of a 3-barrel brewing system.

This operation is so efficient that brewer Eric Harms—who has a background in chemical engineering, by the way—can brew nine batches a week and still take two days off. It has become the stuff of legend around Michigan. Mention the name Dragonmead to a brewer, and he'll react with a combination of disbelief and awe.

This compact but highly efficient brewery stocks fifty-five different grains from seven countries, as well as fifteen strains of yeast. Dragonmead takes an unusual approach to yeast, using a strain only once rather than reusing it for future batches of beer. Its owners also insist on country-specific grain. Using Wisconsin malt in a Bavarian hefeweizen is a definite no-no.

Everything is brewed to style here. It's all about the detail and the process. Let's take a look at mashing, for example. The grain is cracked directly into the mash tun, the mash tun has steam jackets around it, there's an infusion port and even a series of paddles that stirs the mash without aerating it. You get the idea. This is precision engineering.

On to the beer. It's possible to find as many as fifty-two beers on tap here. As you might expect, most of their names are inspired by the Middle Ages—like their flagship ale, Final Absolution Trippel. It'll take even the most dedicated beer drinker a while to sample everything the brewery has to offer. One reason is that except for fifteen or so year-rounders, the beer selection changes every week. Another is that Dragonmead doesn't pour lawn-mower beer. Perusing the menu, we found numerous selections that checked in at 6.0 percent ABV or higher. To help you along, Dragonmead issues passports that your server stamps with the brewery logo and a description of what you just ordered. At the end of the night, you hand it back to the bar staff for safekeeping.

Lately, Dragonmead has been working to boost sales to tap accounts and, especially, sell more bottled beer. Thanks to legal and economic barriers facing small breweries—a pet peeve of a number of brewery people we talked to—distributing beer in Michigan is the modern-day equivalent of slaying a dragon. But the "Big Three of beer" are confident that they'll succeed. Their first two bottled beers are Final Absolution and Kilt Lifter Wee Heavy. That's just the beginning. They plan to roll out two new labels every six months over the next ten years. Unless our math is wrong, that's forty beers.

Fittingly, Dragonmead has embarked on an Arthurian quest. Its owners aim to brew a beer in every style and substyle recognized by the

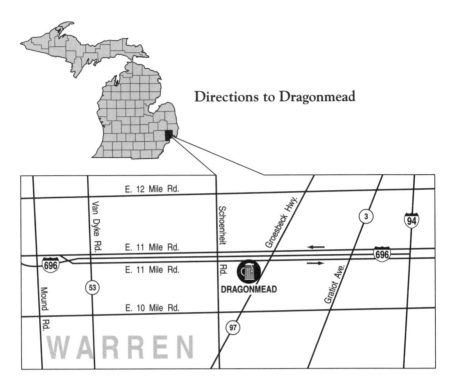

Directions to Dragonmead

Great American Beer Festival. That's about a hundred beers in all, and the judging committee seems to create new categories every year. And they intend to have every one of them on tap. They're almost halfway there, and they have the rest of the task planned out. Given Larry's gift for organizing things, we'd be fools to bet against them.

Class of license: Microbrewery.
Opened: May 1997.
Owners: Larry Channell, Earl Scherbarth, Bill Wrobel.
Brewer: Eric Harms.
System: 3-barrel Heavy Duty Systems with a grain cracker, seven open primary fermenters, nine secondary fermenters, and five lagering tanks. Capacity is 1,400 barrels per year.
Production: 900 barrels in 2004, 1,000 barrels estimated in 2005.
Distribution: Select stores in southern Michigan.
Hours: Monday through Wednesday, 3 to 11 P.M.; Thursday through Saturday, 11 A.M. to midnight. Closed Sunday.
Tours: Yes, on request.
Take-out beer: Growlers and quarter and half barrels. Some beers are available in 12-ounce bottles.

Food: Limited snack menu. Customers can bring in food bought else-where; there's a binder full of menus from local restaurants.
Extras: Dartboard. Live entertainment Saturday nights. Gathering place for homebrew clubs.
Parking: Lot in front of the building.

Kuhnhenn Brewing Company

5919 Chicago Road, Warren, MI 48092
586-979-8361
www.kbrewery.com

A century ago, a few Detroiters tinkered with cars while the rest got around by horse-drawn vehicles. A journey out of town was an adventure, and Warren was a stop on the journey north. Some stopped here because they needed work done on their wagons. Over the years, the site of that repair shop was the home of a general store, a gas station, and eventually a hardware store.

In the 1970s, the Kuhnhenn family bought the store, known as Lutz's Hardware. It's one of the few buildings left in the area with historical significance. Big-box retailers have made it increasingly hard for family-owned hardware stores to compete. The family business went in a different direction after Eric Kuhnhenn brought a homebrew kit back from a trip to Traverse City. He and his brother, Bret, were soon hooked.

It was "The Hobby That Ate Lutz's." Eric and Bret added homebrewing supplies to their store inventory. They sold so much that it became a bigger and bigger part of the business. They also opened a brew-on-premises operation. We'd seen them in Canada, where locals explained to us that taxes were high enough to make U-Brewing, as

Beers brewed: About sixty beers are on tap any given day. When we dropped by, there were a dozen on the menu. The mildest were a tangerine witbier and a domestic lager; farther up the ladder was Kuhnhenn's flagship beer, a pale ale called Loonie Kuhnie; and at the head of the class were three big beers—we're talking 9.0 percent ABV or better—a Belgian-style ale called Nine, Fourth Dementia Olde Ale, and Simcoe Silly. Also on the menu was a selection of wines and a couple of house meads.

they called it, pay off. On our side of the border, Michigan BOPers do it for the love of beer.

Our Picks: Paul picked the Fourth Dementia Olde Ale, a high-alcohol red ale with lots of hops. Maryanne chose Nine, a smooth Belgian abbey-style ale with a creamy finish.

The brothers decided to brew professionally. Why not? They entered the field with several advantages. Their father was a builder, who could help convert part of the hardware store into a brewery. They grew up around tools and literally could weld a brewing operation together. And they knew the value of a buck. The Kuhnhenns logged thousands of miles in a beery scavenger hunt, buying fermenters and storage tanks for cents on the dollar. They regret a few bargains, like the tank they bought from a food company that used to make peanut butter. Cleaning it out was labor-intensive: enough to drive them to drink. Then there's the mash tun–brewkettle that's a scale. Check it out.

Because they opened a microbrewery, not a brewpub, the brothers didn't have to worry about being in the restaurant business. Their menu is limited to cheeses, snacks, pizzas, and whatever customers bring in from outside. The taproom is where serious beer drinkers gather, not someplace where people come to "be seen." It's dominated by a huge black walnut bar, with a movie screen used to show sporting events. Surrounding it is a group of tables for four. The brewing vessels are part of the decor.

Since they went the microbrewery route, the Kuhnhenns have been busy getting their products into bars and onto grocery and liquor store shelves. As for the homebrew supplies next door, sales are still going strong, providing an extra source of revenue as well as the ingredients Bret and Eric use to expand their collection of beer recipes. And the brothers have done just that.

Kuhnhenn's beer has quickly gained a legion of fans. Now that Bret and Eric have tweaked their brewing skills and equipment, and their distribution plans are a little clearer, expansion will be on the horizon. They credit sites such as RateBeer.com and BeerAdvocate.com for some of their success. They told us that good reviews there can catapult niche beers, and those who brew them, to national fame.

Bret and Eric are hardly resting on their laurels. They've gotten the attention of festival-goers at the last two Michigan Brewers Guild events with a Breakfast Series and a Candy Land Series. We also ran into Bret and his dad at the World Beer Festival in Durham, North Carolina. When the brothers aren't on the road, they're hard at work tinkering with the brewery. Just like the auto pioneers of a century ago.

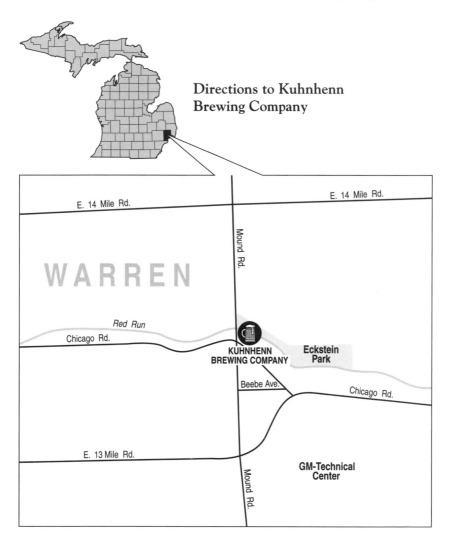

Directions to Kuhnhenn
Brewing Company

Class of license: Microbrewery.
Opened: March 2002.
Owner-brewers: Bret and Eric Kuhnhenn.
System: 8-barrel system fashioned by the Kuhnhenns.
Production: 262 barrels in 2004.
Distribution: Select stores in southeast Michigan.
Hours: Monday through Thursday, noon to midnight; Friday and Saturday, noon to 2 A.M.; Sundays during football season, noon to 6 P.M.
Tours: Yes, call in advance.
Take-out beer: Growlers, some beers available in bottles.

Food: Limited menu. Customers can bring their own or have something delivered.
Extras: Big-screen TV for sporting events. No smoking. Brew-on-premises operation.
Parking: Small lot in the back.

Great Baraboo Brewing Company

35905 Utica Road, Clinton Township, MI 48035
586-792-7397
www.greatbaraboo.com/menu.asp

Okay, Baraboo is in Wisconsin, not Michigan, and there aren't any breweries in Baraboo. But doesn't the name bring a smile to your face? We thought so. The brewery's name and logo—which features a cover girl from a century ago—evoke the pre-Prohibition era of fancy saloons where the town's leading gentlemen would gather.

A lot has changed in a hundred years: Licensed establishments aren't called saloons, ladies are now welcome in them, and city neighborhoods have given way to suburbs and subdivisions. But every community still needs a gathering place, and Great Baraboo has filled the bill since 1995.

Michigan is unusual in that the big pub chains haven't established a foothold here. That's partly the result of a state law limiting an owner to three establishments. But people in the industry also believe that the chains have had a hard time competing with family-operated establishments. At Great Baraboo, staff and customers are part of the family.

Years ago, a "windowless dive" called the Moravian Lodge stood at this location. Our fathers, who were part of the World War II generation, drank at places like that, but we never found them appealing. Neither did Great Baraboo's owner, Harry Kourelis. He gave the lodge an extreme makeover, turning it into a lively restaurant with inviting wood-and-

Beers brewed: The menu beers are Shark Tooth Bay Golden Ale, Kings Peak Caribou Wheat, Snake Eye Canyon Red Ale, Boston Blackstone Porter, and Hoppy Heartland Pale Ale. There's also a rotating special.

brick decor, booths in the shape of beer barrels, and a big T-shaped bar off to one side. It's a cross between a hunting lodge and a sports bar.

The brewing system is part of the scenery at Great Baraboo. The brewkettles stand behind glass in a front corner where customers can see their beer being made. In an unusual twist, four of the fermentation tanks have been incorporated into the dining-area decor. Some patrons who aren't familiar with the brewing process have reportedly used the tanks as coat racks—and worse.

Our Picks: Talk about role reversal. Paul's top choice was Boston Blackstone Porter, a smooth, medium-bodied version of the style. Maryanne decided to opt for the hops and picked the Hoppy Heartland Pale Ale.

Not surprisingly, this is a place where fans converge for big and not-so-big games. About thirty television sets are scattered about, and manager Mike La Branche assured us that there isn't a bad seat in the house when the opening whistle blows. There's other electronic entertainment as well, including Keno, video games, and NTN trivia.

The owner describes Great Baraboo's menu as upscale family fare, with an emphasis on Angus beef, baby back ribs, and fish and chips. There are nightly food specials, including specially priced chicken wings when the local teams are playing. Great Baraboo offers a special kids' menu, and their meals are served in little classic cars. A magician performs on Saturday, and fun characters roam the dining room on Monday.

The man in charge of the brewhouse is Andrew Stroble, yet another pro brewer who started making his own while a cash-strapped college student. Aware that many of his customers were raised on mass-market American and Canadian lagers, he specializes in "comfort beers" and emphasizes clean taste and consistency. Andrew's five year-rounders are familiar styles that won't frighten anyone off. He also brews a rotating monthly special; past offerings included a Scottish ale, a Belgian-style trippel, and an imperial stout—not to mention a pumpkin ale every fall. And those who insist on their regular brand will probably find it on the menu.

An evening out is all about having a good time with friends and family. That is what Great Baraboo offers, and it's been a winning formula with the people of Macomb County.

Class of license: Brewpub.
Opened: July 1995.
Owner: Harry Kourelis.
Brewer: Andrew Stroble.
System: 7-barrel DME. Capacity is 800 barrels.

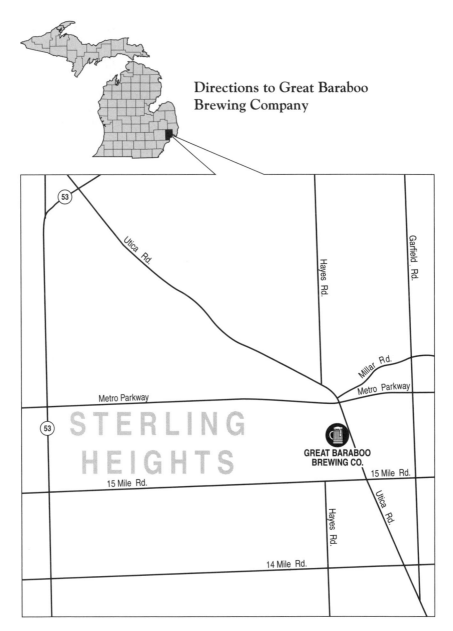

Directions to Great Baraboo Brewing Company

Production: 575 barrels in 2004.

Hours: Open until 2 A.M. daily except Christmas.

Tours: Yes, ask if the brewer is available. You're most likely to find him early in the day.

Take-out beer: Growlers.

Food: Daily specials.

Extras: Full bar service. Outdoor patio. Costumed characters on Monday evenings. Live entertainment Thursday through Saturday. Jukebox with more than a hundred thousand songs. NTN trivia.

Happy hour: Discounted pints when local teams are playing. Happy hour 3 to 6 P.M. weekdays and 11 P.M. to 1 A.M. Saturday through Wednesday. Boomba Day Tuesday, with reduced 35-ounce Boomba mugs.

Mug club: Yes.

Parking: Lot adjacent.

Woodward Avenue Brewers

22626 Woodward Avenue, Ferndale, MI 48220
248-546-3696

Older Michiganders recall the fifties with fondness. The auto industry was humming along, and nothing was more fun than going out for a drive. One night a year, those magical days return in the form of the Woodward Dream Cruise. More than a million people line Woodward Avenue to watch a huge fleet of classic cars pass in review. A good vantage point for watching the Dream Cruise is Woodward Avenue Brewers.

The WAB, as regulars call it, was the idea of Grant Johnson, who trained at the Siebel Institute, and fellow owners Chris and Krista Johnson. The Johnsons bought a two-story brick corner building, which has an offbeat history. Built in the 1920s, it served as a polio clinic, a dance studio, and an Asian massage parlor, where other services were rumored to be on the menu. The trio started the WAB on a shoestring, even building parts of it themselves. They built the brewpub at about the time young people realized the potential of Ferndale, a working-class town that had seen better days.

The WAB is a place that walks to its own beat. The first of its many oddities you'll notice is that there's no entrance on Woodward Avenue; the front door is around the corner. As you go in, there's a "Joe sent me" speakeasy ambience; a blackboard in the entrance points you to the elevator, said to be

Beers brewed: The menu beers are Custom Blonde, Custom Porter, Hefe-Weizen, Pale Ale, Raspberry Blonde, and Vanilla Porter. Seasonals include a pumpkin ale, winter ale, a Märzen in the spring, and an occasional brown ale or cream ale.

the first one installed in the county, which is furnished with a couple of ratty old chairs.

Downstairs looks like a cross between the inside of a garage and a high school cafeteria. During the warm months, the garage door is open, and there's plenty of outdoor seating behind a white picket fence lined with flower boxes. Inside, you'll find exposed ductwork and stucco ceilings, blue-topped stainless tables with seats that once saw service on buses, and a bar in the corner lined with high stainless steel chairs.

Our Picks: Paul had the Pale Ale, made with four kinds of malt. It was agreeably hoppy, a good choice for a warm late-summer afternoon. Maryanne had the Vanilla Porter. It's the WAB's flagship beer, Custom Porter, with vanilla flavor added.

There's also an auto theme downstairs. Rows of old Michigan license plates decorate the walls. They're a reminder of the days when the secretary of state issued new plates, with a different color scheme, every year. Even the menus are bound with blue vanity plates reading "THE WAB" and the motto "The Great Beer State."

At night, the action moves upstairs, where the activities include watching the world go by through the windows overlooking Woodward Avenue, admiring the works of local artists on display, and listening to one of the area's most famous jukeboxes. It has been likened to an urban loft, a fitting venue for the artistic-minded customers, many of whom live within walking distance and party on at home after last call.

It can get crowded here, but take a few minutes to look at a couple more WAB oddities: a display window full of globes halfway up the wooden stairs and photos of Woodward Avenue from Detroit to Pontiac—the route of the modern Dream Cruise—annotated with historical references.

Oh, about the beer. Grant Johnson developed the house beers, but in 2002, he turned the brewing duties over to Dan Shannon. Dan earned a degree in botany from Michigan State and worked at a laboratory before becoming a professional brewer. He follows Grant's original recipes for the six WAB Custom Ales, the flagship of which is Custom Porter, but he gets creative with seasonal and specialty beers.

You'll find more artists than beer geeks in attendance, but the WAB is a brewery and a fun one. It started as a micro but switched to brewpub status in order to offer a full bar menu. It's a funky establishment, one in keeping with the city's new "Fashionable Ferndale" image. And like the Dream Cruise, it offers a trip back in time to Michigan's automotive golden age.

Class of license: Brewpub.
Opened: May 1997.
Owners: Chris and Krista Johnson, Grant Johnson, Tom Voss.

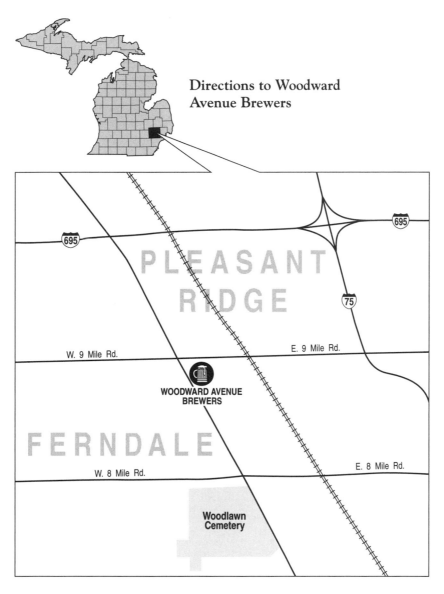

Directions to Woodward Avenue Brewers

Brewer: Dan Shannon.

System: 15-barrel DME.

Production: N/A.

Hours: Monday through Friday, 11 A.M. to 2 A.M.; Saturday and Sunday, noon to 2 A.M.

Tours: No big groups. Ask if the brewer is available and has time.

Take-out beer: Growlers and kegs.

Food: Pub menu with a Tex-Mex accent; also includes pizza, soups and salads, and a variety of sandwiches. Food is half price on Monday nights.

Extras: Beer is available in half-pints as well as pints. Custom root beer brewed on the premises. The upstairs jukebox has everything from Latin salsa to forties show tunes to classic folk rock. Patio is open May to October.

Parking: Metered street parking.

Lily's Seafood Grill and Brewery

410 South Washington Avenue, Royal Oak, MI, 48067
248-591-5459

It seems that everyone in Michigan has a friend who can fix anything, a neighbor who works for a car company, and a relative who lives in Florida. And there's a Florida angle in the story of Lily's Seafood Grill and Brewery.

Our visit to Lily's got off to a great start: Bob Morton came out to meet us wearing a Dr. Seuss fish tie. "If I've got to wear one, I might as well have some fun," he told us. We had fun, too, listening to the story of Lily's. Our first question, of course, was who is Lily? It turns out that she was the Mortons' maternal grandmother, an immigrant from Scotland and one considerable lady.

For years, we'd dropped by the Lily's Seafood booth at the Michigan Brewers Guild summer festival and came away amazed. Why, we asked ourselves, was the beer from a seafood restaurant so good? We were about to find out. And here's where the Florida angle comes in.

There are five Morton brothers. Bob and his brother Scott started a seafood restaurant and brewpub in Florida, then opened a second one. Both were successful, and the brothers eventually sold them to the Big River brewpub chain. Bob went back to Michigan and took a job with DME, a manufacturer of brewing systems, leaving the Florida brewpub operations in Scott's hands.

Beers brewed: There are six beers on tap. The four menu beers are Lily's Light Pilsner, Reggie's French River Red, Strange Stout, and Whitefish Bay Wheat. Seasonal beers include Barnacle Bob's Boatyard Ale; Big Summer; Black Lager; Bock; Honey Brown; People's Choice Pale Ale and Sven & Ollie's IPA, aged in bourbon barrels. There is also cask beer from time to time.

At DME, Bob racked up thousands of miles visiting breweries. In our travels, we heard many a brewer lament that "this brewery wasn't designed by a brewer." Well, Lily's was. Bob learned from what he saw while on the road. He also learned professional brewing thanks to the DME people, who arranged apprenticeships for him at several breweries.

Our Pick: The Strange Stout was the best of a strong lineup. No, the name isn't a comment on the style. It's the last name of the Mortons' grandmother. The beer is a rich and chewy oatmeal stout brewed with 25 pounds of rolled oats.

Bob told us that he and Scott wanted to open a microbrewery in Royal Oak, but city officials were afraid that downtown would turn into a mini–French Quarter. The city fathers were open to an upscale restaurant, however, so they were willing to compromise on a brewpub. That was fine with the Mortons, who love the restaurant trade as much as the brewing business. And since seafood and craft beer were a winning combination in Florida, they replicated it in Michigan.

Lily's is in a building that was an S. S. Kresge store, then a Silver's Office Supply store, and after that a fitness center, before the Mortons brought it back to life. They've worked wonders. One wall is painted an oceanic dark green, and the opposite wall is exposed firebrick with a logo in one corner that will remind Michiganders of Detroit's brewing history. The works of local artists hang on the walls; each month, the artwork changes and Lily's holds a miniexhibition of the new items. The decor also includes photos of the Morton family. If you make your way to the back, beyond the kitchen, you'll find one of Lily herself on the outside of the glass surrounding the brewery.

Lily's is a fun place and not your typical brewpub. The first thing we saw on the way in was a row of fish tanks lining the bar area. The dining area is decorated in a lighthearted nautica-and-nature motif. And the waitstaff wear T-shirts with the slogan "That's Ale, Brother," the same slogan Ballantine used for its famous ale.

Scott Morton is a man of few words, but his beer speaks volumes. He leans toward pale ales and India pale ales, both British and American. He recently brought out an India Pale Ale aged in bourbon barrels, as well as a bold and malty beer he called Big Summer. On the food side, Lily's signature dishes are seared sesame tuna, Creole soup, and tuna burgers.

The Lily that the brewpub honors kept a home where dinner guests were welcome, even groups of friends who dropped in at the last minute. That is the feeling the Mortons want to create at Lily's. They've certainly done it.

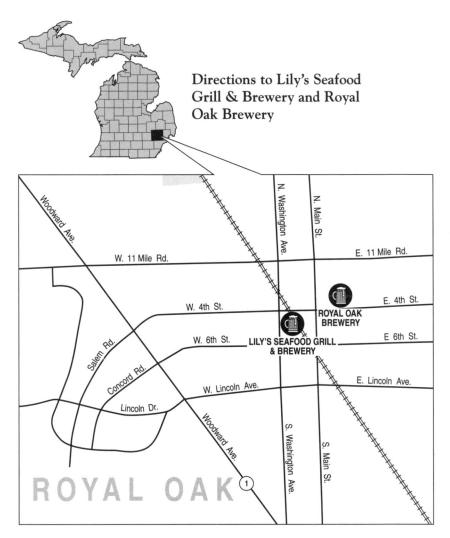

Directions to Lily's Seafood Grill & Brewery and Royal Oak Brewery

Class of license: Brewpub.

Opened: November 1999.

Owners: Bob and Scott Morton. The corporate name is Morton Brothers, Inc.

Brewer: Scott Morton.

System: 5-barrel DME. Capacity is 2,000 barrels.

Production: About 500 barrels in 2004.

Hours: Monday through Friday, 11 A.M. to 10:30 P.M.; Saturday and Sunday, 11 A.M. to 12:30 A.M. These are kitchen hours; the bar may be open a little longer.

Tours: Yes, by request.

Take-out beer: Growlers, kegs, and quarter and half barrels.

Food: Seafood, of course, but some meat and pasta dishes as well. Sunday brunch features crab cakes, salmon hash and eggs, and quiches and omelets.

Extras: Five-course brewer's dinners twice a year. Small outdoor seating area. Children's menu; on Tuesdays, kids under twelve eat free. All-you-can-eat fish fry on Mondays. Oktoberfest beer dinner. Occasional live entertainment.

Happy hour: Monday through Friday, 2 to 7 P.M., and Saturday, 11 A.M. to 7 P.M., with reduced pints. Also, reduced beer during Monday Night Football.

Mug club: Lifetime membership is $35. Benefits include a T-shirt, half a growler, a monthly newsletter called *The Lily Pad* with discount offers, and reduced growler refills.

Parking: Structure behind the rear entrance of the restaurant. Surface lot nearby. Parking can be a problem on weekend nights.

Bastone Belgian Brewery and Restaurant

419 South Main Street, Royal Oak, MI 48067
248-544-6250
www.michiganmenu.com/bastone.html

The brewpub's name is a corruption of Bastogne, the Belgian town where, in 1944, Allied forces turned back the German offensive in the Battle of the Bulge. So it's hardly surprising that Bastone is a Belgian-style brasserie.

The brewpub is part of a four-establishment complex that also includes a DJ dance club, a Latin-themed restaurant, and a wine bar. It's part of the Schelde-managed family of restaurants.

Bastone started out as a grocery store in 1939, and its owners have restored it to Art Deco perfection. The interior has high ceilings, white tile walls, exposed ductwork, and thirties-style posters from Belgium. Bastone draws a business crowd for lunch and an eclectic, smart-casual clientele for dinner and drinks afterward. In the summer, many customers prefer the outside seating along Main Street.

Cuisine à la bière, a Belgian institution, has become popular in the States, and the investors who own Bastone are fond of it. The menu incorporates such French and Belgian specialties as pommes frites with a choice of eight different mayo dips, mussels, Niçoise salad, and Belgian waterzooi with seafood. And the house beers find their way into the food menu.

Unlike most brewpubs, where the brewery takes center stage, Bastone's is in the basement, where quarters are cramped, the vessels are open fermentation, and spent grain has to be hauled up the stairs. More than one brewer we talked to winced at the idea of brewing there. The brewery was originally at the Arena Brewing Company, a short-lived brewpub venture in Grand Rapids.

We were shown around by Kim Schneider, one of only a handful of women who brew professionally in the state. An older brother got her interested in homebrewing, and despite being handed the grunt work, she became hooked. After earning a degree in microbiology at Eastern Michigan University, she worked as a researcher for a pharmaceutical company. But brewing remained her first love, and she went professional in 2004, coming to Bastone after stops at Big Buck and Dragonmead.

Kim had been devoting her brewing to German lagers and English ales, so when she came to Bastone, the first order of business was getting up to speed on Belgian-style ales. She hit the books, asked other brewers for pointers, and said a little prayer when she pitched the yeast. Her efforts paid off; we tasted her private-reserve dubbels and trippels and were more than a little impressed.

After our visit, Rockne van Meter joined the Bastone staff as brewer. Kim continues to brew but also works on marketing. By the time you read this, Kim will have moved, but she won't be hard to find.

Most of the beers are Belgians, but Bastone has a couple of "fun taps" to experiment with. The brewers have included pale ales and India pale ales, a stout for St. Patrick's Day, and a cream ale for summer. Cask-conditioned ales are tapped on Saturdays. Look for lambics and vertical tastings of vintage beer too.

Perhaps because the brewery is downstairs, not everyone who comes here is aware that Bastone is a brewpub. The owners are taking steps to raise the profile of the house beers. They're also trying to educate cus-

Beers brewed: The five menu beers are Belgian Pale, Blonde, Dubbel, Pilsner, and Wit. There is also a rotating seasonal. The house beers are available throughout the complex.

Our Picks: Maryanne chose a Belgian Dubbel, a mahogany-colored beer. Paul went with the Belgian Pale Ale, a very hoppy take on pale ale with a 7.5 percent alcoholic punch.

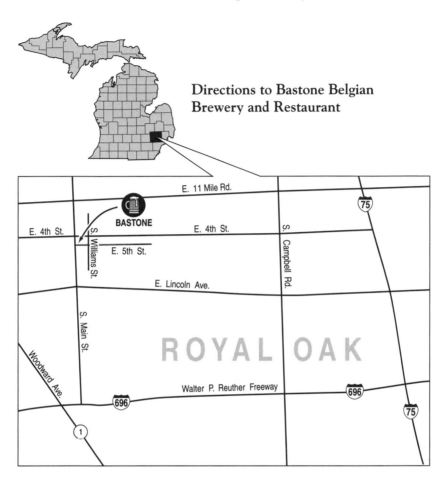

Directions to Bastone Belgian
Brewery and Restaurant

tomers about the beer with events such as brewer's dinners, themed tasting, and Meet the Brewer nights.

Royal Oak is a comeback story. Once a down-at-the-heels suburb, it has sprung back to life, offering bars and restaurants that attract visitors from across metro Detroit. Bastone adds to downtown Royal Oak's diversity and offers some of the region's most underappreciated beers.

Class of license: Brewpub.
Opened: April 2003.
Owner: Union Brewery, LLC. The restaurant is managed by Schelde
    Enterprises.
Brewers: Kim Schneider and Rockne van Meter.
System: 10-barrel Global, with a combined mash–lauter tun, four primary fermenters, seven serving tanks, and three conditioning tanks.

Production: 600–700 barrels estimated for 2005, less than half the
brewery's capacity.

Hours: Sunday through Thursday, 11 A.M. to 11 P.M.; Friday and Saturday, 11 A.M. to midnight.

Tours: Call ahead and arrange.

Take-out beer: Growlers, "fresh kegs" (which resemble keggys), Cornelius
kegs, and half barrels. Gift boxes of bottled beer are also available.

Food: French brasserie menu.

Extras: Full bar service and an excellent selection of wines. Valet parking in the evening. "Kids Eat Free" promotion on Sundays. Smoking is allowed at the bar only. Meet the Brewer night the first
Tuesday of the month, from 6 to 8 P.M.

Happy hour: 3 to 6 P.M., with reduced drink prices. There's also a tap of
the day, with discounts on pints and growlers of one of the seven
draft beers. Frugal customers can find happy-hour prices on the
house beers from 6 to 9 P.M. at Cinq, the downstairs dance club
that's part of the complex.

Mug club: The Bastone Brasserie Beer Club charges $20 for a lifetime
membership. Benefits include discounts on pints and special events.

Parking: Nearby metered surface lots.

Royal Oak Brewery

215 East Fourth Street, Royal Oak, MI 48067
248-544-1141
www.royaloakbrewery.com

It's word association time: What comes to mind when we say "Drew
and Mike"?

If you're like most Detroiters, you're thinking of a couple of local
drive-time radio guys. But there's another Drew and Mike in town.
They're Drew Ciora and Mike Plesz, who founded the Beer Companies.
The Royal Oak Brewery, which recently celebrated its tenth anniversary, was their first venture.

Our state's brewing community is mostly homegrown, but there's a
California connection to the Beer Companies. Mike's sister, Michelle,

moved from Michigan to California, where she took a job at a brewpub in Huntington Beach and fell in love with Drew. Mike, who was homebrewing in his spare time in Michigan, persuaded the two to leave California and start a brewpub with him.

The Beer Companies started modestly. Drew and Mike found a building that used to be a hardware store and did a lot of the renovation work themselves. Somewhere along the line, they met up with Stan Sommers, a breweriana collector, who furnished much of the decor. Some of the items made us do a double take: As kids in New Jersey, we saw them in corner taverns when our fathers took us with them.

We dropped in early in the afternoon. Good thing: With a double row of stools, the bar area makes for a tight squeeze, especially when the brewpub gets crowded, which is the rule on weekend nights. The stainless steel fermenting tanks are mounted above the bar, something customers love but brewers call a nightmare. Farther back—this building is long and narrow—is the brewhouse. It isn't behind glass but out in the open.

Our hosts were Pat Scanlon, the managing partner, and Todd Parker, the brewer. Pat's career pretty much sums up the Beer Companies. He brewed at all three—Michigan law caps ownership at three brewpubs—and moved up from there to an equity position. He couldn't be much more than forty but called himself the "grand old man" of the organization.

Running the Royal Oak Brewery isn't for the faint of heart. Pat said that regulars are knowledgeable about beer and aren't shy about critiquing it. "It keeps us on our toes," he said with a laugh. The man in charge of keeping the customers happy is brewer Todd Parker, another naturalized Michigander. Todd grew up in New Mexico and earned a master's degree in marine biology in California. He took up homebrewing in the early nineties and brewed professionally before coming to Royal Oak.

The owners make sure that Todd goes first-class. They give him the green light to get creative and buy him the best malt and hops they can afford. "I think it pays off. I think it makes a difference," he told us.

Beers brewed: There are six beers on tap. The five menu beers are Royal Oak Red, Fourth Street Wheat, Pappy's Porch Sittin' Porter, Plesz'ures IPA, and the Northern Light, a Kölsch-style beer and the number-one seller. Rotating monthly seasonals are available in bottles. Beer is served in English yards and, during special events, in enormous mugs. Royal Oak Brewery also brews root beer.

Award won: 2005 GABF Gold, Scottish-Style Ale.

Our Picks: Maryanne was in the mood for something hoppy, and that's what she got with Plesz'ures IPA, a play on Mike's last name. Paul's selection was Royal Oak Red, a lushly malty beer based on the Irish red style. He was pleased that the judges at the 2005 Great American Beer Festival saw it his way: They awarded it a gold medal.

Todd brews an all-ale lineup—the brewery is so close to capacity that it can't afford to make lagers—ranging from a Kölsch to a hop-laden India pale ale. But Todd really shines with his seasonals: Scotch ale in the winter; a Belgian early in the year; a high-gravity stout around St. Patrick's Day; and last but not least, Euphoriale, a barleywine-style ale. The day that Todd brews it is a special event. He invites in the regulars and brings out older versions for a vertical tasting.

Pat said that the owners want Royal Oak Brewery to be "a destination that happens to be a brewery." It draws a loyal dinner crowd, with a good representation of families. "We're not a 'last call' bar," Pat told us. The most popular item by far is jambalaya, which goes so fast that it's made in half-barrel vessels. Pizzas are popular, too; they're made with spent grain and baked in a wood-fired oven.

Speaking of destinations, Royal Oak is "the place to be" for party-goers, and anything from the night before Thanksgiving to a Pistons playoff game is an excuse to party. Downtown can get packed, so bring along a sense of humor before you head out.

Class of license: Brewpub.

Opened: September 1995.

Owners: The Beer Companies. Drew Ciora and Mike Plesz are the principals; Pat Scanlon is the managing partner.

Brewer: Todd Parker.

System: 15-barrel Specific Mechanical. Capacity is about 1,000 barrels per year.

Production: 880 barrels in 2004. Expected to be slightly higher in 2005.

Hours: Monday through Thursday and Saturday, 11:30 A.M. to midnight; Friday, 11 A.M. to 2 A.M.; Sunday, noon to midnight.

Tours: When possible. Call in advance.

Take-out beer: Growlers, bottles, and kegs (by arrangement only).

Food: American, with some Southwest and Louisiana specialties. Many dishes are made with the house ales. Most items are made from scratch.

Extras: Guest ales, with regular themed tastings. Outdoor beer garden. Special events, including Barleywine Day February 20, Sunday Sun Splash in July, an anniversary party September 10, and Oktoberfest. Live music one Sunday a month. Occasional pub crawls. Free wireless Internet access.

Happy hour: Monday through Friday, 4 to 6 P.M., with discounts on pints and select appetizers.

Mug club: Membership is $35 a year. Benefits include discounts on beer and free beer on your birthday. The club is so popular that the waiting list is months long.

Parking: Parking can be a problem. There are nine spots on the wall next to the brewpub, but don't count on finding an empty one there. (See map on page 42.) You're more likely to find a space on the street east of the brewpub, but the free lot several blocks away at Eleven Mile and Troy is an even better bet.

Copper Canyon and Restaurant

27522 Northwestern Highway, Southfield, MI 48034
248-223-1700
www.coppercanyonbrewery.com

If there were such a thing as *Sesame Street* for grown-ups, this brewpub would be brought to you by the letter C. First, there's the name Copper Canyon. According to owner Ed Miri—more about him in a moment—he chose it because of the association between copper and high-quality cookware and to honor Michigan's copper-mining heritage.

Then there's the brewer, Chad McDaniels. He was a bit frazzled the day we stopped by, and understandably so. It was the hottest day of the year, and the air conditioner had just decided to quit. But he was a sport, bringing us a sampler and telling us his story. Copper Canyon is his first brewpub job. Until then, he'd worked at micros, including the Detroit and Mackinac Brewery. His beer education also includes working for a wholesaler, where he got acquainted with different beer styles and, of course, homebrewing.

Chad is active in the state's brewing circles. He's vice president of District Michigan of the Master Brewers Association of America, and he has hosted Michigan Brewers Guild beer competitions

Beers brewed: The menu beers are Copper Canyon Alt, Devil's Peak Ale, and Northwestern Gold. There is a rotating seasonal—a stout, wheat, or Scotch ale—as well as the newest, Imperial 7 C's IPA. Two beers are available on hand pull. Copper Canyon also brews Route 696 root beer.

at Copper Canyon. With those connections, it was inevitable that he'd join the "big beer" movement, which has become a signature of Michigan brewing.

Like many of his colleagues, Chad wishes that there were more demand for heartier beers. But he's making progress. Higher-gravity ales are showing up on the beer menu, and there are two cask beers as well. He's thinking about adding Belgians and a perhaps even a nitro-conditioned hefeweizen. And he unveiled a beer surprise, which we'll save for last.

Our Picks: An easy one for Maryanne: Seven C's IPA, which had just the right amount of hop bite. Paul chose McGonigle's Scotch Ale. Ordering a Scotch ale in a brewpub can be a crapshoot, but Copper Canyon's is true to style.

But first, let's go back to Ed Miri. He's part of metro Detroit's large Chaldean Christian population, who emigrated here from Iraq. Ed is a chemist; in fact, he's taught chemistry. And wouldn't you know it? He used to operate a coffee shop. So that explains that coffee grinder amid the comfy chairs in the waiting area.

Ed told us that this building housed a restaurant before he "gutted it to the four walls." The end result is somewhat unusual: blond wood and slate, more evocative of a steakhouse; low ceilings and subdued lighting; and little in the way of breweriana. But there's no doubt that you've come to a brewpub when you see the stainless steel grain silo in front (it works, too) and the brewing equipment in the front window. He told us that plans are in the works to expand both the kitchen and the patio. The brewery is running well under capacity and could easily handle the extra traffic.

There's plenty of potential traffic out there. Copper Canyon is located in the shadow of Southfield's office towers. The local happy-hour culture isn't what it used to be—tough DUI laws and corporate job cuts have seen to that—but it still draws a strong after-five clientele, including fans who come to watch the game over a pint or two as well as the dinner crowd.

We hope Chad's latest offering will lure them in. It's an imperial India pale ale called Seven C's. The beer is brewed with seven different hops, all of which start with the letter C: Centennial, Challenger, Chinook, Cluster, Columbus, and finally, Cascade and Crystal for dry-hopping.

Class of license: Brewpub.
Opened: August 1998.
Owner: Ed Miri.
Brewer: Chad McDaniels, head brewer; Bo Holcomb, assistant brewer.
System: 15-barrel JV Northwest. Capacity is about 1,000 barrels.
Production: 427 barrels in 2004. 500 barrels estimated for 2005.

Hours: Monday through Saturday, 11 A.M. to midnight; Sunday, 1 to 10 P.M. The kitchen closes earlier.

Tours: Yes, just ask.

Take-out beer: Growlers, keggies, and quarter and half barrels. Bottled beer will be added soon.

Food: Casual fare, for the most part. Dishes include salads, sandwiches and wraps, hamburgers, and pizzas. Some menu items are hot and spicy.

Extras: Meet the Brewer Night on Tuesday, with reduced pints. Outdoor patio. Special events, including an anniversary party, a St. Patrick's Day party, and Oktoberfest. Children's menu.

Happy hour: Monday through Friday, 4 to 6 P.M., only at the bar. Also discounted growlers Sundays and Wednesdays.

Mug club: Members get reduced pints and retail merchandise, a free birthday meal, and admission to the annual members-only party, with specially priced beer.

Parking: Lot in front of the brewpub. (See map on page 53.)

Directions: Copper Canyon is devilishly hard to find if you're not familiar with Southfield. Once you find the service drive, it gets easier. The brewpub is between an Asian restaurant and a motel, and there's a grain silo in front.

Etouffee

25333 West Twelve Mile Road, Southfield, MI 48304
248-750-0700
www.mattprenticerg.com/urc/etouffee.asp

Etouffee is Michigan's newest brewpub. The owner, Matt Prentice, is a successful area restaurateur. His first venture, Deli Unique in nearby Oak Park, was a longtime Oakland County icon, and he's been adding to his collection of establishments ever since. Not long ago, Matt broke into the brewpub business with the Thunder Bay Brewing Company, then moved on to Etouffee.

It's located inside the huge Star Theater movieplex, which faces Twelve Mile Road. Since the Star Theater opened, a number of theme restaurants have come and gone at this location. The most recent effort, before Etouffee, never opened its doors. A New York–based restaurant company tried to open a brewpub called the Starlight Brewery. Work progressed to the point where a 15-barrel system was ordered and installed, and construction was 80 percent complete. Then work abruptly stopped, and both the property and brewery stood idle for years.

If you're not familiar with etouffee, it's a spicy stew made with crawfish and vegetables and served over rice that's popular in Louisiana's Cajun country. So it's no surprise that the menu features Cajun and Creole as well as a healthy dose of soul food. The sleek interior is decorated with African American art. And to round out the atmosphere, jazz musicians perform three nights a week.

The brewhouse is located on the second floor—above the kitchen and behind glass. It's beautiful to look up at as you sit at the bar. Unfortunately, it's unfriendly to the brewer, to put it mildly. Etouffee's designers didn't get the concept that spent grains have to be removed. At least they made a last-minute accommodation, creating a hole about the size of a dinner plate that opens up on the floor below. The shoveled grains fall through to a bucket.

Brewer Marty Rapnicki, who's been pulling double duty here and at Thunder Bay, takes all this in stride, though. And the logistics haven't affected his beer. He's offering guests a solid range of five year-round beers and a rotating seasonal.

But sadly, too few of those guests have given the house beers a try. Marty told us that they've been selling more slowly than expected. Perhaps that will change as Etouffee tweaks its operation; we hope they'll do more to showcase the beer. After all, they've invested this much time and money in a brewing system and lined up a first-class brewer.

While very good beer is brewed at Etouffee, it is first and foremost a restaurant—and one consciously attempting to attract an upscale clientele. So if you're looking for somewhere to knock back and watch the game or hang out with friends after a morning of yard work, you might feel out of place here. Etouffee's sister brewpub, Thunder Bay, would be a better bet.

Beers brewed: There are six beers on tap. The menu beers are Dry Stout; Light; Golden Ale, a malt liquor; Pale Ale; and Raspberry Wheat. The sixth tap is a rotating seasonal. So far, Marty has brewed a red ale, an Oktoberfest, and a hefeweizen.

Our Pick: We both chose the Pale Ale, a nice representation of the style.

Class of license: Brewpub.
Opened: September 2005.
Owner: Matt Prentice Restaurant Group.

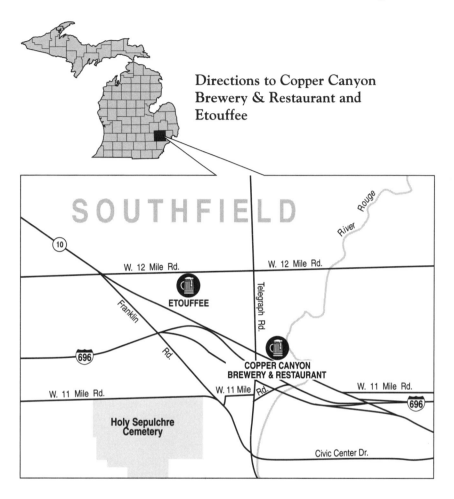

Directions to Copper Canyon Brewery & Restaurant and Etouffee

Brewer: Marty Rapnicki.

System: 15-barrel JV Northwest.

Production: 90 barrels in September through December 2005.

Hours: Monday through Wednesday, 11 A.M. to 10 P.M.; Thursday, 11 A.M. to midnight; Friday, 11 A.M. to 1 A.M.; Saturday, 5 P.M. to 1 A.M.; Sunday, 3 to 9 P.M.

Tours: Yes, ask if the brewer is available.

Take-out beer: Growlers, 5-gallon kegs, and half barrels.

Food: A decidedly upscale menu, featuring Cajun, Creole, and soul food dishes and Memphis-style barbecue.

Extras: Big-screen TVs in the bar area. Private dining room for special parties. Live jazz Thursdays through Saturdays. Dance floor.

Parking: Lot in front.

Big Rock Chop House

245 South Eton Street, Birmingham, MI 48009
248-647-7774
bigrockchophouse.com

Imagine first-class travel: attention to detail, comfort, and fine dining. And so it is at this 1931 Grand Trunk Western train station–turned–restaurant and now a brewpub. Big Rock Chop House is definitely upscale. Customers and customer loyalty are important here.

Some years ago, this was a clubby restaurant named Norman's Eton Street Station, where businesspeople dined on expense accounts. Savvy owners Norm and Bonnie LePage and Mary and Ray Nicholson did some renovating in the mid-nineties. Bowing to the latest trends, they added a martini and cigar bar, and they jumped into the craft-brew movement too.

Big Rock Chop House considers itself a fine-dining restaurant with an extensive wine cellar. The only beer it sells is its own, however. And our hunch is that its high-gravity series will grow rapidly.

The fermentation tanks are stationed behind glass on one side of the barroom, with the names and logos of the house ales in front of them. The O-shaped dark wood bar in the center of the barroom bristles with rows of taps for the house beers. Outside, hop bines grow on the beautiful canopied patio. And the beers brewed here are available throughout the complex.

The man brewing those beers is Dan Rogers, who returned to Michigan after starting his professional career out west. He was originally a chef in California and, later, Las Vegas, where he worked for Big Dog Hospitality. By that time, he'd joined the ranks of homebrewing enthusiasts. When Big Dog opened the Holy Cow! brewpub, he became the brewer there. Dan soon won a Gold Medal at the Great American Beer Festival and has entered his beers in that competition ever since.

Beers brewed: The menu beers are English Mild, Flying Buffalo Oatmeal Stout, India Pale Ale, Norm's Raggedy Ass Pale Ale, Platinum Blonde Lager, Raymondo El Rojo, and Russian Imperial Stout. Seasonals and specialties include Belgian Wit, Maibock, Rye Bock, Weisenheimer Hefeweizen, and a strong version of red ale called Big Rock Scotch Ale. Beer is sold in pints, half-pints, and samplers. Big Rock also brews ginger ale, root beer, and orange cream soda.

Awards won: 2002 GABF Bronze, Coffee Flavored; 2005 GABF Bronze, Imperial Stout.

After several years in Vegas, Dan decided that Michigan would be a better place to raise his two sons. He took a job at the Michigan Brewing Company, where he learned the art of brewing Belgian beers from Pierre Celis, who had come there to help relaunch the Celis brand in this country. Two years later, he moved on to Big Rock when its brewer went back to New York.

Our Picks: Dan's Russian Imperial Stout is a must try. We also awarded high marks to his very traditional Belgian Wit and Czech Pilsner.

Dan likes variety and would like to offer Big Rock's customers a full spectrum of beers. At the same time, he prefers beers that are true to style; he promised us that he'd brew "no marshmallow banana pineapple stout." Dan respects brewing tradition and counts Duvel and Orval, two Belgian classics, among his favorites. He also tries to work local products into his beer; his Belgian witbier is made with unmalted Michigan wheat. And speaking of local products, spent grain from Big Rock's brewing operation feeds a local bison farmer.

The end result of Dan's brewing philosophy is a six- to seven-beer range. It begins with a transition lager for macrobrew drinkers, but for more developed tastes, there's an India pale ale kicked up for hopheads, a reincarnation of the red ale that won him a GABF medal, and an English mild. At the big end of the spectrum, Dan's getting ready to add a Belgian trippel and a cherry trippel, some library beers, and barrel-aged specialties. With extra capacity to play with, he plans to round out his lager selection as well.

Then there's Dan's Russian Imperial Stout. It won a GABF Bronze when he was at Michigan Brewing, and he repeated that feat in 2005 with another version at Big Rock. It's likely to become the signature beer. And fittingly so. Even if you don't go there to close a big deal or celebrate that promotion, a snifter will have you feeling like a million bucks.

Class of license: Brewpub.
Opened: August 1997.
Owners: Norm and Bonnie LePage, Mary and Ray Nicholson.
Brewer: Dan Rogers.
System: 15-barrel DME. Capacity is 2,000 barrels.
Production: 300 barrels in 2004.
Hours: Monday through Friday, 11 A.M. to 2 A.M.; Saturday, noon to 2 A.M.; Sunday, 4 to 9 P.M.
Tours: Yes, just ask.
Take-out beer: Growlers and kegs.
Food: Big Rock is best described as a high-end chop house that specializes in hand-cut steaks and chops. In addition to beef entrees, the

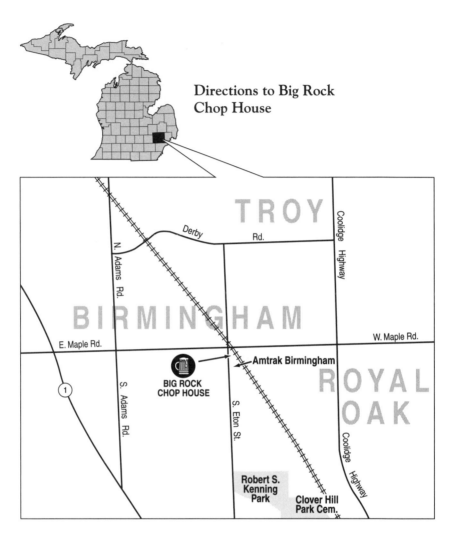

Directions to Big Rock Chop House

menu offers salads, sandwiches, and discounted bar appetizers during happy hour.

Extras: Live bands Wednesday and Thursday nights. Extensive collection of wines and single-malt scotches. A martini and cigar bar called Got Rocks is upstairs. New catering facility, the Reserve, on the premises. Covered terrace and patio.

Happy hour: Appetizer specials only.

Parking: Lot on the premises. Valet available.

King Brewing Company

895 Cesar Chavez Avenue, Pontiac, MI 48340
248-745-5900
www.kingbrewing.com

Pop quiz time. Everyone knows that Bell's is the state's oldest brewery, but which is the second oldest? Okay, time's up. It's King Brewing Company, which opened its doors in August 1994. The eponymous brewery (we couldn't wait to use that word) is owned by Scott King, who has also been at the brewery here since the day it opened.

Scott is the prototype of a hardy species known as the Michigan brewer-owner. He has deep roots in the state, got into the business for the love of beer, and is resourceful. That last quality has helped him endure the ups and downs of Michigan's brewing industry and outlast better-heeled competitors who have come and gone.

In addition to a diploma from the University of Michigan, Scott's credentials include homebrewing experience, beer judge certification, and a stint at several breweries while doing graduate work at the University of Colorado. Fortunately for Michigan craft-beer drinkers, he came back home.

Scott wound up in Pontiac because tonier suburbs said "not in my backyard" to the idea of a brewery. Officials in those communities envisioned noise, pollution, and alcohol abuse and couldn't see the benefits. Besides, in the early nineties, few people understood the concept of a microbrewery. Pontiac was willing to work with Scott, and rents were low. Scott set up shop in a building in the industrial district north of downtown whose past tenants included a collision shop and a lawn-mower dealer.

No, Scott didn't brew lawn-mower beer. His first offerings were English-style ales, and over the years he moved into other styles, including several big beers that have become the rage in this state. Early on, he concentrated on the brewing side of his business. For a brewer, that would seem the log-

Beers brewed: The six menu beers are Continental Lager; IPA; Crown Brown Ale; Irish Red, the biggest seller; King Pale; and Pontiac Porter. Seasonals include Two Fisted Old Ale, Doppelbock, Hefeweizen, Oktoberfest, and King's Cherry Ale, made with Traverse City cherries.

Our Pick: King's Hefeweizen. It is golden-colored and slightly hazy (chill haze), and on the hot afternoon of our visit, it was a welcome smooth thirst-quencher.

ical decision. But around here, beer drinkers expect their local micro to have a taproom as well.

King Brewing was open just twelve hours a week, which was one reason why it hit a rough patch. After boosting production to several thousand barrels a year—which ranked it number two in the state—production fell to a trickle. Some even wondered whether the brewery was going to survive. But Scott turned things around. Drawing on his experience as a chef in Colorado, he designed an expanded food menu and extended its open hours.

The taproom is becoming a bistro where food and beer are both important. On the small side, with room for seventy or so, it's dominated by a bar topped with Italian marble. The interior is painted in pastel colors, with some brewing-themed posters and photos and art reproductions. There's stained glass in the picture windows to make the interior cheerier and soft lighting overhead. The beer is served in matching glassware, as it would be in a Belgian bistro.

With its revamped menu, King Brewing is pulling in a good-size lunch crowd from the huge county government complex nearby. In the evening, the clientele runs toward beer fans who've heard of King via word of mouth plus the occasional beer pilgrim from outside the area. Still, Scott's first priority remains the beer. He told us that his goal is a simple one—namely, "to provide metro Detroit with the freshest, most consistent and genuine beer available." For now, he's content to concentrate on Oakland County, a market that, with a population of more than a million, will keep him busy.

If a genie were to grant Scott three wishes, his first would be for Michiganders to drink locally. As he explained to us: "People here support local car companies. Wouldn't you think they'd support a local beer?" Point well taken, Scott.

Class of license: Microbrewery.
Opened: August 1994.
Owner-brewer: Scott King
System: 15-barrel Criveller.
Production: 1,000 barrels in 2004. King Brewing also produces private-brand beer for local bars.
Distribution: Bottles are available in selected stores in southeast Michigan.
Hours: Monday through Thursday, 11 A.M. to 11 P.M.; Friday and Saturday, 11 A.M. to 1 A.M. Closed Sunday.
Tours: Yes, just ask.
Take-out beer: Bottles, growlers, and kegs.

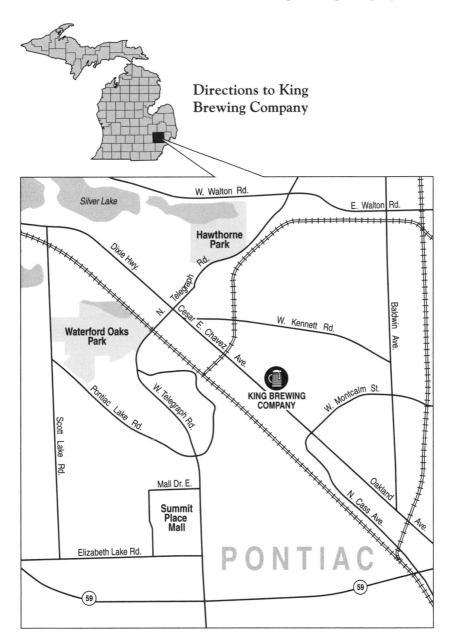

Directions to King Brewing Company

Food: Bistro fare, with international dishes, sandwiches, and wraps among the featured dishes. Children's menu.

Extras: Beer is served in glassware that's appropriate for the style. Several special events every year. The anniversary party is the biggest. Open mike on Wednesday nights.

Happy hour: Daily, 4 to 6 P.M. On Monday, there's a burger and beer
  combo special. On Wednesday, customers get reduced growler refills
  with the purchase of an entree.
Parking: Small lot adjacent to the brewery.
Directions: Oakland Avenue became Cesar Chavez Avenue a few years
  ago, but many locals still use the old name. It's also referred to as
  Business U.S. 24.

Bo's Brewery and Bistro

51 North Saginaw Street, Pontiac, MI 48342
248-338-6200
www.bosbrewery.com

Michiganders enjoy living large. They drive big cars; eat big meals; and
lately, have developed a taste for big beers. It's a trend that we first
noticed a few years ago at the Brewers Guild's annual beer festival. Big
beer is a Michigan brewing trademark, and Bo's Brewery and Bistro
makes the biggest beers in the state.

First, let us introduce you to Bo. His real name is Burgess Young,
the now semiretired owner of the brewpub. If you see a gent inside Bo's
who looks a lot like Kris Kringle, that's him.

Burgess and his sons fell in love with microbrewed beer on a trip to Steamboat Springs, Colorado. The Youngs decided to open their own
brewery in Michigan and settled on Pontiac because
they wanted to be part of a downtown environment.
Once they got into the beermaking business, Burgess
and son Doug decided to "walk the walk": They
took brewing courses. But they've left the brewing
chores to others. Currently, the man with the paddle
is Wayne Burns, who happens to be Michigan's big-
beer king.

When Wayne started brewing, his first love
was Belgian-style beers. He got into big beers soon
after his wedding. It was a story of bride ale in

Beers brewed: The menu
beers are Blond, Seminole
Hills Red, White Lake Wheat,
and North 51 Pale Ale. There
is always one high-gravity
beer on tap. Seasonals include
Boberry Wheat, Oktoberfest,
and Irish Stout. Also brews
root beer.

Our Picks: Paul enjoyed the
Extreme IPA that has four different hops. Maryanne found
the Solar Eclipse Imperial
Stout smooth—incredibly
so for 21 percent ABV.

reverse. Wayne wanted to thank a friend who'd mixed the music for the reception. His friend asked him to brew him a batch of imperial stout. Ever since, he's been scaling higher and higher peaks.

With his Solar Eclipse, Wayne reached Himalayan heights. It's an imperial stout that checks in at 21 percent ABV, putting him in a league with Samuel Adams's Utopias and Dogfish Head's World Wide Stout. In recent years, he also turned out an ultrastrong Grand Cru, an Amber Eisbock, and his most often quaffed big beer, Extreme IPA. It's what Bo's calls "a particularly intense" version of an American imperial IPA, with copious amounts of four different hops and an 11 percent alcoholic wallop.

But Wayne's smaller beers have gained a following as well. Because the brewery has plenty of excess capacity, he can afford to add lagers to the lineup. In fact, the brewpub's flagship beer, Blonde Ale, has been relaunched as a lager.

If you drive down Saginaw Street, it isn't hard to find the brewpub. It's the building with the the copper-clad, steam-fired brewkettle in the picture window. Before the Youngs turned the building into a brewpub, it housed an office supply store and, before that, an Osmun's department store. You can still see the Osmun's logo, inlaid in tile, as you walk in the front entrance. The main level, by the way, used to be the store's bargain basement.

The interior decor, which has been described as eclectic, features brick walls and breweriana, as well as fish tanks, flags, and an odd piñata or three. There's a big second-floor loft with plenty of seating and room for entertainers, a banquet room, and an outdoor patio that's very popular for two annual events: the Woodward Dream Cruise and the Arts, Eats, and Beats festival.

Man does not live by beer alone. Bo's seventy-item food menu features rotating lunch and dinner specials and a wide range of pub-grub favorites, including the signature dish, personal pizzas. House ales go into a variety of menu items, including something out-of-staters might consider an acquired taste: fried pickles.

In recent years, Pontiac has suffered. Factories have packed up or closed down, and to add insult to injury, the Lions fled back to Detroit. But downtown Pontiac has become a destination for nightclubbers. With any luck, it might become a destination for beer aficionados as well.

Class of license: Brewpub.
Opened: August 1996.
Owner: Burgess "Bo" Young.

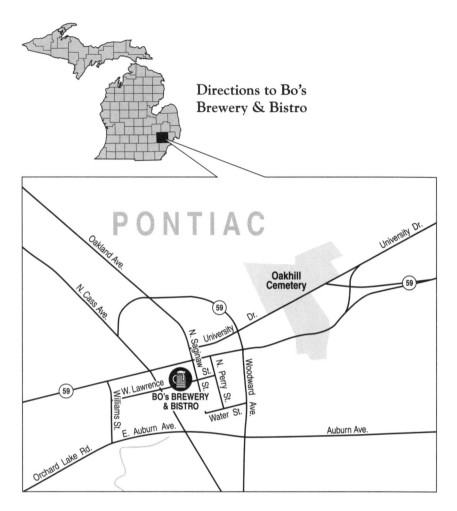

Directions to Bo's
Brewery & Bistro

Brewer: Wayne Burns.

System: 15-barrel Bohemian. Capacity is 1,200 to 1,400 barrels.

Production: 330 barrels in 2004.

Hours: Monday through Thursday, 11 A.M. to midnight; Friday, 11 A.M. to 2 A.M.; Saturday, noon to 2 A.M. Closed Sunday.

Tours: Yes, call ahead.

Take-out beer: Growlers and kegs.

Food: Diverse casual and pub menu, with daily specials.

Extras: Lively crowd gathers to watch Pistons games.

Parking: Metered street parking. Municipal lots within walking distance. During the day, Bo's will validate for the lot on the southwest corner of Huron and Saginaw.

Thunder Bay Brewing Company

Great Lakes Crossing
4362 Baldwin Road, Auburn Hills, MI 48326
248-454-8486
mattprenticerg.com/urc/thunderbay.asp

Sitting on the front porch of the Grand Hotel on Mackinac Island is one of Michigan's great experiences. However, you have to pony up $10 for the privilege. But if you go to the Thunder Bay Brewing Company, you can sit on a replica of that porch for free—and use the ten bucks to buy a couple of pints.

This brewpub started life as part of the Alcatraz chain, which opened along with the mall in 1988. But Alcatraz's fortunes took a turn for the worse, and it pulled out of Auburn Hills. That created an opportunity for a local restaurateur, Matt Prentice, to get into the brewpub business. He recently opened a second establishment, Etouffee, in Southfield.

Alcatraz's San Francisco-esque decor, which included a mini–Golden Gate Bridge and a lighthouse, gave Matt an idea: Why not give it an all-Michigan makeover? The bridge became a replica of the Mackinac Bridge, one of the state's most-beloved icons, and the lighthouse was joined by photographs of Michigan's lighthouses—105 in all. Even the name has a Michigan connection: Thunder Bay, in Lake Huron, is the site of a number of shipwrecks. It's been designated a marine sanctuary, off-limits to curious scuba divers.

Matt didn't stop there. He dedicated a wall to Michigan rockers, such as Bob Seger, Ted Nugent, and Kid Rock, and put in a Motown-themed nook with photos from the "Hitsville U.S.A." era. High up on a back wall are retro picture postcards from Up North. You have heard of the Mystery Spot, right? And Matt didn't forget sports fans: Steve Yzerman, Al Kaline, Ben Wallace, and Barry Sanders

Beers brewed: The five menu beers are Freighters Ale, a red ale; Great Lakes Light; Motorhead IPA; Petoskey Pilsner; and Pewamo Porter. Seasonals include a Kölsch-style beer, a hefeweizen, an Oktoberfest, and a Russian imperial stout.

Our Picks: Paul is always up for an India pale ale, and he had no difficulty choosing Motorhead IPA, an American (read: hoppy) version. Maryanne's pick was the Kölsch, a tough style that American craft brewers have begun to master.

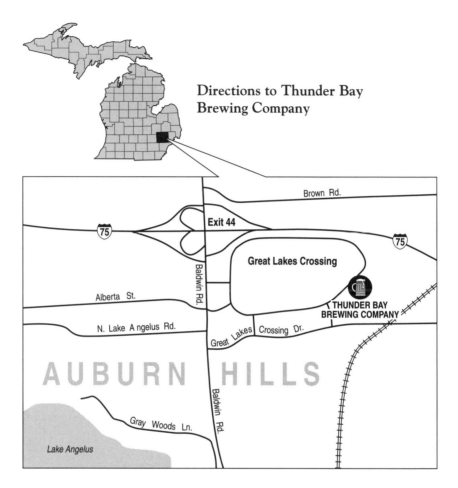

Directions to Thunder Bay Brewing Company

stare back at you from behind the bar. Even the place mats used for beer samplers are filled with Michigan fun facts. Did you know we have a state turtle?

Fittingly, brewer Marty Rapnicki was born and raised in Michigan—Detroit, to be exact. Marty took an unusual road to the brewhouse. He gave up a well-paying job as a plumber to follow his passion for brewing beer. And he's amassed quite a résumé. His first professional job was at the Big Buck Brewery and Steakhouse up the road, followed by stints at the Rochester Mills Beer Company and Royal Oak Brewery, before he came back to Auburn Hills during the Alcatraz days. After helping open Bastone, he came back to Thunder Bay. Why not? He already knew the brewing system.

Marty said that he aims to brew true to style. Thunder Bay's menu beers are very accessible—his rendition of national-brand lager is the leading seller—but his seasonals and specialties run toward German styles. Oktoberfest, he told us, is his favorite style. And yes, the beers are named for Michigan people and places. Marty also admitted that he's a busy man these days, commuting between Thunder Bay and Etouffee.

Thunder Bay's food menu also has a Michigan theme, featuring such dishes as venison chili, turkey salad with Traverse City cherries, Upper Peninsula pasties, Great Lakes perch and whitefish, and bumpy cake. Marty's beers go into some menu items: pilsner in the ribs, India pale ale in the cheddar ale soup, and porter in the chili. Thunder Bay also plans to offer a brewer's dinner four times a year.

Thunder Bay is a Michigan mini–theme park with a brewery inside. It's a place where a visitor can literally drink in the history and lore of our state. You couldn't ask for a more enjoyable form of education.

Class of license: Brewpub.
Opened: June 2004.
Owner: Matt Prentice Restaurant Group.
Brewer: Marty Rapnicki.
System: 15-barrel DME. Capacity is 1,100 barrels per year.
Production: 550 barrels in 2004; 1,100 barrels for the twelve months ending June 2005.
Hours: Monday through Thursday, 11 A.M. to 10 P.M.; Friday and Saturday, 11 A.M. to 11 P.M.; Sunday, 11:30 A.M. to 8 P.M.
Tours: Yes, please call ahead.
Take-out beer: Growlers, 5-gallon kegs, and quarter and half barrels.
Food: Informal family fare with a Michigan theme.
Extras: Beer Night on the second Thursday of the month, hosted by Marty Rapnicki, Bill Wamby of Redwood Brewing, Andy Rathaus of Sullivan's Black Forest Brau Keller, and Rex Halfpenny of the *Michigan Beer Guide*. Quarterly brewer's dinners. Occasional live entertainment.
Happy hour: Monday through Friday, 4 to 7 P.M., with discounts on pints. Specials on Sunday.
Mug club: Annual membership is $35. Benefits include a logo polo shirt, discounts on mugs and growlers, and special previews of new arrival beers with happy-hour prices and appetizers.
Parking: Large lot surrounding the mall. Be sure to park near District 6, at the south end of the mall near the Star Theater movieplex.

Big Buck Brewery and Steakhouse #3

2550 Takata Drive, Auburn Hills, MI 48326
248-276-2285
bigbuck.com

A bit of trivia: The Big Buck Brewery and Steakhouse in Auburn Hills is 202 miles from the original location in Gaylord. But it offers the same cozy Up North feeling amid the shopping malls and office towers of Oakland County. A local restaurant critic described it as "a rustic, autumn kind of place." One that evokes the Michigan ritual of deer season.

Big Buck is the closest equivalent to a brewpub chain in Michigan. At one time, it had three locations in Michigan, but location #2, in Grand Rapids, closed some years ago. The company endured serious financial problems (see the chapter on Big Buck #1 in Gaylord) but survived them and appears to be on the way back.

The look and feel of the Gaylord location have been replicated here. You'll find the giant beer bottle that doubles as a grain silo, the hunting-lodge decor, fixtures made out of deer antlers, and the church-like arrangement of the brewery. But there's one noticeable difference: With a capacity of 651, this brewpub is even bigger than the original.

There are more subtle differences as well. Inside the lobby, there's a cooler filled with party pigs. Big Buck sells about thirty a week, which they say is more than any other brewpub in the state. The bar area, in front, is dominated by a large bar that features a brewkettle on which the taps are mounted and a cluster of TV screens overhead. This is the only place where smoking is permitted. Blackboards near the bar list what's on tap.

Farther back is the dining area. The way in is flanked by two wood carvings, one of a bear, the other of three bears in a tree; they're the work of a northern Michigan artist. Take a look back over your shoulder, and you'll see a row of deer heads on the wall. Jose Ortiz, the general manager, said that

Beers brewed: Menu beers are Antler Ale, an amber ale; Big Buck; Buck Naked; IPA; Redbird Ale; and Black River Stout. Seasonals include Belgian Grand Cru, Doc's ESB, Doppelbock, Hefeweizen, Munich Helles, Raspberry Wheat, and Steam Beer.

Our Pick: We both chose the India Pale Ale, which was unfiltered, moderately hopped, and definitely on the potent side.

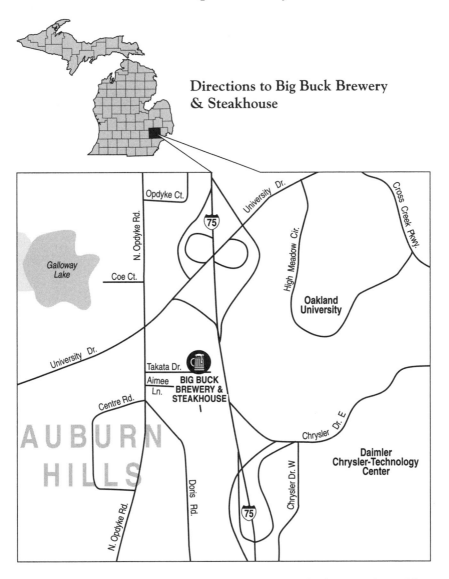

Directions to Big Buck Brewery
& Steakhouse

the heads were donated by deer hunters who got lucky. He also told us that the tables and chairs were made by hand by Michigan Amish craftspeople, and that the barstools are works of art worth $500 apiece.

Finally, you reach the quiet area in the back beneath the service bar and the fermentation tanks. Jose said that even when the room is crowded, noise doesn't interfere with conversation. The brewing equipment is displayed behind glass, with a green neon deer head above it. At night, Big Buck leaves the brewery lights on as a greeting to passing motorists on I-75.

Here, as in Gaylord, the management has gone back to a meat-and-potatoes menu that was so popular in Big Buck's early days. The aim is to offer high-end food, especially steaks, at more reasonable prices than other local restaurants. It has brought in a new executive chef and plans to offer brewer's dinners, food-and-beer pairings, and perhaps even guest speakers.

Which brings us to the brewer. His name is Forrest Knapp, and he was elevated to head brewer shortly before we stopped in to see him. His background is in carpentry, and strangely, he didn't homebrew before going professional. His version of Big Buck, the flagship, is a Kölsch-style ale. Forrest's favorite beer is Belgian Grand Cru, which he makes with local honey.

Forrest describes the brewery as "one of the most brewer-friendly in Michigan." It's a 15-barrel JV Northwest system, with twenty-six fermentation tanks. Capacity is much higher than production—the result of Big Buck's early days as a microbrewery with ambitions of distributing tens of thousands of barrels of bottled beer. The brewery is one of the most impressive in the state to tour.

The brewpub is a short drive from The Palace of Auburn Hills, where the Detroit Pistons play. If you ask the bar staff nicely, they'll tell you how to get there via the "secret backroads." Big Buck has taken a page out of the Pistons' playbook. Through hard work, it has rediscovered the winning formula.

Class of license: Brewpub.
Opened: October 1997.
Owners: Publicly held, no longer traded.
Brewer: Forrest Knapp, head brewer; Jude Audrich, assistant brewer.
System: 15-barrel JV Northwest. Capacity is 15,000 barrels.
Production: 1,802 barrels in 2004.
Hours: Monday through Thursday, 11 A.M. to 11 P.M.; Friday and Saturday, 11 A.M. to 1 A.M. (kitchen closes at midnight); Sunday, 11 A.M. to 10 P.M.
Tours: Yes, just ask.
Take-out beer: Party pigs and quarter and half barrels.
Food: Premium steaks and a variety of chicken, seafood, and pasta dishes. The house beers are used in fish and chips, beer cheese soup, stout cheesecake, and beer-flavored bratwurst. There's a smokehouse for ribs.
Extras: No smoking except in the bar area. Free shuttle to Detroit Pistons games. Wireless Internet hot spot. Annual Oktoberfest. Occa-

sional live entertainment, usually in the late fall and winter. "Little Buck" menu for children.

Happy hour: Daily, 4 to 6 P.M. and 10 P.M. to midnight, with discounts on pints.

Mug club: Management is revamping the program.

Parking: Lot adjacent.

Rochester Mills Beer Company

400 Water Street, Rochester, MI 48307
248-650-5080
www.rochestermillsbeerco.com

One hundred years ago, the Western Knitting Mill was one of the area's biggest employers. Today the mill is the home of one of Michigan's biggest brewpubs, the Rochester Mills Beer Company.

A mill stood on this site since the 1830s, and the present brick building, constructed by Western, dates back to 1896. As you approach from the parking lot, look toward the top of the building; you'll see the company name. By the standards of the time, Western provided a safe and comfortable environment in which employees knitted gloves, mittens, and socks. That kind of work has long since been automated and sent overseas, and the factory eventually stood empty for more than ten years.

In the 1990s, a group of investors realized the potential of a historic building just two blocks from downtown. They restored it to its original design, including hardwood floors, columns, and exposed brick walls. Restored and refurbished, it attracted professionals who have offices here. And Rochester Mills, which is the anchor tenant.

Rochester Mills is the second of the three Beer Companies, and the owners didn't skimp in building it. Its interior evokes the former knitting mill, with high wooden ceilings, exposed brick walls and ductwork, and industrial-style lighting fixtures. Dozens of dark wooden tables that seat two to six are

Beers brewed: There are eight menu beers on tap. The year-round beers are Buckshot ESB, Cornerstone IPA, Harvest Lite, Lazy Daze Lager, Paint Creek Porter, Rochester Red, and Water Street Wheat. Sacri-Licious Stout rotates with Milk Shake Stout. Seasonals include Oktoberfest, Maibock, dunkelweizen, barleywine, and doppelbock. Beer is served in samplers, 12- and 16-ounce glasses, and pitchers.

Awards won: 2005 GABF Bronze, Classic Irish-Style Dry Stout.

arranged around the room. In the middle are five tan-topped pool tables and, above them, a blackboard advertising happy-hour specials.

Brewery posters and photos of the mill in its heyday decorate the interior, along with some hanging plants. To remind us that this is the twenty-first century, not the nineteenth, television screens are everywhere, even inside the restrooms. After looking around, we found a quiet corner table where we talked with Gerry Barnewold, the managing partner, and Eric Briggeman, the brewer.

Our Picks: Maryanne's top choice was Rochester Red, a malty and slightly sweet version of a red ale. Paul gave the nod to Sacri-Licious Stout, a dry stout made in the Irish style and one of the best dry stouts he's had in Michigan.

Eric, who was born in Rochester, brewed at Big Buck Brewery and Steakhouse in Auburn Hills before joining Rochester Mills in 2005. He described himself as largely self-taught and said he'd spent a great deal of time hitting the books. His brewing interests run the gamut; he told us, "I don't order the same beer twice." Like many Michigan brewers, Eric is fond of big beers, but he draws the line at "over-the-top" styles.

Brewing is a business, of course, and Eric offers beer that's true to style yet appeals to customers. His year-round lineup runs mostly toward British styles, but he also makes a lager and a wheat beer, and the seasonals have a strong German accent. Recently, Eric brewed an altbier in an effort to get mass-market-lager drinkers to try craft beer.

Rochester Mills invests in the area's beer culture. The local homebrew club, one of Michigan's largest, meets here, and the staff try to educate customers about beer, even making suggestions about what beers pair well with food. Tutored tastings and brewer's dinners could be in the works as well.

Since this is one of the Beer Companies, Gerry told us, food gets a high priority. The chef makes an effort to work the house beers into the menu, which includes a beer cheese soup, served in a beer-grain mold; marinated pork cutlets and St. Louis ribs marinated in ale; and even gelato topped with stout. The menu is popular with families and has helped attract a loyal, largely thirty-and-over clientele.

In just seven years, Rochester Mills Brewing Company has integrated itself into the community. It is active in local organizations and events, including a family-style Oktoberfest that's become the second-largest such event in Michigan. It's all part of an effort to become "your neighborhood brewpub."

Class of license: Brewpub.
Opened: June 1998.
Owners: Drew Ciora and Mike Plesz.

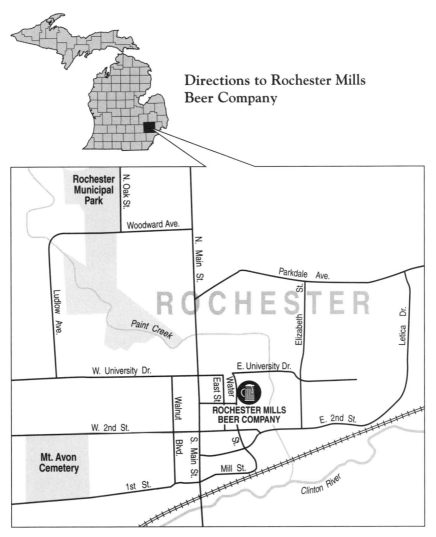

Directions to Rochester Mills Beer Company

Brewer: Eric Briggeman, head brewer.

System: 15-barrel Specific Mechanical for regular production. Capacity is 2,700 barrels per year. Also a 1-barrel Specific Mechanical system for experimental batches.

Production: 1,300 barrels in 2004.

Hours: Monday through Wednesday, 11:30 A.M. to midnight; Thursday through Saturday, 11:30 A.M. to 2 A.M.; Sunday, noon to midnight.

Tours: Yes, please call ahead.

Take-out beer: Bottles, growlers, Cornelius kegs, keggies, and quarter and half barrels.

Food: Eclectic American menu, with some Southwest and Louisiana specialties. Most items are made from scratch.

Extras: Special tastings when new specialty beers go on tap. Special events, including an anniversary party in June, Oktoberfest, a chili cookoff, and the Christmas parade afterglow. Live entertainment, with dancing, on Friday and Saturday nights. Martini and cigar lounge. Outdoor patio. Free wireless Internet access. NTN trivia.

Happy hour: Monday through Friday, 4 to 6 P.M., with reduced prices on pints and select appetizers.

Mug club: Membership costs $35 a year. For $15 more, membership is available at all three Beer Companies. Benefits include reduced-price mugs, an annual party, discounts on merchandise, and free birthday beer.

Parking: Available in the adjoining lot. Please don't park in someone else's assigned space.

CJ's Brewing Company

8115 Richardson Road, Commerce Township, MI 48382
248-366-7979
www.cjsbrewing.com

We've been to dozens of establishments that advertise handcrafted beer, but not many can boast that they're also handcrafted breweries. But one that can make that claim is CJ's Brewery, a gem of a brewpub in Oakland County's lake district.

"CJ" refers to Cary Moore, the founder, who ran several pizzerias before deciding to open a brewpub. A builder by trade, Moore literally built CJ's by hand, down to the brickwork and tables. Take a good look at the interior, and you'll swear that CJ's is a lot more than eight years old. That was certainly our reaction.

Moore decided to offer his hometown a "friendly local." With 180 seats, it's one of the smaller family-owned brewpubs in Michigan. That's just the way Moore wanted it. It's family-friendly, with a "Kids Eat Free" promotion on Sunday; it has hosted high school reunions and corporate outings; and it has become a magnet for the area's craft-beer lovers.

Beers brewed: The menu beers are Golden Lager, Vat 33 IPA, Rich-Hagg Red Ale, Honey Brown Wheat, and Lower Straits Stout. Seasonals include Big Saint Nick Barley-wine, Belgian White, Summer Brew, and Oktoberfest.

Dan Scarsella, the current owner, has been the brewer at CJ's almost from day one. He is a quietly intense individual, and it occurred to us as he told his story that he was probably destined to brew. He grew up almost in the shadow of the Stroh brewery on Detroit's East Side and was guided into home-brewing by his father. A biology major in college, Dan saw brewing as a series of science projects. Heaven, to him, is a plateful of problems to solve.

Our Picks: Maryanne picked the Summer Brew, a golden-colored seasonal flavored with honey and orange peel, so smooth that we didn't realize it carried a 7.5 percent alco-holic punch until we glanced at the menu. Paul really liked the Golden Lager and found it quite refreshing on a hot day.

Dan loves to tinker with his beer recipes, so before setting out, you might want to check out CJ's website to find out what's on tap. As you might expect, he prefers hands-on brewing to the high-tech, fully computerized operations found in some breweries. Recently, Dan has gotten his hands on more tanks, which will allow him to expand his range of beers to a dozen or so. That range starts with a pre-Prohibition-style Golden Lager, a good introduction for those who think they won't like craft-brewed beer. At only 3.8 percent ABV, it's accessible, too. From there, beers get bigger and bolder.

Dan's talents extend to the kitchen, where you might find him when he isn't in the brewhouse. He designed CJ's menu, which features fresh chips and salsa, half-pound burgers, and Voodoo Skins, potato skins filled with blackened chicken and cheese. Then there's the specialty of the house: chicken breast breaded in Cap'n Crunch cereal, pan fried, and topped off with honey mustard sauce. Dan tries to work the house beers into his menu and proudly told us, "Every day is a brewer's dinner here."

One of CJ's most pleasant features is the Hop Garden Patio, where healthy hop vines, which originally grew on Dan's grandparents' farm, shelter customers from the summer sun while providing the ideal backdrop for enjoying good beer. When fall arrives, Dan harvests the hop cones and uses them in a special seasonal beer. Last year, it was an India pale ale.

The brewpub's decor includes the brewing equipment, which you can see from the bar and most of the dining area. It also features the largest collection of breweriana in the state. When the Oldenberg brewery in Kentucky closed down, its huge collection of signs, tap handles, and whatnot went on the auction block. Dan bought some of it for CJ's, then tastefully arranged those items—along with some contributed by customers—on the walls.

Class of license: Brewpub.
Opened: December 1997.
Owner-brewer: Dan Scarsella.

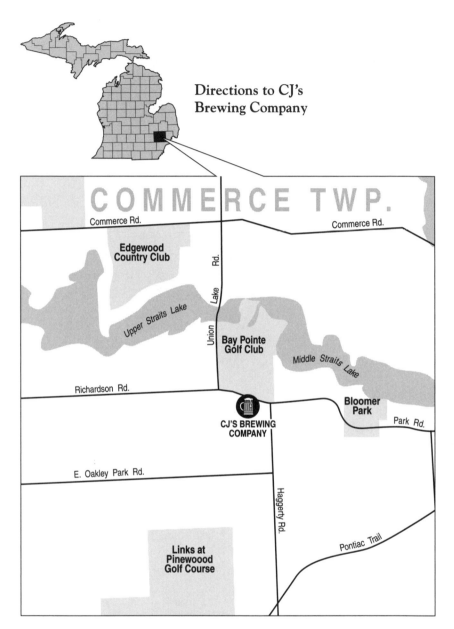

Directions to CJ's
Brewing Company

System: 7-barrel DME. Capacity is 900 barrels.
Production: Slightly over 700 barrels in 2004.
Hours: Monday through Saturday, 11 A.M. to midnight (taproom closes at 2 A.M.); Sunday, noon to 10 P.M.
Tours: Yes, by request.
Take-out beer: Six-packs.

Food: Family-friendly menu, with some spicy dishes to pair with beer. House beers go into a number of menu items.

Extras: Extensive collection of breweriana. Outdoor patio with hop bines. Annual Oktoberfest with pig roast. Live entertainment for special occasions.

Parking: Lot in back. Dan asks that you not park in the adjacent lot, which belongs to another business.

Bonfire Bistro and Brewery

39550 Seven Mile Road, Northville, MI 48167
248-735-4570
www.michiganmenu.com/bonfire.html

Welcome to Detroit's western suburbs, the part of the world we call home. Out here, streets are laid out on an orderly grid, big-box stores and strip malls attract shoppers, and people live in nice, orderly subdivisions. Amid all this development—critics call it sprawl—is the brewpub closest to our home, the Bonfire Bistro and Brewery.

Bonfire's welcome starts with decorative hop bines near the front door and a glimpse of the brewhouse in the window. Once inside, you're greeted by the aroma of burning wood. The brewpub got its name from the way food is cooked here. We're talking open flame and real wood, and not just a wood-fired oven, but a grill and rotisserie as well. Wood-fired cooking is a trademark of brewpubs owned or managed by Schelde Enterprises.

Although it was a brewpub from the day it opened, Bonfire had a reputation as a white-tablecloth bistro. It was slowly transformed from bistro to brewpub, and steps were taken to give the house beers a more prominent role. Recent changes include tearing down dividing walls to make the

Beers brewed: Bonfire has eight beers on tap. The five menu beers are Burning Brand Bitter, Firelight Lager, Promethean Porter, Roaring Red Ale, and Vulcan's Vienna Ale. There are two seasonal beers; in the past, they've included a doppelbock, a Maibock, a pale ale, an American IPA, an Okoberfest, an imperial stout, and barrel-aged Scottish ale. There's a rotating cask ale as well. Bonfire also brews root beer, and one of the ingredients is sassafras.

interior less formal and directing staff to say, "Bonfire Brewery," when they pick up the phone.

Vance Powell is in charge of brewing here. We caught up with him on the back patio on a pleasant July afternoon. He grew up just a mile away, when this area was largely undeveloped. Vance took an unusual path to the head brewer's position. He worked in the food industry for years and learned to appreciate good beer while working at Arbor Brewing Company.

Our Pick: Vulcan's Vienna Ale Over the years, it has been the pint we most often ordered, so that settles it. You're probably asking, what's a "Vienna ale"? It's a bit like an altbier, a bit like a Vienna lager. See for yourself why we like it.

His big break at Bonfire was like that scene in a movie when the star gets hurt and the understudy has to step in. When the brewer at Bonfire left, the Schelde people needed a replacement, and fast. Vance persuaded them to give him the job, and he was given a crash course by another Schelde brewer, Ron Jeffries. Until then, Powell told us with a laugh, "the only thing I brewed was coffee."

Vance might look laid-back, but he frequently puts in fourteen- to sixteen-hour days, often starting early in the morning before Bonfire opens. He also describes himself as a clean freak and says that his brewery is so spick-and-span that some customers don't believe beer is actually made there. (He's willing to show skeptics, or anyone else, that it is.)

Although many Michigan brewers have gravitated to bold, powerful beers, Powell hasn't followed the trend. He prefers flavorful beers with relatively low alcohol content. His beers don't just refresh customers, but they also show up in quite a few menu items, including onion soup, the marinade for pulled pork, fish and chips batter, and Gorgonzola dip.

There aren't many brewpubs in the western 'burbs, thanks in part to tough zoning restrictions and the high price of real estate. As a result, Vance has had to ease the locals into craft beer. He says he's making progress; they're advancing from his entry-level Firelight Lager to his more distinctive beers. Now customers eagerly await his monthly firkin tapping.

The clientele tends to be thirty and up, with a heavy representation of business customers and couples who come for dinner. The atmosphere is low-key and friendly, with a minimum of electronic distractions and music that doesn't overpower conversation, though there are a few TVs handy for sports fans.

Bonfire is an old friend of ours. It's a place we've visited often, whether to unwind after shopping or try to get past a bout of writer's block. But we're happy to share it with our beer friends, old and new alike. Come on down. The beer is great and so is the food.

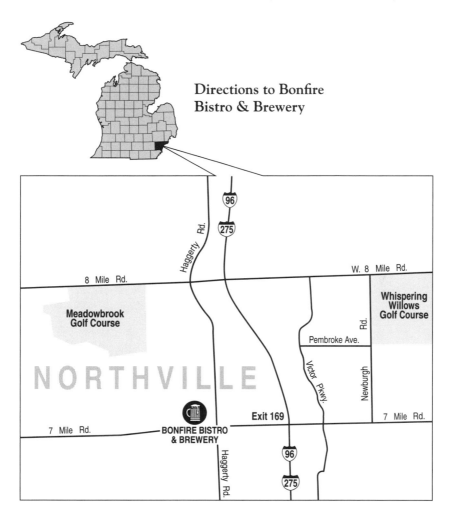

Directions to Bonfire
Bistro & Brewery

Class of license: Brewpub.

Opened: March 1999.

Owner: Schelde Enterprises.

Brewer: Vance Powell III.

System: 10-barrel Global. Capacity is somewhere between 800 and 1,000 barrels.

Production: 660 barrels in 2004.

Hours: Monday through Saturday, 11 A.M. to midnight; Sunday, 11 A.M. to 10 P.M.

Tours: Yes, call ahead. Bonfire is considering scheduled tours with tasting.

Take-out beer: Growlers, kegs, and keggies.

Food: The menu features wood-fired dishes, including steaks, pizza, and rotisserie chicken. It's kid-friendly, and kids love the pizza and cheese sticks.

Extras: Wheelchair accessible. Outdoor patio in back.

Happy hour: One of the best brewpub happy hours in the state, 3 to 6 P.M. and 9 P.M. until closing daily, with discounts on pints, chicken wings, and cheese sticks. Discounts on growlers on Wednesdays and Sundays. Also, buy six growlers and get the seventh for $1.

Mug club: Benefits include members-only tastings, 25-ounce mugs for the price of a pint, and pub quizzes.

Parking: Large parking lots on either side of the brewpub.

Michigan Icons

Ask a Michigander where he or she lives, and if it's outside the metro Detroit area, the person will answer your question by holding up the right hand, palm facing toward you, and pointing to a place on the hand. Michigan's Lower Peninsula very closely resembles the inside of your right hand. Our official state name is the Great Lake State, but don't be surprised if you hear someone refer to the "mitten."

Now, about those Great Lakes. Michigan borders four: Michigan, Superior, Huron, and Erie. There are 38,375 square miles of Great Lakes and three thousand shipwrecks in them. They're beautiful to look at and there's lots of recreational enjoyment—fishing, sailing, and swimming—but beware of the temperature before you go in. Lake Superior is so cold that most people simply dip their toes in the water.

The Mackinac Bridge, which connects the Lower and Upper Peninsulas, is the state's most recognizable icon. At 5 miles in length, it is one of the longest suspension bridges in the world. It opened on November 1, 1957. On Labor Day, Michigan's governor traditionally leads a walk across the bridge to salute our state's labor roots.

Don't miss the opportunity to visit Mackinac Island. At the center of the Great Lakes waterway, this little island, 3 miles long and 2 miles wide, has an important place in the history of North America. It first served as a tribal gathering place and later was visited by French fur traders and Jesuit missionaries. After the French and Indian War, the British moved their camp from the upper shores of the Lower Peninsula to the island and established a military fort. Following the War of 1812, British troops were forced to turn over the island to the Americans. Fur trading gave way to fishing, which gave way to tourism after the Civil War.

Today the island is preserved in 1890s grandeur, the era when the nation's wealthy built summer homes there. Much of the land is dedicated to a park. Motorized vehicles are not permitted on the island; visitors travel from place to place by horse-drawn carriage or ride bicycles. In addition to the old military fort, the most famous landmark is the Grand Hotel, with its legendary front porch. Those not lucky enough to stay at what's been called the world's most expensive hotel are charged for the privilege of sitting on its porch. Access to the island is by ferries that leave from Mackinaw City and St. Ignace or by private boat.

Mother Nature may have connected the Great Lakes with rivers, but she didn't necessarily make it easy to get from one lake to another. The rapids of St. Mary's River drop 21 feet between Lake Huron and Lake Superior. The Soo Locks, the first of which was built in 1855, have solved that problem. Today there are four locks, and 95 million tons of freight pass through them every year. They are actually in the town of Sault Sainte Marie, the oldest in the state.

No article about Michigan icons or unusual attractions would be compete without mentioning the "mystery spot." Located not far from St. Ignace, there's a plot of land that seems to defy gravity. In the 1950s, several surveyors discovered an area where optical illusions trump reality. You appear to be leaning in one direction but actually are standing straight.

Lighthouses are an important part of culture by the sea, and Michigan has more than a hundred. They dot the coastline around the state, including the banks of the Detroit River. Huge efforts are in progress to restore and preserve these structures and document their place in Michigan maritime history. A number are open to the public, and some even allow visitors to climb to the top outside and view the surrounding area.

The Dunes is the term Michiganders use to describe the shoreline of Lake Michigan on the western coast of the state. Much of the land is a series of coastal dunes, hence the nickname. The state has preserved the area, which includes hiking and cross-country ski trails in addition to the beachfront.

Every state has a state bird, and a movement is under way to reconsider Michigan's. Birders are supporting an effort to replace the robin, our state bird since 1931, with the Kirtland's warbler. This tiny bird, weighing in at only half an ounce, is on the endangered species list. Its only consistent breeding ground since it was discovered in the 1850s is a 100-mile stretch of dense pine trees along the Au Sable River drainage area.

You can celebrate Christmas 361 days a year at Bronner's in Frankenmuth. Filled with more than fifty thousand decorations and other items for the holiday, it's said to be the "world's largest" Christmas store.

In the 1920s and 1930s, Ford Motor Company's Rouge plant was the largest industrial complex in the world, as well as the most advanced architecturally and technically. It was built to keep Ford self-sufficient and independent of suppliers. They literally started with iron ore and the end result was an automobile. It's still an active production facility, today for F-150s. Visitors can tour the facility, which has five parts, one of which is the assembly plant. The plant is part of the tour only during nonproduction hours.

Nearby, you can also visit the Henry Ford Museum and Greenfield Village. The museum is dedicated to preserving and celebrating American innovation. You can learn the stories of many of the country's industrial pioneers, including Ford, Edison, and the Wright Brothers. Greenfield Village is 90 acres filled with buildings of historical significance. Costumed tour guides will answer questions.

Don't worry, you're not hallucinating when you head east on I-94 from Metro Airport and see a giant tire. It was originally a Ferris wheel, the Uniroyal exhibit at the 1964–65 World's Fair in New York City. Where better to put a giant tire on the side of the highway than outside Detroit?

Finally, those sleek towers you see glistening on the Detroit Riverfront are the Renaissance Center. The four-tower thirty-nine-story office complex and seventy-story hotel was intended to anchor the downtown area's revival, or renaissance if you will. General Motors is now the main tenant. From the observation deck and lounge atop the Ren Cen, visitors can enjoy a view of the area, including the city of Windsor, Ontario. The view includes another notable bridge—the busy Ambassador Bridge, linking two countries.

Big Ten Country

Well live in the heart of Big Ten country, where people are serious about their football. Saturdays in the fall mean getting up early, grabbing a prime tailgating spot, then firing up the grill. Not to mention quaffing a few beers to set the mood for kickoff.

Michigan is home to two Big Ten schools, the University of Michigan and Michigan State University. As you might have guessed, the two schools are bitter rivals. Harvard vs. Yale might be older, and Florida State vs. Miami might have more of a bearing on the national championship, but for good old-fashioned trash talking, this rivalry ranks as number one. You can find stores with names like the Great Divide all over the state. They stock a full line of apparel and knickknacks for Wolverine and Spartan fans.

In planning our travels around the state, we noticed that if you take what we call the Great Circle Route from Ann Arbor, the home of U-M, to East Lansing, the home of MSU, and back to Ann Arbor, you'll pass within a short drive of no fewer than seven breweries.

Let's start in Ann Arbor. Many of the city's leading attractions are connected with the university. Michigan Stadium (201 South Main Street, 734-647-2583), known as "The Big House," is America's largest college-owned football stadium. A number of the university's museums are open to the public, including the Museum of Art (525 South State Street) and the Museum of Natural History (1109 Geddes Avenue). The Power Center for the Performing Arts (121 Fletcher Street) and Hill Auditorium (825 North University Avenue, 734-764-8350) attract world-class musical and theatrical performances. A family favorite is the Ann Arbor Hands-On Museum (220 East Ann Street, 734-995-5439, aahom.org), which has more than 250 interactive exhibits for children of all ages. Ann Arbor has a wealth of restaurants offering a variety of cuisines, specialty shops, entertainment of all kinds, and of course, bars and clubs.

83

The road leads west along I-94. Chelsea, some 20 miles west of Ann Arbor, is the home of the Purple Rose Theatre Company (137 Park Street, 734-433-ROSE, purplerosetheatre.org), founded by actor Jeff Daniels, who starred in *The Purple Rose of Cairo*. I-94 intersects I-127 at Jackson, where in 1854 a convention of antislavery men chose a slate of candidates for office. Michiganders consider "Under the Oaks" to be the birthplace of the Republican Party. The site is at the intersection of Second Street and Franklin Street.

I-127 leads north to Lansing, the state capital. The city's best-known landmark is the recently renovated Capitol Building (100 Capital Avenue, 517-373-2353). Tours are available, and as our state has a full-time legislature, you might see lawmakers in action. The Michigan Historical Museum (702 West Kalamazoo Street, 517-373-3559) features a walk-through copper mine, along with a one-room schoolhouse and a 1957 Auto Show.

Next door is East Lansing, which is dominated by Michigan State University, America's pioneer land-grant college. MSU's football team plays its home games at Spartan Stadium, but it's basketball—both the men's and women's teams—that's been in the national spotlight in recent years. They play at the Breslin Student Events Center (517-432-1989), which is also a venue for concerts, circuses, and other events. Other on-campus attractions include the Abrams Planetarium (517-355-4676), the Kresge Art Museum (517-353-9834), and the MSU Museum (517-355-2370), which concentrates on the natural and cultural history of the Great Lakes region.

The route heads east from East Lansing along I-96 through fast-growing Livingston County, then turns south on U.S. Route 23 at Brighton. South of Brighton is Liquid Manufacturing, LLC (6150 Whitmore Lake Road, 810-220-2802, www.liquidmfg.com), which used to be the Local Color Brewery. We didn't profile Liquid Manufacturing in this edition because its owners hadn't finalized all the details, including what they were going to call their beer. By the time you read this, Liquid Manufacturing beer might be available and their taproom might be open. But do call ahead.

Not far away is the entrance to the Huron Meadows Metropark, one of thirteen in southeast Michigan operated by the Huron-Clinton Metropark Authority (www.metroparks.com). The parks offer a variety of activities, including picknicking, golf, watersports, and cross-country skiing.

East of Ann Arbor, U.S. 23 intersects with M-17, or Washtenaw Avenue. The road west leads back to Ann Arbor. To the east is Ypsilanti, which earns a spot on Michigan's craft-brewing map because it's the site of the annual Michigan Brewers Guild Summer Festival. The annual event at Riverside Park in Depot Town draws some five thousand festival-goers and has recently earned a reputation for big beers. Really big ones.

Convention and Visitors Bureaus
Ann Arbor: www.annarbor.org
Lansing: www.lansing.org

Recommended Beer Bars
Ann Arbor
Ashley's Restaurant and Pub, 338 South State Street, 734-996-9191, www.ashleys.com. Offers more than sixty-five beers on tap, including a decent representation of Michigan micros.

East Lansing
Crunchy's, 254 West Grand River, 517-341-2506. Student hangout with a good selection of Michigan microbrews on tap.

Okemos
Old Chicago Pasta and Pizza, 1938 West Grand River Avenue, 517-347-1111, www.oldchicago.com. The first Michigan location for this chain of beer bars. More than a hundred beers are on the menu.

Jolly Pumpkin Artisan Ales

3115 Broad Street, Suite A, Dexter, MI 48130
734-426-4962
www.jollypumpkin.com

Although suburban sprawl is encroaching, Dexter retains much of its village charm. And that makes it a perfect location for an American version of a French farmhouse brewery. It is a dream come true for Ron Jeffries and his wife, Laurie, who took over a building that once housed a bank and established a unique craft brewery.

Ron told us that he's had a hankering to run his own brewery since, as he put it, "1991-ish." He started homebrewing while a graduate student. And when time permitted, he hit the library and devoured stacks of books about the science of brewing. His professional career started in 1995, and he spent most of it working for the Schelde family of brewpubs, most recently at Grizzly Peak in Ann Arbor.

Beers brewed: The menu beers are Bière de Mars, Calabaza Blanca, La Roja, Luicernaga, Maricabo Especial, and Oro de Calabaza.

Ron struck out on his own in July 2004, and his beers were an instant hit. His Oro de Calabaza won a Gold Medal in the Belgian- and French-style Ales category at the Great American Beer Festival. Not many breweries have won a GABF Gold Medal for their first batch of beer. In 2005, Oro de Calabaza won a bronze.

Awards won: 2004 GABF Gold, Belgian- and French-Style Ale; 2005 GABF Bronze, Belgian- and French-Style Ale.

The name, Jolly Pumpkin Artisan Ales, says a lot about Ron and his brewery. It bubbled up during a brainstorming session with Laurie and stayed put in their minds. "Jolly Pumpkin" is the fun part of the name. Everyone likes Halloween, Ron told us, and the smiling jack-o'-lantern that symbolizes it. And yes, the name, like the beer, brings a smile to our faces.

Our Pick: All Ron's beer is outstanding. If you like this style of beer, each one will delight you. The very first we tried was Oro de Calabaza, and it's won two medals at the Great American Beer Festival. Need we say more?

But the rest of the name, "Artisan Ales," is the serious part. Even the bottle labels, which feature the fantastic, almost surreal work of illustrator Adam Forman, are part of the brewery's artisanal bent. While Ron aspires to a "slow-food" existence, making just enough beer to pay the bills, he'll never cut corners at his brewery. When he sat down with us, Ron spoke about his beers in almost loving terms. They don't fit into style guidelines, and Ron likes it that way. His ambition is to make complex, out-of-the-ordinary beers—beers that will leave an impression on the drinker.

Jolly Pumpkin definitely isn't your mass-market lager house. The emphasis is on quality, not quantity. Ron open-ferments and then barrel-ages his beer, bottle-conditioning it before it leaves the brewery. He doesn't filter his beer, either. The brewing equipment once saw service in a Montana brewery. The fermenters have been added as demand and production increased, and Ron added a bottler and a stockpile of bourbon barrels—more than fifty by the time you read this. Ron has done all of the refurbishing and retrofitting work himself, including the plumbing. He's going to need those barrels, because word has gotten out about Jolly Pumpkin. Even if you don't live in Michigan, its products might be coming to a store near you.

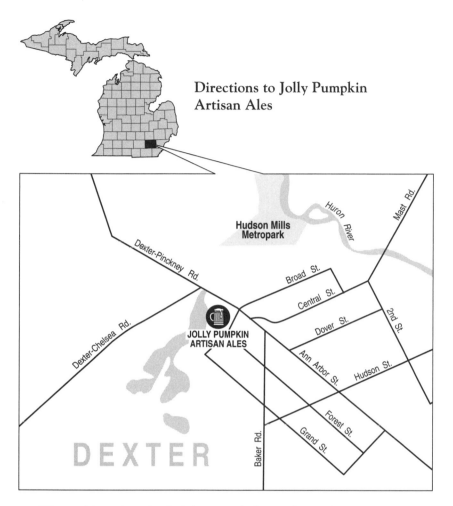

**Directions to Jolly Pumpkin
Artisan Ales**

The golden Oro de Calabaza and the amber-colored La Roja are both strong ales in the bière de garde tradition. The third member of Jolly Pumpkin's original lineup, Calabaza Blanca, is a less potent bière blanche. Ron hasn't stood pat. This year he brought out Luciernaga, a slightly gentler version of a Grand Cru, and Maricabo Especial, a strong brown ale inspired by the Belgian monks.

By now you're probably wondering about the Spanish names Ron has given his beers. There's a simple explanation: He loves the tropics, and one of his favorite places is the Spanish Main, where pirate ships of legend once roamed. Which gets us back to Halloween: Ron said that every kid wants to dress up as a pirate and go trick-or-treating.

The brewery has no taproom, but there is a retail area where customers can purchase beer and Jolly Pumpkin merchandise. The decor, as you might expect, is fun. Ron's GABF medals are on display on a monkey-themed tapestry, not far from the plastic palm tree decked out in Christmas lights or the stuffed parrot in an open cage.

Beer drinkers raised on American lager will find Jolly Pumpkin beers an acquired taste. And that's fine with Ron, who's creating his own niche in the beer world, much like Sam Calagione at Dogfish Head in Delaware. We hope we're not jinxing him, but we won't be surprised when Ron joins Sam in the ranks of craft brewing's stars.

Class of license: Microbrewery.
Opened: July 2004.
Owners: Ron and Laurie Jeffries.
Brewer: Ron Jeffries.
System: 10-barrel Jeffries.
Production: 100 barrels in the last six months of 2004, 365 barrels in 2005.
Distribution: Select retail outlets in Michigan as well as Connecticut, Florida, Illinois, Iowa, Massachusetts, Ohio, Tennessee, Virginia, and Wisconsin.
Hours: Thursday through Saturday, 12 to 6 P.M.
Take-out beer: 750-milliliter bottles.
Food: None.
Extras: 5 percent discount on cases.
Parking: Municipal lots within walking distance. One space in front of the brewery.

Arbor Brewing Company

114–118–120 Washington Street, Ann Arbor, MI 48104
734-213-1393
www.arborbrewing.com

Of all the establishments near our home, Arbor Brewing Company comes closest to being our friendly local. Since it opened in 1995, we've gone there for business meetings, postgame pints, and get-togethers with friends. This is Ann Arbor's first brewpub, and one of the first in Michigan to pour what used to be called hard-to-find styles.

For all this time, our hosts have been Matt and Rene Greff. When we sat down with them—over their beers, of course—Matt told us, "We never dreamed we would get to this point." Today they're leaders in their community and respected by their brewing peers.

The Greffs fell in love while they were students at Kalamazoo College. Soon after they graduated, Matt fell in love again. He picked up a copy of Charlie Papazian's *The Complete Joy of Homebrewing*, and he was hooked. What started as Matt's homebrewing hobby threatened to overrun their entire house.

Starry-eyed and still in their twenties, the Greffs had a vision. They wanted to build something like the pubs of the British Isles, a place where a family with young children could feel as much at home as a Michigan alum back in town for his or her twenty-fifth reunion. They've done just that, perhaps with the help of Ninkasi, the goddess of beer. Their dream became reality in less than a year—amazing when one considers how many things can go wrong when renovating an old building.

Beers brewed: The menu beers are Red Snapper, Huxtell's Best Bitter, Sacred Cow IPA, Faricy Fest Irish Stout, Old #22 Altbier, and Big Ben English Mild. There's also a wide variety of seasonals, including several stouts around St. Patrick's Day. Recently, Arbor Brewing added the Phat Abbot line of Belgian ales, available in 750-milliliter bottles.

Our Picks: Paul loves Düsseldorf-style altbier and was impressed with Old #22 since he first tasted it. Maryanne was pleased to see a Kriek on the menu and was delighted with Arbor Brewing's version, which is made with Michigan's famous Balaton cherries.

The building dates back to 1876, when Ann Arbor was a small German town and the beverage of choice was beer. Legend has it that the city's first police officer to be gunned down met his fate here. Many believe that his ghost inhabits the brewery. One night after they'd first opened the brewpub, Rene told us, he made such a racket that she and Matt fled the building.

Arbor Brewing's main room is cozy and traditional, with exposed brick walls, a high tin ceiling, and wooden floors. There's a smallish bar in the middle, and behind it is the glass-enclosed brewhouse, which looks like tight quarters for brewer Dug Jakubiak. Wooden tables and booths take up most of the room, and that's a good thing: Arbor Brewing does a brisk lunch and dinner business and attracts its share of businesspeople, families, and couples on dates.

The decor features posters for European breweries along with other breweriana. The items include signs from Brasserie Greff, a brewery that operated in Nancy, France, until World War II, which led Matt to tell us an "it's a small world" story: While tracing his family tree, he discovered that the brewery's proprietors were distant relatives of his.

The original five menu beers have kept their original names, though Matt told us that the recipes have been tweaked over the

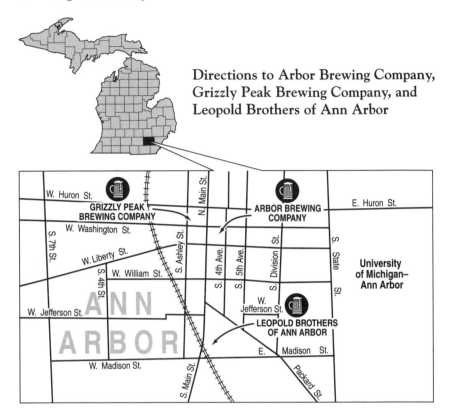

Directions to Arbor Brewing Company,
Grizzly Peak Brewing Company, and
Leopold Brothers of Ann Arbor

years—a luxury that a brewpub enjoys. Arbor Brewing also turns out a
dozen or more specials and seasonals, including several varieties of stout
for St. Patrick's Day. Some seasonals have semi-year-round status, such
as No Parking Pilsner, brewed in "honor" of Ann Arbor's decision to
tear down and renovate the parking structure across the street. For a
while, that project made Ann Arbor's already legendary parking woes a
nightmare for Arbor Brewing's customers.

Arbor Brewing has expanded several times since it opened. A few
years ago, the Greffs acquired space in an adjoining building, doubled
their brewing capacity, and acquired a bottler. They also expanded down-
ward, building a European-style beer cellar. More recently, they broad-
ened their range of beer, brewing and cellaring the Phat Abbot line of
Belgian-style beers. Inspired by a visit to a beer bar in Antwerp, the
Greffs plan to cellar those beers and bring them out for vertical tastings.

Fittingly for a college town, Arbor Brewing offers continuing education in the form of monthly tastings. They feature up to thirty beers,
many of them not often seen, plus an appetizer buffet and "course mate-

rials"—namely, notes on the beers. The brewpub is also a driving force behind the city's Oktoberfest celebration.

Good corporate citizenship is important to Arbor Brewing. The Greffs are active in charitable and civic efforts and support independent businesses like their own. They've reacted to corporate farming practices by turning to a supplier of vegetable-raised beef, and they're looking for other local purveyors as well. The menu is kind to vegetarians, offering meatless pierogies, pasta, burritos, and tacos, but pub favorites like chicken wings and hamburgers are available as well.

Recently, we caught up with Matt and Rene, who told us that they're going ahead with plans to open a second establishment, the Corner Brewery, in the neighboring city of Ypsilanti. It will include a tree-shaded, European-style beer garden, along with a production brewery that will allow for statewide distribution of several menu beers as well as the Phat Abbot dubbel and trippel. If all goes well, the Corner Brewery will be up and running by the time you read this. Check its website, www.cornerbrewery.com, to find out whether Ninkasi is smiling on their efforts. We're sure that she is.

Class of license: Brewpub.
Opened: August 1995.
Owners: Matt and Rene Greff.
Brewer: Dug Jakubiak.
System: 7-barrel DME. Capacity is just above 1,000 barrels per year.
Production: 1,300 barrels in 2004.
Hours: Monday through Saturday, 11:30 A.M. to 1 A.M.; Sunday, 1 P.M. to 1 A.M.
Tours: Yes, call ahead.
Take-out beer: Growlers, six-packs, and 750-millileter bottles of Belgian ales.
Food: Pub menu with a wide selection of vegetarian dishes.
Extras: Monthly themed beer tastings. Annual Oktoberfest. Outdoor seating. Kid-friendly menu. No smoking in main bar area.
Mug club: No.
Parking: Structure across the street; several other structures and lots within walking distance.

Grizzly Peak Brewing Company

120 West Washington Street, Ann Arbor, MI 48104
734-741-PEAK
www.michiganmenu.com/grizzlypeak.html

Germans have been influential since Ann Arbor's earliest days. Thanks to them, the town supported several breweries and more than its share of licensed establishments. One of them, the Old German restaurant, survived until the 1990s. Its closing saddened locals—we feel your pain— but the spirit of gemutlichkeit lives on at the Grizzly Peak Brewing Company. Its name comes from a mountain range in Wyoming, but its roots are in west Michigan.

Grizzly Peak, which recently celebrated its tenth anniversary, is owned by a group of investors led by Jon Carlson. Jon is a University of Michigan graduate with roots in Traverse City and a knack for finding historic structures and refurbishing them. The group, called GPBC, signed a management contract with Schelde Enterprises, Inc., of Grand Rapids, which owned and was already running the successful Grand Rapids Brewing Company.

Grizzly Peak's interior reminds us a bit of the beer halls we've been to in Germany. The interior is furnished with wood and more wood, with exposed brick walls and a mixture of outdoor and maritime decor and a fair amount of breweriana. The busy barroom, which gets chaotic on weekend nights, stands in the front, with quieter dining rooms farther back.

Before Jon Carlson and his partners made Grizzly Peak a reality, an Ann Arbor couple, Barry Seifert and Jennifer Kirscht, tried to make a go of it. Tragedy ended their dream, when Jennifer fell victim to cancer. But they did bring British brewery consultants Peter Austin and partners into the picture. As a result, the distinctive brick-lined Peter Austin brewkettle stands in the picture window.

The man in charge of the brewery is Duncan Williams. After graduating from Eastern Michigan

Beers brewed: The menu beers are Bear Paw Porter, Grizzly Peak Pale Ale, Steelhead Red Ale, and Victors Golden Ale. The fifth and sixth taps are rotating seasonals and might include barleywine or Christmas white beer in the winter; bock in the spring; Helles, white ale, or hefeweizen in the summer; and Oktoberfest or altbier in the fall. One of the menu beers is available in cask as well. Grizzly Peak also brews root beer.

University with a degree in theater, he managed a Kinko's store and spent his spare time homebrewing. A few batches convinced him that he was good enough at it to brew for a living. After studying at the Siebel Institute, he got a part-time job at CJ's Brewing Company, then came to Grizzly Peak as an assistant to Ron Jeffries before getting the top job. Duncan has two assistant brewers and told us that they're needed here because the equipment has to be cleaned by hand.

Our Picks: Paul chose Victors Golden Ale based on the number of growlers he brought home after trips into Ann Arbor. Paired with grilled chicken, this is heaven. Maryanne went with the Irish Amber. Some brewers mail this style in, but Grizzly Peak's version had plenty of substance.

The menu beers at Grizzly Peak have kept their names since opening day, but their recipes have evolved as brewers came and went. Asked to describe his brewing style, Duncan called it "American-style and British-inspired," a good fit, given the brewing system. The Ringwood yeast strain is British, Duncan prefers British malts, and he said that he grows East Kent Goldings hops at home and would like to dry-hop a batch of ale with them.

Though he's not as enamored of big beers as some Michigan brewers, Duncan works a few into the lineup, along with occasional Belgian beers. You can count on finding a traditional German beer, too. Duncan also brews a Scottish wassail ale with local Gala apples, which are roasted and put into the cask. And he uses honey from a local beekeeper—who's a Grizzly Peak regular—in his honey porter.

From the time it opened, Grizzly Peak has attracted a lunch and dinner crowd, so much so that its beer hasn't gotten the recognition it deserves. Wood-fired pizzas and rotisserie dishes are popular, and quite a few items on the menu incorporate the beer brewed here. Kitchen staff try to make dishes from scratch and buy their food from local suppliers.

Another chapter of the Grizzly Peak story is unfolding. The owners have expanded into what used to be the Del Rio Bar, a place we remember well, and turned it into the Grizzly Den. And yes, they've preserved the best of the old hangout—down to the music that was played there.

Class of license: Brewpub.
Opened: August 1995.
Owner: GPBC, Inc.; managed by Schelde Enterprises, Inc.
Brewers: Duncan Williams, head brewer; Jeff Hancock and Dave Julander, assistant brewers.
System: 7-barrel Peter Austin. Capacity is about 2,000 barrels. Uses proprietary Ringwood yeast from the Shipyard Brewing Company of Portland, Maine.

Production: 992 barrels in 2004.
Hours: Monday through Thursday, 11 A.M. to 11 P.M.; Friday and Saturday, 11 A.M. to midnight; Sunday, noon to 11 P.M.
Tours: Yes, call ahead a week in advance please.
Take-out beer: Growlers, keggies, and quarter and half barrels.
Food: American cuisine featuring pizza, burgers, ribs, fresh fish, pasta, sandwiches, and salads.
Extras: Wood-fired oven. St. Patrick's Day and Oktoberfest celebrations, with special dinners, special logo mugs, and reduced pints. Smoking is allowed in the Grizzly Den only. Sidewalk dining in warm weather.
Happy hour: Discounted pints and appetizers, 4 to 6 P.M. daily.
Mug club: Lifetime membership is $60. Benefits include reduced pints, admission to club events, and an invitation to the annual Polar Bear Day outside in the middle of February.
Parking: City lots and structures within walking distance. Parking can be tight on Friday and Saturday nights. Free parking on Sunday. (See map on page 90.)

Leopold Brothers of Ann Arbor Brewery and Distilling

529 South Main Street, Ann Arbor, MI 48104
734-757-9806
www.leopoldbros.com

As Todd and Scott Leopold tell it, the story of their brewery began with a conversation over beers in their hometown of Boulder, Colorado. They concluded that they could build one that generated zero waste: an "eco-brewery," one might say. The brewery would also carry on a family tradition: The brothers' great-granduncle, Aldo, was a famous conservationist.

Todd and Scott chose Ann Arbor because it, like Boulder, was a progressive community whose residents were likely to embrace their idea. They also had the skills to pull it off. Scott was an environmental engineer, and Todd was a brewmaster who'd studied in Germany. And they could call on their father, an architect, to design the brewery.

The brothers found what they were looking for just south of downtown Ann Arbor: a building that dates back to 1914 and at one time housed an ice cream factory. After they finished renovating the building—and that was a story in itself—they had a beer hall with 30-foot-high ceilings, brick walls, and exposed truss work. Much of what you find inside has been recycled. For example, the tables saw service at a monastery before they were brought here, and the bar front is made of old oars.

The ambience is hard to describe; it's an amalgam of styles. A row of long wooden tables along the south wall is reminiscent of a German beer hall. But on the other side, there's a collection of chairs you'd likely find at a campus-area coffeehouse, and the bar in back is typical of an American brewpub. Outside, there's a small beer garden. The brewery is atypical in one more respect: The brewing vessels aren't part of the decor but instead are kept behind doors that bear the brewery logo.

Beers brewed: The menu beers are Golden Lager, Red Lager, Hefeweizen, and Schwarzbier. Seasonals and specialties include Dunkelweizen, Imperial Stout, Kölsch, Nut Brown Ale, Porter, Radler (a German-style mixture of beer and lemonade), and Winter Lager.

Our Picks: Paul chose the Schwarzbier—"just like in Germany," he said. Maryanne chose the HefeBock, a seasonal beer so smooth that the bartenders warn people about its alcohol content.

Unfortunately, Todd and Scott were prevented from reaching their goal of zero waste. Their original plan called for recycling carbon dioxide into a greenhouse, where herbs and spices would be grown for local restaurants. But city officials demanded design changes the brothers couldn't afford, and they put the greenhouse on hold. That was the bad news. The good news is that the brewery wastes less than one-fifth the water of the average brewery, and their spent grain has made a local flock of chickens so happy that egg production has soared.

By this point, you're probably wondering about the beer. Here, too, Todd and Scott have chosen not to follow the crowd. Following the lead of small German breweries, they specialize in unfiltered lagers. "We're proud to be a lager house," Todd told us. The original lineup included Red Lager, still the flagship beer; Schwarzbier; and Pilsner. All of these are German versions of session beers; the brothers are content to leave big beers to other brewers.

Because it's a healthy walk from campus, Leopold Brothers draws a slightly older crowd, largely grad students and young professionals. Much of the entertainment these days is nonelectronic, ranging from billiards and foosball to board games like Sorry and Clue. These diversions, and the long communal tables, make for an atmosphere conducive to meeting new friends and conversing with old ones. That said, it can get crazy on football Saturdays. Located less than half a mile from Michigan Stadium, it's the closest place for Wolverine fans to celebrate—or drown their sorrows—as they head back toward campus.

Lately, Todd and Scott have been following Yogi Berra's advice: "When you come to the fork in the road, take it." Leopold Brothers recently got a distiller's license, acquired a pot still, and branched out into flavored gins and vodkas—more than twenty in all. Their line of spirits has become so popular that the Leopold Brothers logo now reads, "Brewing and Distilling."

Meanwhile, the beer end of the business chugs along, and the brewery continues to be a pleasant gathering place. The Leopold Brothers' story didn't follow the plan that Todd and Scott sketched out on a restaurant menu in Boulder. But to borrow a phrase, perhaps "all's well that ends well."

Class of license: Microbrewery.
Opened: October 1999.
Owners: Todd and Scott Leopold.
Brewer: Todd Leopold
System: 20-barrel DME, custom designed by the Leopolds. Capacity is 1,500 barrels.
Production: 800 barrels in 2004.
Distribution: Select stores in Ann Arbor area.
Hours: Monday through Thursday, 4 P.M. to 1 A.M.; Friday and Saturday, 4 P.M. to 2 A.M. (10 A.M. to 2 A.M. home football Saturdays); Sunday, 6 P.M. to 1 A.M.
Take-out beer: Bottles and kegs.
Food: Limited bar menu featuring wraps, sandwiches, and quesadillas.
Extras: Outdoor beer garden. Board games, pool tables, and foosball. Distilled spirits.
Parking: Small lot adjacent to brewery. Municipal lot and structure within walking distance. (See map on page 90.)

Michigan Brewing Company

1093 Highview Drive, Webberville, MI 48892
517-521-3600
www.michiganbrewing.com

It's been a long, strange trip for Celis Beer. A trip that began in Belgian Flanders, wound through the hill country of Texas, and ended in Webberville, Michigan, the home of Michigan Brewing Company.

The Celis saga began when Pierre Celis, a Flemish dairyman, saw the brewers of his beloved witbier—a wheat beer flavored with orange peel and coriander seed—close their doors one by one. Pierre joined forces with a retired brewer to revive the style. Their beer became so popular that Pierre took it commercial and named it for his hometown of Hoegaarden.

Pierre sold Hoegaarden to the brewing giant Interbrew and later moved to Austin, Texas, to start another brewery specializing in witbier and Belgian-style beers. This time he put his own name on the brewery. After Celis's beers earned a national following, he sold his brewery to Miller Brewing Company. But the Celis brand languished in Miller's hands, and production stopped in 2001.

Bobby Mason, the founder and owner of Michigan Brewing, saw an opportunity to take his business in a new direction. In 2002, Bobby bought Celis—lock, stock, and vintage brewing system— and organized a twenty-seven-truck convoy to haul everything to Webberville.

Owning Celis was quite a triumph for someone who got into brewing somewhat by accident. Let's go back to the nineties. Bobby decided that he wanted to own a factory. He looked at soda pop, potato chips, and even beef jerky, before he got intrigued with microbrewed beer while on a trip to Oregon. When he got back home, he talked to the owner of a homebrew supply shop about starting a brewery. After boning up on brewing, he fashioned his first

Beers brewed: The old taproom offered a dozen beers on tap, and the new one should offer at least that many. There are four beers in the Celis line: Pale Bock, Grand Cru, Raspberry, and White (GABF Gold, 2003). The Michigan line includes High Seas India Pale Ale; Michigan Nut Brown Ale; Mackinac Pale Ale; Michigan Golden Ale, a Vienna-style lager; Peninsula Porter; Petosky Pilsner, a Bohemian-style lager; Sunset Amber Lager; Superior Stout; and Wheatland Wheat Beer.

Awards won: 2002 GABF Bronze, Imperial Stout; 2003 GABF Gold, Belgian-Style White.

system out of beer kegs. Bobby still has the system and sometimes lends it out to homebrew clubs.

In the years that followed, he steadily grew his business, upgrading to a 30-barrel system and getting his beer into bars and stores throughout the state. The Michigan brand is known for a wide range of styles and distinctive packaging that features Michigan symbols. The brand was popular enough to make the brewery one of the state's top brewers even before it added Celis. The Michigan line is very much alive, accounting for almost one-third of total production.

Our Picks: Celis White got the nod from Paul. Belgians call the beer white because unfiltered protein from the wheat malt gives it a cloudy appearance. Dozens of craft breweries emulate this style, but Celis still is the gold standard. Maryanne's choice was the Celis Grand Cru, a strong (8 percent ABV) version of witbier with a decidedly spicy flavor.

After closing the Celis deal, Bobby enlisted Pierre's help in relaunching the beer in the States. Pierre took him on a tour of Flemish breweries and, once they got back to Webberville, brewed several batches of Celis with Bobby to make sure he'd gotten the recipe right. Currently, Michigan Brewing brews four beers from the Celis line, and Bobby is thinking of expanding it with both year-round and seasonal beers. Bobby also discovered that he'd not only bought Celis, but acquired its fans as well, some of whom are distributors. That should improve his chances of making Celis a national brand.

Buying Celis wasn't the end of Bobby Mason's ambitions. He's been hard at work on the next round of changes. He bought the factory next door, which he's transforming into Michigan Brewing Company 2.0. It will be anchored by Celis's 100-barrel system, which features two huge copper kettles that were manufactured before World War II. They were so large that Bobby wondered whether they'd fit through the doors of his new quarters (they did, but just barely).

Bobby's new facility won't be just a brewery. He plans to expand his homebrew supply and breweriana shop, as well as his retail beer store; put in a small brewing museum; and open a beer garden with hop bines and wrought-iron tables and chairs. And of course, he'll have a taproom.

The new taproom will be bigger than the old chaletlike structure in the original brewery; offer a full menu; and have as its centerpiece a hundred-year-old bar, complete with brass rail, that Bobby bought from a brewery in Ohio. But Bobby assured us that he'll preserve the old place's rustic, North Woods ambience. It had become a hangout for locals and passers-by alike. On the day we visited, a few lucky hunters who'd bagged their deer had dropped by to celebrate.

Bobby's near-term plans also include expanding the tap selection, adding a hand pull or two and branching into more offbeat styles. One

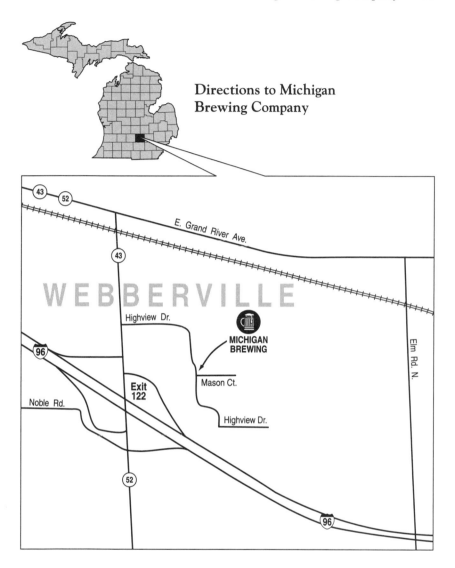

Directions to Michigan
Brewing Company

of them, a beer he calls Renaissance, is made with 100 percent malted spelt. He'd also like to join the trend toward higher-end beers. He plans to add a small winery license and, last but not least, distilled spirits. Bobby showed us his latest acquisition, a Christian Carl pot still that originally was used at Michigan State University. He intends to use it for educational programs as well as commercially. Speaking of education, don't be surprise if a brewing school gets started in Webberville.

By the time you read this, Bobby Mason will have taken Michigan Brewing to the next level. He hopes that his new quarters will become a destination along the busy I-96 freeway. And with expanded production capacity, he'll be able to bring Celis beer to even more Americans.

Class of license: Microbrewery.

Opened: December 1995.

Owner-brewer: Bobby Mason.

System: 30-barrel Century and 100-barrel manufactured in Belgium acquired with the Celis brand. Capacity is 24,000 barrels per year.

Production: 5,800 barrels in 2004.

Distribution: Michigan-brand beers are distributed in-state. Celis is available in Massachusetts, New York, Oregon, and Texas, and distribution will expand to other states.

Hours: Monday through Thursday, 10 A.M. to 9 P.M. (11 P.M. in summer); Friday and Saturday, 10 A.M. to midnight; Sunday, noon to 9 P.M.

Tours: Yes, call for availability.

Take-out beer: Bottles, growlers, Cornelius kegs, and full kegs. Michigan Brewing is experimenting with plastic bottles and might add 16- and 32-ounce bottles.

Food: The current limited menu of chili, sandwiches, and burgers will be expanded. Michigan Brewing has hired a chef for the new location and is considering adding a more upscale, rotating menu.

Extras: The new facility will feature a taproom; Things Beer, a homebrew supply and breweriana store; and an outdoor beer garden.

Parking: Lot outside the brewery.

Travelers Club International Restaurant and Tuba Museum/ Tuba Charlie's Brewpub

2138 Hamilton Road, Okemos, MI 48864
517-349-1701
www.travelerstuba.com/travelersclub_001.htm

Will White believes "music and food are international languages" that can tear down linguistic and cultural barriers. So it's no surprise that bringing the world together is the guiding principle behind Travelers Club International Restaurant, which he and his partner, Jennifer Byrom, have operated since 1982. It offers a wide, and constantly changing, menu inspired by their years of seeing the world.

The restaurant is located in one of the oldest parts of town, where Chiefs Okemos and Pontiac once lived and the plank road between Detroit and Lansing once ran. It occupies a building that dates back to 1950, formerly a hardware store and, later on, a Miller's ice cream parlor. It has retained some of its soda-fountain ambience, with circular stools at the bar—where adult beverages are now served—and little tables along the sides. Miller's ice cream is still sold out of a display case.

From an early age, Jennifer traveled the world and experienced other countries' cuisine. Will grew up in an ethnically mixed neighborhood and later did some traveling of his own. But every time they came home, they had the same problem: Local restaurants didn't serve the dishes they enjoyed overseas. Their solution? Make them at home and share them with friends. That provided the inspiration for their restaurant.

"International cuisine" hardly begins to describe what's served here. The menu is more than twenty pages long and has its own table of contents; the featured items include Latin, Middle Eastern, and stir-fry dishes. But the Travelers Club is best known for an entree and a vegetarian sampler from a partic-

Beers brewed: Rotating Tuba Charlie's Ale of the Month.

Our Pick: Actually, it was Will's pick—the bar has only one of its beers on tap at a time. He served us Medieval Maibock, a pan-European beer brewed from wild yeasts and local maple syrup. Despite the name, it was similar to a Belgian lambic but even sourer.

ular country or region, which changes every month. Most of the food, even the soup stock, is made from scratch and often includes herbs from the extensive garden.

The second part of this establishment's name, the Tuba Museum, comes from Will's high school days, when he played tuba in the school band. It led to a lifelong love of music—he's still an owner of the music store next door—and the tuba in particular. If, like us, you're not conversant with the tuba, pick up the menu and learn about its history.

Will has collected about sixty tubas, some of which go back to John Philip Sousa's day, along with "a baker's dozen of sousaphones." Some, he told us, are still in playing condition. The tubas are displayed on the walls of the restaurant, along with ethnic and fabric art and curios that Jennifer found while traveling. A couple of them have even been turned into a fountain that serves as the centerpiece of the outdoor patio.

At long last we come to Tuba Charlie's, which is Will's nickname and the name of the brewery. Will has been homebrewing since the days before he opened the restaurant and continues the tradition by hosting the local homebrewing club. He has wanted to go professional for some time. His first step in that direction was to buy a three-quarter-barrel system. When the spirit moves him, he brings it out on the porch and fire-brews a new batch. His favorite beers are Belgian, but he loves to brew distinctive, style-bending beers and share them with customers. Some house beer finds its way onto the restaurant's extensive menu.

Will said that his current brewery, which he described as "an advanced homebrew system," is merely part one of his grand plan. A while back, he bought a 15-barrel system in anticipation of opening a professional-grade brewery. As he put it, "six months turned into six years." But the last time we spoke to Will, he said that he's on track for a late 2006 opening of an environmentally friendly operation certified by Leadership in Energy and Environmental Design (LEED). Once he gets up and running, he'll offer six to eight house beers. As you might expect, they'll be named after tubas.

Class of license: Brewpub.
Opened: The first batch of beer was racked in September 1999.
Owners: Will White, Jennifer Byrom.
Brewer: Will White.
System: Three-quarter-barrel Pico.
Production: About 5 barrels a year.
Hours: Monday through Thursday, 8 A.M. to 10 P.M.; Friday and Saturday, 8 A.M. to 11 P.M.; Sunday, 9 A.M. to 9 P.M.

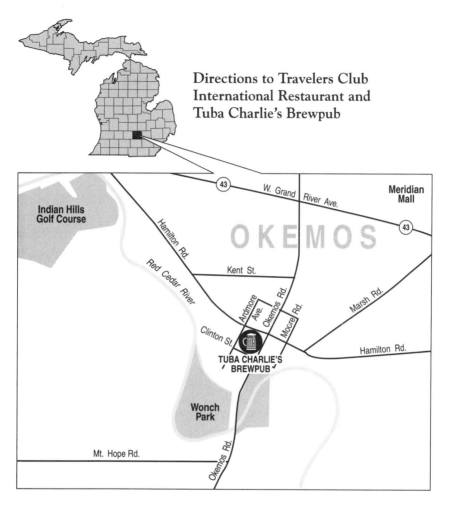

Directions to Travelers Club
International Restaurant and
Tuba Charlie's Brewpub

Take-out beer: Bottles of imported beer are available, but all of the house beers are consumed on premises.

Food: Ethnic and international cuisine, including rotating monthly specials.

Extras: More than 120 imported beers from thirty countries, and not just the usual suspects; we found beers from Finland and Lebanon. Michigan microbrews on draft. Kid- and vegetarian-friendly. Smoke-free.

Happy hour: Reduced-price Belgian beers on Thursday. Reduced pints Monday through Wednesday.

Parking: Free parking in front, in the unpaved lot next door, and in the back.

Harper's Restaurant and Brewpub

131 Albert Avenue, East Lansing, MI 48823
571-333-4040

Once upon a time, eighteen-year-olds could drink in Michigan, and college towns—East Lansing in particular—were famous for their parties. At Michigan State University, the place to party was Dooley's Restaurant and Bar. But things gradually got ugly. After an accumulation of offenses involving noise, fights, and liquor code violations, the city ordered Dooley's to close.

Enter Pat and Trisha Riley, a local couple who headed a group of investors who bought the building. They relaunched it as a brewpub and dance club, which not only solved the long-standing "Dooley's problem," but also brought a much-needed restaurant to downtown East Lansing.

Harper's is a large establishment—capacity is upward of five hundred—and with the MSU campus virtually across the street, it's busy almost every night of the year. But the atmosphere here is much different than it was during Dooley's era. To begin with, floor-to-ceiling windows in front brighten the mood, and the brewing equipment has been given top billing. The brewery stands proudly behind the windows, and the serving tanks have a prominent place by the bar.

The dining area has bistro-style blond-wood tables and wrought-iron chairs, along with green walls, tables, and carpeting (Michigan State's colors are green and white). Exposed ceilings and retro lighting fixtures provide a vaguely industrial ambience, and vintage photos add a bit of nostalgia. During the warm months—yes, we get those in Michigan—customers flock to the patio, which spans three sides of the building.

Harper's is often stereotyped as a sports bar, but its owners would like to break out of that mold. To draw a bigger dinner crowd, they've recruited a

Beers brewed: There are six beers on tap. The four menu beers are Burning Couch Hefe-Weizen, Grove Street Pale Ale, Harper's Light, and Raspberry Wheat. There is also a rotating seasonal, either a stout or a porter, and a brewer's choice. Scott said that he planned to add cask beers to the rotation.

Our Picks: Paul went with the Spartan Wheat, a seasonal, and one of the better American-style wheats he sampled for this book. Maryanne's top choice was the Grove Street Pale Ale. Those who enjoy fruit beer will find the Raspberry Wheat outstanding.

new chef from the Northwest, who's working at upgrading the menu and incorporating beers into more dishes. One unusual item we spotted on the menu was the Peppered Burger, topped with pickled hops.

Musicians perform four or five nights a week—there's a stage in the corner—and some good local acts have appeared here. During the day, an interesting mix of oldies music plays on the sound system. Downstairs is Club 131, a dance club frequented by singles, some of whose parents might have met here. And sports fans haven't been forgotten: There's a large-screen television behind the bar and smaller monitors elsewhere. As you might expect, things get hectic on MSU game days.

Scott Isham, who grew up in west Michigan, has been the brewer at Harper's since September 2000. He started homebrewing after he finished his hitch in the army and resumed his studies in college. Isham fell in love with British-style ales, and if he had his druthers, he'd offer an all-British lineup of ales. Although the Rileys have given him a free hand in brewing, he's a realist who said to us, "I'm in business to sell beer."

The typical beer drinker at Harper's is more likely to be a student who recently turned twenty-one than a hard-core beer geek. For Isham, that isn't all bad. He's discovered that younger customers are willing to try something other than mass-market lager and to judge beer on taste rather than advertising hype. He's also encouraged by the fact that older MSU alumni show up, especially before and after football games, and some take growlers to tailgate parties.

With production topping 1,000 barrels a year, Harper's is a big brewpub. Isham joked to us that Harper's is "the biggest brewpub in the state that no one has heard of." As the regulars tell their friends about it, that distinction isn't likely to last much longer.

Class of license: Brewpub.
Opened: September 1997.
Owner: Harbrinel, Inc. Pat and Trisha Riley are its main shareholders. The brewpub is named for Trisha's late father.
Brewer: Scott Isham.
System: 15-barrel DME system, with five fermenters and serving tanks.
Production: 976 barrels in 2004; expected to be slightly higher in 2005.
Hours: Monday through Saturday, 11 A.M. to 2 A.M.; Sunday, 11 A.M. to 11 P.M.
Tours: Ask if brewer is available or call ahead.
Take-out beer: Growlers, Cornelius kegs, and kegs.
Food: Bistro fare, with good variety, including upscale pub grub, pizzas, and a variety of entrees.

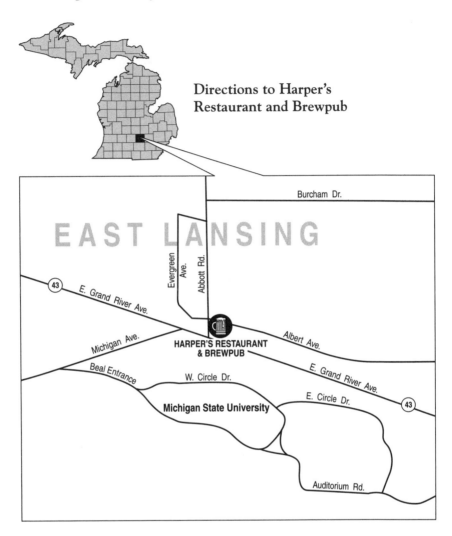

Directions to Harper's Restaurant and Brewpub

Extras: Dance club downstairs. Live entertainment.
Happy hour: Monday through Friday, 4 to 7 P.M., with reduced pints. Wednesday is half-off day for both food and drinks. Reduced pint specials on Monday, Tuesday, and Thursday nights.
Parking: Structure and surface lot facing the brewpub.

A word about . . .

Microbreweries, Brewpubs, and Michigan Beer Laws

W hen beer is involved, regulation is sure to follow. That's been true as far back as the Code of Hammurabi, the oldest known compilation of laws. In those days, disorderly conduct in a tavern could earn you the death penalty.

Michigan's liquor code isn't quite that strict, but it does impose significant restrictions on the brewing industry. Like most states, Michigan legislated a three-tier system—which entailed brewers, distributors, and retailers—after the repeal of Prohibition. That means that a brewer could not sell directly to a retail outlet but instead had to sell its product to a distributor, which in turn sold it to bars and liquor stores.

One objective of the three-tier system was to prevent big brewers from controlling the market by either owning or controlling taverns. But the brewing industry of the late twentieth century was radically different from that of the 1930s: Laws originally designed to stop abuses by big breweries had the opposite effect, making it difficult, if not impossible, for new craft brewers to enter the market.

Starting in the eighties, state lawmakers carved out narrow exceptions to the three-tier system that allow craft breweries to operate. Michigan changed its laws somewhat later than states in the West, where the craft-brew movement began. In 1992, the legislature allowed brewpubs to operate.

Today Michigan law recognizes three categories of brewery licenses: *brewery*, *microbrewery*, and *brewpub*.

Brewery

A brewery license is issued to a brewery that manufactures more than 30,000 barrels per year. Only one Michigan brewery, Bell's, falls into that category.

A brewer may sell beer at an on-premises taproom or in containers for customers to take home. However, it may not sell directly to retailers such as bars and liquor stores. A brewer may operate more than one facility, but each requires a separate license and only one may have a taproom. In 2002, Bell's Brewery opened a production facility without a taproom in Comstock Township; its other brewery in downtown Kalamazoo has a taproom called the Eccentric Café.

In addition, brewers are allowed to contract-brew—that is, make beer whose brand name and recipe are owned by someone else. A brewer that does so is responsible for complying with all the laws governing brewing. A brewer also may produce private-label beer to be sold at a retail establishment such as a restaurant—through a distributor, of course.

Microbrewery

A microbrewery license is issued to a brewery that manufactures 30,000 barrels or less per year. According to the Liquor Control Commission (LCC), twenty-seven microbrewery licenses were in force as of late 2005. A microbrewer, like a brewer, may sell beer at an on-premises taproom or in containers for customers to take home. The law doesn't require a microbrewer to operate a restaurant in connection with the taproom, but most serve at least a limited menu. Some, like Arcadia Brewing Company in Battle Creek, decided that it made business sense to operate a full-service restaurant.

Like a brewer, a microbrewer may not sell directly to retailers. It may have multiple brewing facilities, but each requires a separate license. For example, New Holland Brewing Company has two facilities in Holland: a production brewery and a smaller brewery downtown that has a taproom. Like a brewer, a microbrewer may contract-brew or produce private-label beer.

Brewpub

A brewpub license is issued to a brewer that manufactures 5,000 barrels or less per year. According to the LCC, fifty-one brewpub licenses were in force as of late 2005.

To be licensed as a brewpub, a business must already have a license to sell liquor on the premises. Nearly all brewpubs have Class C licenses, which allow them to sell beer, wine, and hard liquor. As a result, the vast majority provide full bar service. Some offer guest ales, typically imports, national-brand craft beers, or Michigan microbrewed beers. A few brewpub owners confessed that they keep a supply of national-brand beer on hand "for those who insist." State law also requires a brewpub to be in the restaurant business: It must be licensed to sell food and derive at least 25 percent of its sales from food and nonalcoholic beverages. Like brewers and microbrewers, brewpubs may also sell beer in containers to go.

In an effort to prevent big chains from dominating the market, the law forbids a person to have an interest—which includes being a shareholder or a landlord as well as an owner—in more than three brewpubs. Currently, Schelde Enterprises and the Beer Companies each own three brewpubs. Additionally, the 5,000-barrel limit applies to the total production of multiple brewpubs owned by the same person.

Brew-on-Premises Operations
Several Michigan microbrewers have brew-on-premises operations, in which customers participate in the brewing process. The LCC has ruled that brew-on-premises operations are not homebrewing, because brewing takes place outside the customer's home. As a result, these operations are legal only if the customer makes beer under the supervision of the microbrewer's staff. By the way, the microbrewer is considered to have sold the final product to the customer.

Wine and Liquor Manufacturing
For another annual fee, a microbrewer may also obtain a small winemaker license, which allows it make wine and sell it to wholesalers, retailers, and customers. Most microbrewers in Michigan have gotten or are in the process of getting their license. If a microbrewer operates a restaurant—it doesn't have to—it may sell wine by the glass as well.

In addition, some microbrewers have obtained distiller's licenses from the federal government. New Holland and Leopold Brothers Brewing and Distilling are among the brewers that also distill.

Other Michigan Laws
Here are a few other laws that a visitor should be aware of:

• Beer isn't hard to find in Michigan. It can be sold in liquor stores; supermarkets, drugstores, and delis; convenience stores, which are called "party stores" in much of Michigan; and gas stations in many communities outside the Detroit area. The selection you'll find there is another matter. Most drug and convenience stores, and some liquor stores, stock only the usual suspects. In our experience, high-end stores like Whole Foods Markets offer a wider selection of local microbrews than big supermarket chains. We've also found that better wine shops often carry a good selection of beer.

• Serving hours are limited to 7 A.M. to 2 A.M. Monday through Saturday and noon to 2 A.M. Sunday. Some communities enforce an earlier last call, and a few ban sales on Sunday. A new law allows establishments to offer entertainment and dancing, but not alcohol, after 2

A.M. Alcohol may not be served after 9 P.M. on Christmas Eve or at any time on Christmas Day.

• Michigan has a deposit law that applies to both bottles and cans. Unlike other states, the deposit is a dime rather than a nickel, which inspired the *Seinfeld* episode in which Newman wanted to drive a truck-load of used cans to Michigan. Had he done so, he would have run into problems: By law, stores have the right to limit customers to $25 worth of bottles and cans.

• The legal age for buying beer is twenty-one, same as everywhere else in the country, and many establishments enforce it strictly. In fact, some grocery chains have a "card everyone" policy, so please don't take it personally.

• Finally, there's the "growler controversy." A number of brewpub owners won't refill growlers from other establishments, and some have told us that it's the law. Actually, it isn't. There's no law or Liquor Control Commission rule against filling another's growler, so long as the filling establishment sanitizes it and places a label on the growler that meets federal requirements. Having said that, nothing in the law requires a brewpub to fill someone else's growler, either. We suggest that you ask in advance, and be a sport about it if you're told no.

West Michigan
Heartland

An oddity about Michigan is that most of its people live in the southeast but most large microbreweries are found in the west. Some of this has to do with the politics and economics of beer distribution. For a variety of reasons, it's tougher for a small brewery to crack the huge Detroit-area beer market than it is to break into markets in the rest of the state. Another big reason is Bell's Brewery. In talking with the state's brewers, we were surprised to discover how many had crossed paths with Larry Bell—a number had worked for him at one time—or were influenced by his brewery.

Bell's is located in Kalamazoo, whose name comes from a Native American word meaning "the place where the water boils." They were referring to the Kalamazoo River, not brewkettles. Located halfway between Detroit and Chicago, Kalamazoo has been used as a test market for new products. And for political ideas as well. Its diverse population is almost evenly divided along party lines, a fact that hadn't escaped the attention of those who conduct political focus groups. One of the city's leading attractions is the Kalamazoo Air Zoo (6151 Portage Road, 866-524-7966, www.airzoo.org), one of the nation's premier military aircraft museums.

One axis of the West Michigan heartland is U.S. Route 131, which extends from the Indiana line almost to Traverse City. Less than an hour's drive north of Kalamazoo on U.S. Route 131 is Grand Rapids, which, logically enough, got its name from the rapids of the Grand River, on which millions of logs were once floated downstream to be milled in the city. The city has been known for its furniture industry ever since. Today it's the headquarters of the office furniture maker Steelcase.

Downtown Grand Rapids has gotten a facelift with the help of some wealthy locals: the Meijer, DeVos, and Van Andel families. Long before the first Wal-Mart opened in Michigan, shoppers were familiar with the

111

"hypermarket" concept because they'd been shopping at Hendrik Meijer's stores, which he originally called Meijer Thrifty Acres. One of the city's attractions is Frederick Meijer Gardens (1000 East Beltline Road, N.E., 616-957-1580, www.meijergardens.org), which include a tropical conservatory and a large collection of sculptures. Richard DeVos and Jay Van Andel made their fortune with Amway Corporation, whose headquarters are in nearby Ada. Members of the DeVos family are a powerful force in Michigan Republican politics. Van Andel's name appears on the Van Andel Arena (130 West Fulton Street, 616-742-6600, www.vanandel arena.com), where Grand Rapids' minor-league hockey and Arena Football League teams play, and the Van Andel Museum Center (272 Pearl Street, N.W., 616-456-3977, www.grmuseum.org), an educational complex with a bit of a theme park atmosphere.

Parts of town were wide open during logging days, but that didn't last very long. For most of its history, Grand Rapids was inhabited by hardworking, clean-living Republicans. For years, it was represented in Congress by Gerald R. Ford, who found himself in the White House after scandals forced both Spiro Agnew and Richard Nixon to resign. Grand Rapids is home to the Gerald R. Ford Museum (303 Pearl Street, N.W., 616-254-0400, www.geraldrfordfoundation.org), which has a life-size replica of the Oval Office and hands-on, interactive video and holographic displays. The Christian Reformed Church has its headquarters in this city, and many residents belong. There are also Polish American, African American, Asian, and Latino populations.

The other axis of the west Michigan heartland is I-94, the busy east-west freeway connecting Detroit and Chicago. East of Kalamazoo is Marshall, which boasts an outstanding collection of Greek and Gothic Revival homes from the mid-nineteenth century. These homes have attracted travel writers from across the country, not to mention visitors who come to the annual home tour offered by the historical society (www.marshallhistoricalsociety.org) in early September. One notable building is the Honolulu House, built by a Marshall resident who served as U.S. consul to Hawaii in the days before it was American territory.

Between Marshall and Kalamazoo, you'll find Battle Creek, where the number-one industry used to be health resorts that put its patients on strict diets. If you read T. Coraghessan Boyle's novel *The Road to Wellville*, or watch the movie based on it, you know what we're talking about. One of Battle Creek's sanatoriums was run by John Harvey Kellogg, a Seventh-Day Adventist who developed corn flakes as part of his regimen. The city is still home to the Kellogg Company and its Cereal City USA (171 West Michigan Avenue, 800-970-7020, www.kelloggs

cerealcity.com), a combination museum, factory tour, and theme attraction where you can meet Tony the Tiger and have your photo placed on a box of cereal. Post and Ralston Purina cereals are also made there. In June, the city invites the world to sit down at the "world's longest breakfast table."

West of Kalamazoo, you enter the state's fruit-growing region—and the snowbelt. Lake-effect snow, the result of cold air crossing the warmer waters of the Great Lakes, can add up to a foot or more in parts of west Michigan—even though places farther east get only a dusting. The upside is that the same lakes that turn on the snow machine in winter lengthen the growing season in fall, making it possible to grow a variety of fruit, including wine grapes. You'll find a number of wineries along the Southwest Michigan Wine Trail (www.miwinetrail.com).

Convention and Visitors Bureaus
Battle Creek: www.thatclose.org
Kalamazoo: www.discoverkalamazoo.com
Grand Rapids: www.visitgrandrapids.org

Recommended Beer Bars
Battle Creek
Griffin Grill & Pub, 38 Michigan Avenue West, 269-965-7206. A Celtic-themed bar on the city's main drag.

Dowagiac
Zeke's, 109 South Front Street, 269-782-5070. Thirty taps, many of them microbrews from the Great Lakes, and more than 250 bottled beers.

Grand Rapids
Cambridge House, 600 Monroe Avenue, N.W., 616-356-1622, www.we luvbeer-wine.com/cambridgehouse/index.html. British ales and some local microbrews on tap.
Logan's Alley, 916 Michigan Street, N.E., 616-458-1612, weluvbeer-wine.com/logansalley. Good and unusual selection of beers, with nearly twenty taps and a wide selection of bottles.

Kalamazoo
Corner Bar and Grill, 1020 East Vine Street, 269-385-2028. A Chicago-style hangout with more than a dozen microbrews on tap and an interesting collection of breweriana.

Pilsen Klub, 1408 West Michigan Avenue, 269-349-2020. In the lower level of Waldo's, a campus bar near Western Michigan University. Good beer selection.

Shakespeare's Pub, 241 East Kalamazoo Avenue, 269-488-7782. A sports bar that offers a wide selection of tap beers, including local micros. Close to Eccentric Café and Kraftbräu.

Lawton

Big T, 155 North Main Street, 269-624-1200. Across the street from the Old Hat brewpub. Has more than two hundred bottled beers.

Marshall

Stagecoach Inn, 201 West Michigan Avenue, 269-781-3571.

Founders Brewing Company

648 Monroe Avenue, N.W., Grand Rapids, MI 49503
616-776-1195
www.foundersbrewing.com

Here's a lesson in Grand Rapids brewing history. This brewery's official name is the Canal Street Brewing Company, which honors the street where the city's breweries clustered in the late nineteenth century. Its original labels bore a picture of the men who founded those breweries, and locals started calling the beer Founders.

Now, let's talk about another set of founders. They are Mike Stevens and Dave Engbers, friends who grew up in Grand Rapids and attended Hope College. Interestingly, they belonged to the same fraternity as Jason Spaulding and Brett VanderKamp, who went on to start New Holland Brewing Company. Did we mention that Michigan's brewing community is close-knit?

After graduating from college, Mike and Dave decided to go into the craft-brewing business. They recruited a group of local investors, lined up financing, and found a building that once was a brass-stamping factory. They brought the red brick building back to life—complete with a black-and-gold sign bearing its original name—and put in a brewery and bottling line.

A year after brewing its first batch of beer, Founders opened a taproom on the second floor. That's where we found Nate Walser, who was at the time half of the two-headed brewing team. Nate has since left to start a business cleaning draft lines— Founders was his first customer—and the head man is now Jeremy Koznicki, who's been brewing here since 2001.

Nate was on the same page as Jeremy, as well as the owners, when it came to Founders' brewing philosophy. "We're an American brewery," he told us, "so you won't find European-style beers here." Founders is one of the leaders of Michigan's big-beer movement. As Nate put it, "Americans like to live large, and we intend to indulge their appetites."

That "living-large" approach represented a big change of heart. At first Founders brewed a fairly tame assortment of beers: an amber, a wheat, and a pale ale. They were modestly successful, but Mike and Dave asked themselves that famous question, "Is that all there is?" They decided it wasn't. "That's it. We're going to make beers we want to drink," Mike said. That is now Founders' slogan.

Founders ditched most of its conventional products and concentrated on big and unusual beers. Enthusiasts noticed the change and spread the word over the Internet. Mike credits sites like RateBeer.com, whose contributors rank Founders one of America's best breweries, and BeerAdvocate.com for putting the brewery on the map, not just among beer drinkers, but among distributors as well.

If Canal Street's beer barons were brought back to life and transported to the taproom, they'd hardly recognize what's on tap. Take Devil Dancer, for instance. It's a double India pale ale that weighs in at 13 percent ABV and is brewed with ten different hops. Lawn-mower beer it's not. The taproom's twelve-beer selection includes year-rounders like Breakfast Stout and Red's Rye as well as experimental beers. Founders is still small enough to take big chances.

Hard-to-find beer is the taproom's main attraction, but not the only one. It's a comfortable, laid-back place that attracts a mixed crowd,

Beers brewed: The lineup includes Black Rye; Breakfast Stout; Centennial IPA; Curmudgeon Old Ale; Devil Dancer, a double IPA; Dirty Bastard Scotch Ale, Founders' flagship beer; Imperial Stout; Kentucky Breakfast, a barrel-aged stout; Pale Ale; Red's Rye; Rubaeus, a raspberry pale ale; and seasonals and specialties too numerous to mention. Before heading out, check the brewery's website for the list of what's on at the taproom. Beer is served in appropriate glassware. Founders earns an extra pat on the back for making liberal use of Michigan products, including maple syrup, cherries, and honey.

Our Pick: We rarely eat breakfast, but how could we not choose the Breakfast Stout? You've got to love Founders' attitude. The label for this beer features a baby, and its slogan is "You can't drink all day unless you start in the morning." Breakfast Stout is brewed with oats, imported chocolate, and Sumatra and Kona coffee, and it wields a deceptive 8.3 percent alcoholic hammer.

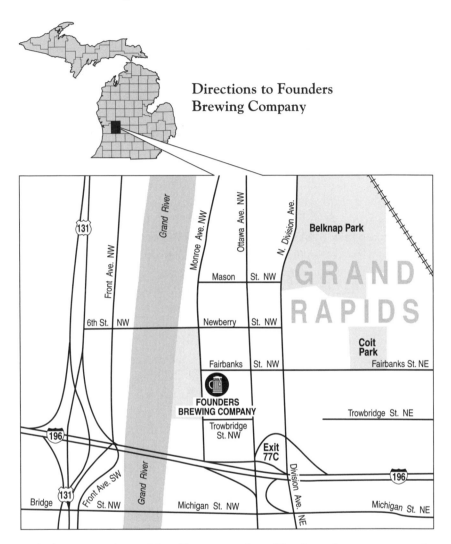

Directions to Founders Brewing Company

including a steady trickle of beer travelers. The furnishings consist of a small bar, tables built by Mike and Dave themselves, a pool table, a few televisions, and a first-class jukebox. The front windows overlook Grand Rapids' industrial district; the windows in the back of the taproom allow customers to watch the beer being brewed.

Not only is Founders operating in the black, but its owners face a problem other brewers wish they had: It's running at capacity and has no room to expand. The owners have their eye on a nearby building, and when we last spoke to Mike, they were in the process of closing a loan for the project. If all goes well, the new facility, which ultimately will turn out upward of 20,000 barrels, should be up and running by now. And yes, the owners intend to maintain a taproom—in the name of science, of course.

Class of license: Microbrewery.
Opened: Brewing operations began October 1997. The taproom opened in August 1998.
Official corporate name: Canal Street Brewing Company.
Owners: Mike Stevens and Dave Engbers.
Brewer: Jeremy Koznicki, head brewer.
System: 30-barrel Sprinkman. Capacity is 5,000 barrels.
Production: 5,000 barrels in 2005. If all has gone according to plan, production will rise to 10,000 barrels a year at the new facility.
Distribution: Throughout Michigan as well as portions of Illinois, Indiana, Ohio, and Wisconsin. Founders distributes four-packs of the most popular "big beers" to select retailers.
Hours: Monday through Saturday, 11 A.M. to 2 A.M.; Sunday, 3 P.M. to 2 A.M.
Tours: Yes, please call ahead.
Take-out beer: Four- and six-packs, growlers, and kegs.
Food: Deli menu 11 A.M. to 2 P.M.; snacks only the rest of the day.
Extras: Free wireless Internet. Jazz and blues on Tuesdays. Open mike on Wednesdays. Rock bands, mainly on weekends. Special events, including pub crawls, festivals, and holiday parties. Founders is licensed as a small winery and offers hard cider in the fall.
Happy hour: Monday through Friday, 3 to 6 P.M., with reduced pints. Nightly specials, including "bartender's choice" on Monday and reduced pitchers on Tuesday.
Parking: A limited number of metered spaces on nearby streets. Free parking in the Brass Works lot after 5 P.M.

Grand Rapids Brewing Company

3689 Twenty-eighth Street, S.E., Grand Rapids, MI 49512
616-285-5970
www.michiganmenu.com/grbrewing.html

Its fans insist that Grand Rapids Brewing Company is the state's oldest brewpub. They point out that beer has been brewed there continuously since November 3, 1993, a claim that no other brewpub can make.

First or not, Grand Rapids Brewing Company is a first-class operation in every respect. As you enter, you'll see a large outdoor deck decorated with international flags and ivy growing on the side of the building. Inside, a large vestibule holds a wide selection of brewpub merchandise and gift items. To the right is the dining area, which draws families and a substantial business clientele. It's decorated with vintage beer-themed photos, some of them donated by customers, and breweriana from the original Grand Rapids Brewing Company, which opened a century before the current version.

The earlier Grand Rapids Brewing Company was formed when six of the city's breweries joined forces to stave off competitors, financial problems being as old as commercial brewing itself. The brewery turned out a pilsner called Silver Foam, which became quite popular in the area. Silver Foam survived until 1917, when statewide prohibition took effect.

To the left is a barroom dominated by a large wooden bar. Behind it, along with the bottles of spirits, are mugs belonging to mug-club members—some seven hundred in all. This is a place to have a beer and a conversation; distractions are limited to a couple of television sets at the bar and some electronic games off to the side. In the corner is the Hall of Foam, a collection of photos of regulars taken in exotic locales.

It was there that we caught up with John Svoboda, who's been the head brewer since 1998. John

Beers brewed: The menu beers are Boleyn's Bitter, California Common, Centennial Silver Foam, Grand Rapids Light, Lumberman Dark, and River City Red. There's a rotating pale ale, available on draft and on hand pull, and a rotating seasonal. A specialty of the house is a range of six stouts that run the gamut for the style.

Our Picks: It was hard to choose among John's many fine offerings, but Maryanne went with California Common, not the easiest style for brewers to nail. Paul chose the Lumberman Dark, which was described as a stout-porter hybrid.

got interested in brewing after a fellow bicycle racer introduced him to homebrewing. He was a science major in college but told us he has an artistic side as well, one that expresses itself in the brewery.

John applied for a job here when he learned that the owners wanted to open a brewpub. He's been on the brewing staff since day one. His many interests include cooking, which also serves as an influence on his brewing. It has led him to brew a variety of beers—"whatever tastes good," he said—rather than concentrate on a particular style. There's an effort under way to "bring food and beer closer together," so it's no surprise that the house beers go into a variety of items, ranging from mussels and sausage to marinara sauce to fish batter.

His flagship beer is Centennial Silver Foam. It's a pilsner-style beer, but unlike the original, it's made with all German ingredients. Silver Foam and River City Red used to be the two biggest sellers, but customers have lately upped their consumption of seasonals and specialties. A rotating "brewer's choice" tap allows John to roam brewing's frontiers. "We go all over the place," he said. "It could be anything from a heather ale to a Maibock to a Belgian grand cru." He considers himself "more of a grain and yeast guy than a hop guy."

John told us that his recipes have evolved substantially over the years, and more changes are in the offing. He's one of the state's many brewers of "big beers." With the help of assistant brewer Dan Mariage, he's branched out into lambics (we saw a barrel of faro tucked away in the cooler). And he's also gotten into barrel-aged beer, which he intends to offer in four-packs.

With John Svoboda wielding the paddle, Grand Rapids Brewing Company has been one of the state's most innovative establishments. If you find yourself in town, take a seat at the bar and taste the future of Michigan beer.

Class of license: Brewpub.
Opened: November 1993.
Owner: Schelde Enterprises, Inc.
Brewer: John Svoboda, head brewer; Dan Mariage, assistant brewer.
System: 7-barrel DME. Capacity is 900 barrels.
Production: About 675 barrels in 2004.
Hours: Sunday through Thursday, 11 A.M. to 10 P.M.; Friday and Saturday, 11 A.M. to 11 P.M.
Tours: Yes, just ask.
Take-out beer: Growlers and kegs, as well as gift boxes of bottle-conditioned ales.

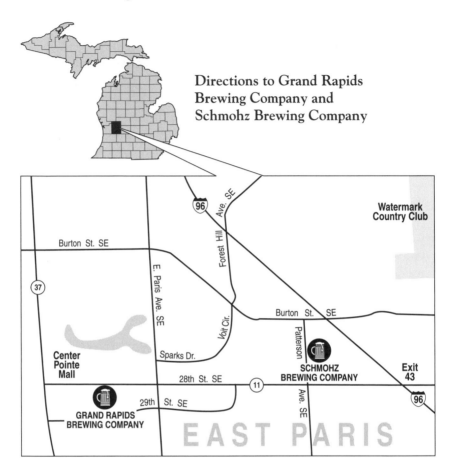

Food: Full menu, with a range of entrees as well as lighter bar fare.

Extras: Brewer's dinners, including an annual "Night Out with Stouts," with beer and food pairings. Oktoberfest, a pig roast–wheat beer event, and other special events. Occasional live entertainment. Outdoor deck. "Kids Eat Free" promotion on Sundays.

Happy hour: Monday through Friday, 3 to 6 P.M.

Mug club: Onetime membership fee. Benefits include discounts on pints, growlers, and merchandise and notice of special events.

Parking: Large lot adjacent.

Directions: Twenty-eighth Street is a nightmare, but the brewpub's two grain silos are handy landmarks.

Hideout Brewing Company

3113 Plaza Drive, N.E., Grand Rapids, MI 49225
616-361-9658
www.hideoutbrewing.com

Online mapping programs have come a long way, but the directions to the Hideout Brewing Company made us wonder if our luck had ended. It sent us through an endless apartment complex and into the parking lot of a tacky seventies-era building with a "Hubba Bubba" sign on the outside. A dead end? Hardly. Turned out we'd come to the right place. It really is hidden.

The building opened in the late seventies as a fitness center, and the business next door still rents hot tubs by the hour. The half of the building occupied by Hideout had been home to two other breweries: the Homebrew Kitchen, a brew-on-premises operation, and more recently, the Hair of the Frog Brewing Company.

We talked with Ken McPhail, the brewer-owner, inside the smallish (capacity forty-nine) downstairs taproom. The furnishings are spartan: a tiny U-shaped bar in the middle, a dozen or so homemade barstools, and chairs along the walls, along with a television set in one corner and a small popcorn machine. Decor consists of a cabinet that will be used to display merchandise and some photos that we'll get to in a moment. Upstairs, there's a large-screen television, a foosball table, and darts.

Ken explained that the brewery and taproom were hand-me-downs from the Hair of the Frog. When that brewery closed its doors, he managed to negotiate favorable terms and got "essentially a turnkey operation," down to the taps on the wall. Low overhead here will give him the financial breathing room he needs to improve things. His plans include an expanded food menu, live entertainment and special events, an outdoor patio, and last but not least, signage to make the brewery easier to locate.

Beers brewed: There are six menu beers: Purple Gang Pilsner, Crusaders' Weizen, Bootleg IPA, Cement Shoe Stout, Nitro Stout, and Smuggler's Hazelnut. Seasonals include F.D.R.'s ESB, Tommy Gun Red, dunkelweizen, and Oktoberfest. Hideout also makes mead, which contains local honey.

Our Picks: Paul chose the Smuggler's Hazelnut Stout, a hearty black ale that uses locally roasted hazelnut coffee beans. Maryanne's pick was the F.D.R. Extra Special Bitter, which, at 6.8 percent ABV, was much stronger than she'd ever had in English pubs.

Ken said that he has wanted to own a microbrewery for years. As head man, he does a little of everything, including tending bar and packaging his beer. His interest in brewing goes back to his days as a business major at Western Michigan University, where one of his case studies was Bell's Beer. He also worked at Bell's, managing the home-brew supply store and learning the brewing business from the bottom up. Ken's first pro job was at the Big Buck brewpub in Grand Rapids. When it closed, he managed a restaurant until the Hair of the Frog went on the market.

Hideout's brewery is a 5-barrel combination system assembled by the Hair of the Frog's owners. Ken, who brewed his own for years, pro-nounced the system "homebrew-friendly," though he's upgraded it to where it can turn out decent-size professionally brewed batches. He still considers himself part of the area's "grassroots brewing tradition" and hosts monthly meetings of the local homebrew club.

Ken concentrates on traditional, true-to-style beers. He plans to supplement his six year-round beers with the likes of ESB, Oktoberfest, and Belgian abbey-style beers, along with "some really big beers." He has a small winemaker's license and also offers hard cider made from local apples and mead made with local honey.

In the first few months of operation, Hideout won back many Hair of the Frog customers who, Ken said, prefer things "a little different from the mainstream." He's also attracted a new clientele and told us that on a given night, you'll find anyone from twenty-two-year-old college students to retirees, and a good representation of women and couples.

The brewery's dead-end location is one reason why it's called Hide-out. The other reason is Ken's interest in Prohibition days. He's deco-rated the walls with Library of Congress photos from that era—you might have seen them elsewhere—and his beer names evoke the speakeasy era.

When we visited, Hideout was, admittedly, a work in progress. But Ken has experience in both the brewing and restaurant sides of the business and a degree in entrepreneurship. With those credentials, he's no doubt mapped out Hideout's route to success.

Class of license: Microbrewery.
Opened: May 2005
Owner-brewer: Ken McPhail.
System: 5-barrel McPhail system.
Production: Three batches a week, which adds up to 180 barrels a year.
Distribution: Hideout has begun to line up distributors.
Hours: Tuesday through Thursday, 4 P.M. to 1 A.M.; Friday, 4 P.M. to 2

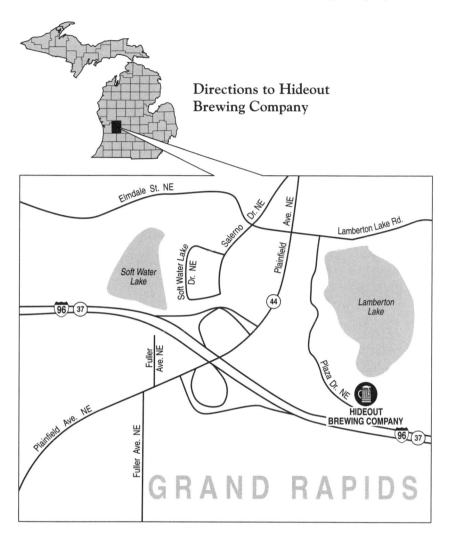

Directions to Hideout
Brewing Company

A.M.; Saturday, 2 P.M. to 2 A.M.; Sunday, 4 to 10 P.M. Closed Monday. Shorter hours in the summer.

Tours: Ask if possible.

Take-out beer: Growlers and kegs.

Food: Snacks including sandwiches, nachos, chili, and soup.

Extras: Sunday NFL Ticket, with reduced pints during games. Monthly Primetime Brewers' meetings. Christmas and New Year's Eve parties. Smoking permitted upstairs only.

Mug club: $45 per year. Benefits include a 20-ounce personalized mug, discounts on mugs and growlers, and a members-only potluck dinner with reduced pints.

Parking: Lot adjacent to the brewery.

Schmohz Brewing Company

2600 Patterson Avenue, S.E., Grand Rapids, MI 49546
616-949-0860
www.schmohz.com

"From one beer lover to another, Stroh's." That jingle is hard-wired into the brain of every Michigander over forty. Stroh's was the biggest-selling beer in Michigan history, the sponsor of Detroit Tigers broadcasts, and a Detroit landmark.

We suspect that Stroh's has something to do with Schmohz Brewing Company's name. Its owners, Jim and Laurie Schwerin, were a little cagey about its origin. All Laurie would tell was that they picked it "four hours and four pages into a road trip." But here are a couple of hints: It starts with the same letters as their last name. And it rhymes with you-know-what.

Schmohz isn't the first brewery to make a go of it at this site, an industrial building east of downtown. It was once the home of the Robert Thomas Brewery, which couldn't survive the craft-brewing slump of the early twenty-first century even after merging with another brewery.

For the Schwerins, Robert Thomas's closing was a classic example of good news, bad news. First the bad news: They lived in southeast Michigan and Jim worked there. Running a brewery in Grand Rapids meant a nasty commute and logistical problems. For now, Jim's juggling two jobs.

Now the good news: The Schwerins inherited a turnkey operation. As Laurie said, "Why did we put it here? Because it was here." All they had to do was give the brewery a good scrubbing, slap on a fresh coat of paint, and redesign the bar to their liking. And wait for bureaucrats to move the paperwork for their license.

Beers brewed: The menu beers are Amber Tease; Gypsy's Kiss Bock; Hopknocker India Pale Ale, the number-one seller; Mad Tom's Robust Porter; and Valley City Cream Ale. Seasonals included a stout, an Oktoberfest, and a weizen. Schmohz also offers beer mixtures and brews its own root beer.

Our Picks: Paul chose the Amber Tease, a good rendition of a California common beer. "Tease," by the way, is a near anagram for "Steam." Maryanne chose Gypsy's Kiss Bock, a sweet and somewhat less alcoholic version of the style.

Schmohz's website describes Jim as a "midlife crisis brewer." Jim went to Northern Michigan University, where he met Laurie. He started homebrewing when his company sent him to Hannover, Germany, where, according to Laurie, he was disappointed in the local beer. Now there's a man with high standards. Later the Schwerins decided to open their own brewery but got a "not in my backyard" reaction from local officials, which led them to look at areas farther from metro Detroit.

The taproom has low ceilings, concrete floors, and reddish walls with wood. There's a big-screen television in the corner, a poster from the German town of Schwerin (the owners have distant relatives there), and few quarter barrels scattered about. That's about it for decor. Entertainment includes darts, a pinball machine, a pool table, and board games available at the bar.

Farther back is the copper-topped bar. Behind it is a classroom-issue blackboard promoting the "Weekly Deals" and another board listing what's on tap. If you look through the small window in the corner, you'll see part of the stainless steel 20-barrel brewery that might induce envy in other brewers. There's a selection of merchandise, a television set, and regulars' mugs as well.

Schmohz's beer menu has a couple of unusual twists. One is its beer mixtures, which include Milkman (India pale ale and porter) and SNC (cream ale, bock, and stout). The other is Breakaway Bay Root Beer, which has gained a following in its own right. Even people who don't drink beer stop by for root beer floats. The name, by the way, was suggested by a nine-year-old.

The Schwerins not only took over the Robert Thomas Brewery, but also inherited many of its regulars, who've known each other for years. Schmohz has also attracted newcomers, many of whom are in their twenties. The regulars range from airport workers to schoolteachers to golf course greenskeepers. It's the kind of crowd that flocks to a Sunday potluck dinner, which is one of the perks of belonging to Schmohz's mug club.

If you're old enough to remember the Stroh's jingle, Schmohz will remind you of your father's basement den. It's a down-to-earth kind of place, one where a euchre tournament is liable to break out. You can't get any more into Michigan culture than that.

Class of license: Microbrewery.
Opened: December 2004.
Owners: Jim and Laurie Schwerin.
Brewer: Jim Schwerin.

System: 20-barrel Century.

Production: N/A.

Distribution: Tap accounts in the Grand Rapids area. Schmohz is gearing up for bottled beer production.

Hours: Monday and Tuesday, 2 to 10 P.M.; Wednesday and Thursday, 2 P.M. to midnight; Friday and Saturday, noon to midnight. Reserved for private parties on Sunday.

Tours: Call in advance. No tours Monday or Tuesday.

Take-out beer: Six-packs, growlers, Cornelius kegs, and kegs.

Food: Only snack foods are available, but you can bring in any food you want.

Extras: Wireless Internet hot spot. Smoking is strictly forbidden.

Happy hour: On Tuesday, reduced pints for those who fill up their growlers. On Wednesday, reduced pints on Brewer's Choice beers. On Thursday, reduced pints.

Mug club: Membership costs $40 a year and entitles the member to reduced pints, growlers, and kegs.

Parking: Small lot in front and street parking within walking distance. It can get tight, especially on Friday nights, when Schmohz is the busiest. (See map on page 120.)

Middle Villa Inn

4611 North M-37, Middleville, MI 49333
616-891-1287
www.middle-villa-inn.com

MIDDLE VILLA INN
AND MICRO BREWERY

BOWLING   BANQUETS   CATERING   DINING   DANCING

Middleville's history reaches back to stagecoach days, when this little town was a stop on the Kalamazoo–to–Grand Rapids route. Despite the encroachment of suburbia, Middleville retains its small-town character. That's certainly true at the Middle Villa Inn, a family-owned business since 1962, which became a brewpub in 2003.

Owner Steve Wiersum escorted us into "his booth" in the bright and airy Garden Restaurant. He and his wife, Susan, decorated it with farm and garden implements, with little plaques next to each—their way of gently poking fun at the rock memorabilia in a popular restaurant chain. Above us were lamps in the shape of birdhouses. In the corner were flowers and knick-knacks that Susan changes with the seasons.

The Middle Villa complex also has four banquet rooms; a sixteen-lane bowling alley with all the electronic bells and whistles; a bakery offering bread, cookies, and pastries (Steve somehow finds time to bake); the restaurant, which has a salad bar and slow roaster; and the bar. This is a gathering place for community groups, families, and friends.

The Wiersums bought Middle Villa in 1969 and have gradually expanded it, including little touches like soft ice cream here, wireless Internet access there. The latest addition is the brewery, which stands behind the bar in back of a window with the legend "Middle Villa Brewery." The brewing vessels are visible from the bar; at night, Steve said, they give the barroom added character.

Steve told us that he got into the brewing business after he met a sales representative at a bowling proprietors' convention. He concluded that the idea made sense for Middle Villa and ordered a system. Steve showed it to us, and it's quite ingenious: a 4-barrel system consisting of a stainless steel brewkettle and two copper-jacketed fermenters and chillers. It's a turnkey system, too: The manufacturer ships all the ingredients, making the brewing process low-maintenance. (The same can't be said about Middle Villa getting licensed: The feds demanded paperwork going back to 1969 before they gave the okay to brew.)

Full disclosure: Middle Villa is an extract brewery. The state of the art has improved greatly since the early nineties, however, when we ran across extract houses whose beers were a crapshoot. In our opinion, Steve's beer compared favorably with national-brand lagers. But you need not take our word for it. In terms of sales volume, the house beers more than hold their own with what the big guys turn out.

Steve is still wending his way through the thirty or so recipes the manufacturer offers and hasn't finalized his menu. Eventually, he plans to offer two year-round beers and two rotating specialties. Beer brewed on the premises "makes us a little different from the guys down the street," Steve explained. He also let us in on a little secret: Middleville, it turns out, was voted as having the best water in Michigan.

Beers brewed: Four beers on tap. We tasted Beetle Bug Light, a light crisp lager similar to a Canadian light lager; Toad House Ale, an amber-colored Scottish-style ale; Down n' Dirty, a porter with a brown to black color; and Harvest Wheat, a North American wheat beer. Steve also brought out his variations of wheat beer—raspberry, peach, and black currant—along with regular wheat.

Beer is available in pints, pitchers, and samplers. Middle Villa also brews root beer.

Our Picks: This is an extract house, but Wiersum's turnkey system pretty much assures consistency. Paul chose Down n' Dirty, a porter, and Maryanne's pick was the Peach Wheat. Both were refreshing on a warm summer afternoon.

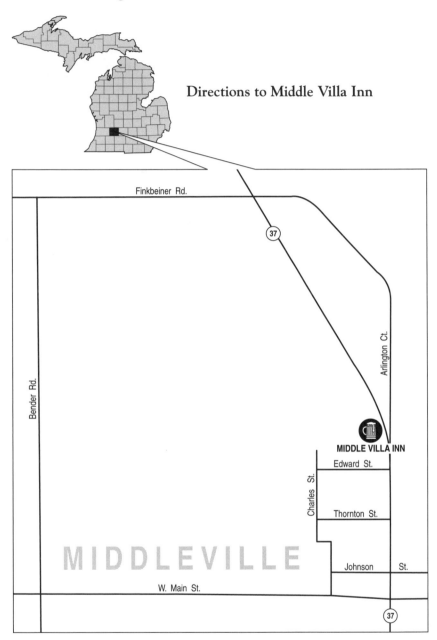

Directions to Middle Villa Inn

Finkbeiner Rd.

37

Bender Rd.

Arlington Ct.

MIDDLE VILLA INN

Edward St.

Charles St.

Thornton St.

MIDDLEVILLE

Johnson   St.

W. Main St.

37

    Steve drew samples of beer from the tap handles mounted on a cask and shared them with us. Each of the sample glasses was a tiny mug. As for the beer, it's best described as entry-level craft beer: a Canadian light lager, an amber ale, a porter, and a wheat beer. Their names were suggested by customers and reflect the restaurant's garden theme. Speaking of the garden, Steve said that he takes his leftover beer and trub out there to fight slugs. "At least they die happy," he said with a laugh.

We've read enough books on financial planning to know that diversification is the key to investment success. The Wiersums have done just that. Their brewery is part of Middle Villa Inn's well-rounded portfolio. It's a pleasant place to stop for a bite to eat and a quick quaff if you're traveling between Kalamazoo and Grand Rapids.

Class of license: Brewpub.
Opened: April 2003.
Owners: Steve and Susan Wiersum.
Brewer: Steve Wiersum.
System: 4-barrel MicroPub Systems.
Production: N/A
Hours: Daily, 11 A.M. to 10 P.M.
Tours: Yes, please ask.
Take-out beer: Growlers and Cornelius kegs.
Food: The menu leans heavily toward comfort food. Soup, salad, and ice cream bar with thirty-one items. Nightly early-bird and all-you-can-eat specials. Lunch is served until 5 P.M. Fish fry on Wednesdays.
Extras: Sixteen bowling lanes. Free wireless Internet access. Big-band performance once a quarter. Keno and pull tabs. Smoking is permitted.
Happy hour: Discounts on pints on Mondays.
Parking: Lot outside.

The Old Hat Brewery

114 North Main Street, Lawton, MI 49065
269-624-6445

To most travelers on I-94, Lawton—population 1,859—is just another name on an exit sign. But beer lovers know it well. On one side of downtown is The Big T, a beer bar with more than 250 bottled selections. Across the street is The Old Hat Brewery, one of Michigan's more characterful brewpubs.

The Old Hat's story began in 1994, when Phil Balog, a retired crop duster, opened a brewery called Duster's. His crotchety personality was legendary; locals said his brewery's slogan should have been "Where the Ale Is Better than the Attitude."

Larry Bell, the founder of Bell's Brewery, took a liking to the little brewery. He bought it in 1998 and renamed it The Old Hat because he was fond of hats and he'd been making beer so long that it was old hat to him. He put it in the hands of Tom Fuller, who had worked at Bell's for ten years. In 2003, Bell's production between his two locations rose to the point that he had to sell it. And he did, to Tom and his partners.

We caught up with Tom and his assistant brewer, Danielle Osborn, on a sunny summer afternoon. Tom's name sounded familiar, and we soon found out why: His byline had appeared in "brewspaper" stories about the Michigan brewing industry. He hung up his pen a while back and now splits his time between the brewery and running a farm nearby.

Beers brewed: You might find as many as twelve beers on tap. The menu beers are Bitter Lager, Copper Red Lager, Light Gold, Kolsch, and Stubbins Stout. Seasonals include Altbier, Billy Bock, Cherry Weissbier, Hefeweizen, India Pale Ale, Maibock, Oatmeal Stout, Strawberry Wheat, Stinger Honey Brown, and Triple Bock. Old Hat also has two or three homemade sodas; flavors may include green apple, grape, orange, cream, or root beer.

Our Pick: Two thumbs up at The Old Hat. Both of us chose the Copper Red Lager, which is a roasty Vienna-style lager. We're glad that Michigan breweries are warming up to this style.

Tom told us we were inside a building that was more than 125 years old and has been "a million different things" over the years. Its claim to fame, he said, is the Lost Finger. While renovating the space, Phil Balog sliced off part of a finger and never recovered it. The finger gets blamed for the inevitable brewing mishaps.

Danielle grew up around here, left, and came back. "This place seems to be a sucking vortex that brings you back," she said. She started out as a winemaker—Lawton is in the middle of a wine-producing region—but pitched in on the brewing side when Tom needed an extra pair of hands. It didn't take her long to get up to speed. With a laugh, she said, "I want to see how many beer style rules I can break for one beer."

Like Tom and Danielle, The Old Hat has a sense of humor. It's on the small side, with exposed brick walls and lots of wood. Behind the bar are rows of mugs—about five hundred in all—and opposite it a row of wooden booths. The ceiling is covered with dollar bills, about 100 bucks' worth. How did they get there? Tom described the technique, which involves two quarters and a thumb tack.

Asked to name a dominant influence on the brewing, Tom said it was German styles; even their American beers are made with German

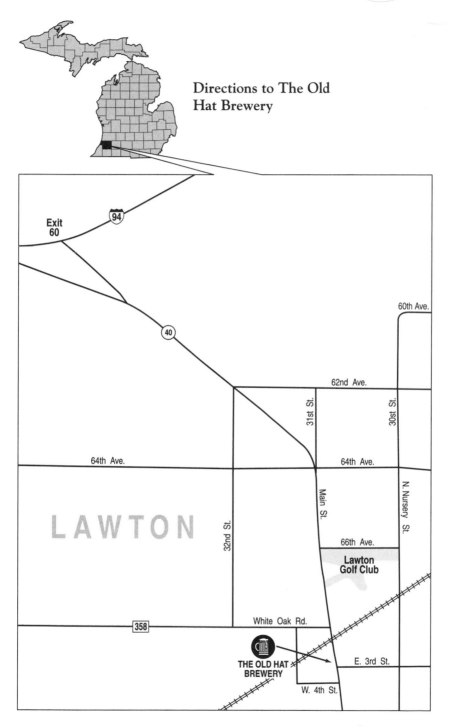

Directions to The Old
Hat Brewery

yeast. But they're not locked into style guidelines. They try to give their customers a variety of beers, offering up to twelve different ones, and their seasonals run the gamut. They also like to tweak their recipes. As Tom told us, "I go back and forth between making what people like and what I want to drink."

In the back corner is a stage, with the Duster's logo above it, where bands play on many evenings. Most of the acts are what Tom called "roots rock": blues, country and western, and rockabilly. Which brings us back to hats. Larry Bell is gone, but the hat collection is still here. When the band is playing, you're welcome to take one off the wall, wear it, and trade with your friends. Contributions are welcome, too, but real hats only, no baseball caps.

Class of license: Microbrewery.
Opened: October 1998 under current ownership.
Owners: Tom and Annette Fuller, John Aker.
Brewers: Tom Fuller, head brewer; Danielle Osborn, assistant brewer.
System: 10-barrel Specific Mechanical. Capacity is 500 barrels.
Production: 300 barrels in 2004.
Distribution: The Old Hat plans to resume bottling.
Hours: Monday through Thursday, 4 to 11 P.M.; Friday, 4 P.M. to midnight; Saturday, noon to midnight; Sunday, 1 to 9 P.M.
Tours: Yes, just ask.
Take-out beer: Growlers, Cornelius kegs, and quarter and half barrels. Soda is also available in kegs.
Food: Pub food, including pizza, burgers, soups, and salads. Old Hat's beer turns up in stout burgers, drunken shrimp, ale dip, and black bean chili—a year-round favorite here.
Extras: Annual party with polka band to celebrate the arrival of Bock beer. Old Hat is also a small winery.
Mug club: Club has some five hundred members, who get reduced-price beer and a break on the entertainment cover charge.
Parking: On nearby streets.

Bell's Brewery, Inc.

Production Facility and Office
8938 Krum Avenue, Galesburg, MI 49053
269-382-2338

Eccentric Café
355 East Kalamazoo Avenue, Kalamazoo, MI 49007
269-382-2332
www.bellsbeer.com

Larry Bell grew up in the Chicago area and attended Kalamazoo College during the seventies. He's been in Kalamazoo ever since and has been brewing beer for more than twenty years. His business began in 1983 as the Kalamazoo Brewing Company, a homebrew shop. It was named after a brewery that closed in 1915 when the city voted itself dry.

By 1985, Larry was brewing commercially using a 15-gallon commercial soup kettle. He rented three rooms from a plumbing-supply warehouse for his makeshift brewery. His first year's production was 135 barrels. Business was a little different in those days. Part of the reason was that Michigan's liquor code didn't have classifications for micros or brewpubs then—the only classification was brewery—so in addition to brewing and bottling, Larry was able to self-distribute his beers, meaning that he even delivered beer to accounts. Production continued to inch upward during the eighties, reaching several hundred barrels a year. In 1989, Larry lined up his first wholesaler when his production went past the 500-barrel mark.

The year 1993 brought major changes to Michigan's liquor laws. It was also then that Larry moved his operation to new quarters just east of downtown Kalamazoo. There, on June 11, 1993, Kalamazoo Brewing Company became the first Michigan brewery to serve beer by the glass to the public. The facility still belongs to Bell's, but most of the beer

Beers brewed: The year-round beers are Amber Ale; Bell's Beer, sold only to draft accounts; Kalamazoo Stout; Pale Ale; Porter; Third Coast Beer, a pale ale; and Two Hearted Ale, an India pale ale. The seasonals are Best Brown Ale; Cherry Stout; Expedition Stout; Double Cream Stout; Java Stout; Oberon Ale, an American wheat ale; Third Coast Old Ale; and Winter White Ale. Consecrator Doppelbock and Sparkling Ale are annual single-batch releases. Bell's produces a number of one-time-only beers, including a special beer to commemorate each thousandth batch brewed. Batch 7,000 was a double stout with 12 percent ABV.

brewed at the downtown facility is distributed to local draft accounts. It's now known as the Eccentric Café and offers ten tap handles as well as food and entertainment. The brewing facility sometimes turns out experimental batches that are sold only to café customers.

Production steadily increased, hitting 20,000 barrels in 1996. About this time, Larry was quoted as saying that his ambition was to reach 30,000 barrels a year and stay there. We find it difficult to blame him for continuing to grow and suspect most Michigan beer drinkers are glad that he has.

Larry hit the 30,000-barrel mark as he opened a new 32,000-square-foot production site located in Comstock Township (the post office address is Galesburg) in December 2002. Now Larry had a facility built from the bottom up as a brewery instead of a building that had to be retrofitted. He bought a 50-barrel Steinecker brewing system from Anheuser-Busch, which had used it only a handful of times in a venture with Wolfgang Puck before closing it down. The new facility also has a Krones bottling line.

In conjunction with the brewery's twentieth anniversary last fall, Larry had its name officially changed to Bell's Brewery, Inc. We doubt that the average customer even noticed the change; for years, the brewery was referred to on the street as Bell's.

Overall, more than forty different beers have borne the Bell's name, with Amber, Pale Ale, Porter, Kalamazoo Stout, Third Coast Ale, and Two Hearted Ale offered year-round. A much larger list is produced seasonally, including Oberon Ale, a warm-weather favorite throughout Michigan.

Bell's is the oldest craft brewery east of Boulder and the largest in Michigan. It also has the largest distribution network, which currently reaches ten states, with two more expected by time you read this. Larry projects 22 percent growth for 2006. That's an awful lot of soup kettles.

Awards won: 1995 GABF Silver, Strong Ale; 1998 GABF Bronze, German-Style Pilsner; 2001 GABF Bronze, German-Style Doppelbock.

Our Picks: Paul's all-time favorite is Deb's Red Ale, which used to be brewed for the annual Eugene V. Debs Kazoo night at Tiger Stadium. Maryanne looks forward to the Oberon in the summer and has been enjoying it since the days it was called Solsun.

Class of license: Brewery.

Opened: September 1985. The Kalamazoo Avenue facility opened in June 1993. The Galesburg production facility brewed its first batch of beer in December 2002.

Owner: Larry Bell.

Brewers: Bell said he doesn't want special emphasis given to his brewers, as he thinks all parts of the operation are just as important.

System: 50-barrel Steinecker in Galesburg. Kalamazoo has a 15-barrel BRD, an ancestor of DME (parts of the equipment have been modified over the years, and the original kettle is now a whirlpool).

Production: 47,370 barrels in 2004; 57,379 barrels in 2005.

Distribution: Bell's beers are distributed in Illinois, Indiana, Kentucky, Michigan, Minnesota, Missouri, North Dakota, Ohio, Pennsylvania, and Wisconsin and should be available soon in Iowa and South Dakota.

Hours: Eccentric Café hours are Sunday through Wednesday, 11 A.M. to midnight; Thursday through Saturday, 11 A.M. to 1 A.M. There is no taproom in Galesburg.

Tours: No public tours. Private tours can be arranged in advance by calling the office. You can take a virtual tour online.

Food: The Eccentric Café currently offers lunch, light meals, and Eccentric Snacks but will become a full-service restaurant after expansion.

Extras: At the Eccentric Café, live music Thursday through Sunday nights. Annual Eccentric Day in December, with a specially brewed high-gravity Eccentric Ale. A cider and two wines are also available.

Parking: Lot on Porter Street, just off Kalamazoo Avenue. (See map on page 140.)

Olde Peninsula Brewpub and Restaurant

200 East Michigan Avenue, Kalamazoo, MI 49007
269-343-2739

Our state's motto is "If you seek a pleasant peninsula, look around you." So it was inevitable that some brewpub would use the word *peninsula* in its name. That brewpub is the Olde Peninsula Brewpub and Restaurant in Kalamazoo.

The brewpub, Kalamazoo's first, is named for the Peninsula Building, which it occupies. The building, in turn, was designed for the Peninsula Restaurant, which opened in 1874. It later was home to a clothing store, a stove company, a book bindery, a hotel, and finally, an advertising agency, before Stephen Blinn and his wife, Marie, took it over.

Stephen went to college at Western Michigan University and later worked for a beer distributor. As an insider, he saw craft brewing's potential. And with the city's Haymarket district, once a slum, coming back to life, he saw an opportunity to attract downtown's office workers before the competition got started. He also thought that a brewpub would blend with the district's historic character.

Beyond the front entrance, which sells merchandise along with bread from a nearby bakery, you'll find the bar. In classic brewpub style, the walls are exposed brick and the floors are made of wood, except for a tiled area around the pre-Prohibition-style wooden bar. The walls are decorated with breweriana, along with signs that advertise gasoline and soda pop. Opposite the bar, behind glass, is the brewing equipment.

The rest of Olde Peninsula is a dining area, with a little game room in one corner. The Blinns have tried to make it a place where people from all walks of life can get together. Not a bad idea, considering that Kalamazoo is so diverse that it serves as a test market for new products. The dining-room decor is somewhat lighthearted and is highlighted by brightly colored beer-themed murals by local artist Linda Valentino.

Dan Kiplinger is the brewer. He grew up in Kalamazoo and went to Michigan State University. He discovered good beer when a friend who homebrewed handed him an India pale ale. It was the farthest thing from Bud Dry, which at the time was the fad beer on campus. After getting his hands on a copy of *The Joy of Homebrewing*, which he read cover to cover in one sitting, he said to himself, "I've got to make something." That something turned out to be a mead.

Like many west Michigan brewers, Dan's first professional job was at Bell's. After hours, he continued homebrewing in order to get a better feel for the brewing process. His next stop, before coming here, was the now-closed Mystic Brewing Company, where he developed the beer recipes. At Olde Peninsula, his goal is to achieve consistency, just like the big brewers do.

Dan considers Kalamazoo a great town in which to brew, thanks to its history of craft brewing and a steady supply of students turning twenty-one. As he put it, "The beer drinker in Kalamazoo isn't afraid of

Beers brewed: The menu beers are Sunset Red; Haymarket Light; OP IPA, the biggest seller; Midnight Stout; and Rockin' Raspberry Stout. Seasonals include a hefeweizen, an imperial IPA, a pumpkin ale, a vanilla porter, a honey cream ale, and Tornado Pale Ale. Olde Peninsula also offers combination brews: Black 'n Tan, 1-2-3 Ale, Black Raspberry, Midnight Apple, and Red Raspberry.

Our Picks: Paul liked both India pale ales, but his first choice was Batch 100, a special beer that has reentered the lineup as an imperial IPA. Maryanne chose the Sunset Red. No bland beer, this one had a prominent caramel malt flavor and real overall character.

Directions to Olde Peninsula
Brewpub & Restaurant

anything." His biggest seller is an India pale ale, and his most popular seasonal is a pumpkin ale brewed with spices from Kalsec, a longtime provider of spices and flavors based in Kalamazoo. Other seasonals include a vanilla porter and a honey cream ale, with an imperial IPA on the way. Those choices say a lot about the customers' tastes and the quality of the beer.

There's one more piece of Kalamazoo that Olde Peninsula commemorates: the 1980 tornado that ripped up downtown and severely damaged the Peninsula Building. Every May 13, Dan marks the occasion by bringing out a batch of Tornado Pale Ale. It's good enough to blow away any doubts that Michigan brews excellent beer.

Class of license: Brewpub.
Opened: March 1996.
Owners: Marie and Stephen Blinn.

Brewer: Dan "Gonzo" Kiplinger.

System: 7-barrel DME. Capacity is 800 barrels.

Production: 529 barrels in 2004.

Hours: Monday and Tuesday, 11 A.M. to 11 P.M.; Wednesday and Thursday, 11 A.M. to midnight; Friday and Saturday, 11 A.M. to 1 A.M.; Sunday, noon to 11 P.M.

Tours: Yes, just ask.

Take-out beer: Growlers and kegs.

Food: The entrees run toward beef and chicken. Also on the menu: grilled pizzas, calzones, sandwiches, and bar appetizers. House beers are incorporated in much of the menu—vinaigrettes, marinades, barbecue sauce, soup, and even beer bread.

Extras: Darts and electronic games. Customers can help themselves to a free cookie on their way out.

Happy hour: Daily late-night happy hour, 9 P.M. to closing, with reduced pints.

Parking: Most of the nearby lots are private. Metered spots are rare, and Kalamazoo's finest watch the meters like hawks. By now, however, there should be a structure a block south of the brewpub on Portage Street.

Kraftbräu Brewery

402 East Kalamazoo Avenue, Kalamazoo, MI 49007
269-384-0288
www.kraftbraubrewery.com

As you might have guessed, the name was inspired by the German electronic band Kraftwerk. Quite appropriate for a brewery that specializes in German-style beer and where who's on stage is as big an attraction as what's on tap.

On the way in, we passed tables full of alternative publications, then found ourselves inside a room with high ceilings and a stage with a full sound system. It looked like a place where garage bands play, one that would appeal more to members of MoveOn.org than the College Republicans.

There was good news and bad news on the day we arrived. First the bad news: Jim Quinn, the owner-brewer, had to divide his time between us and a batch of doppelbock he was brewing. And even though it wasn't yet noon, it was already hot and sticky outside. Now the good news: Once we started talking to Jim, we discovered that the ceiling fans and cross ventilation made things bearable.

Between trips to the brewkettle, Jim told us the story of Kraftbräu. He founded the brewery with John Gabriele, who from the beginning emphasized live entertainment. He was followed by Steve Berthel, who's now in charge at The Livery, and then by current partner Andre Ellison.

The ownership has changed, but one thing hasn't: Kraftbräu books live entertainment most nights of the week. It's so important that the brewery has a marquee facing the traffic that lists upcoming acts. For that reason, Jim said, his brewery draws "a cross section of people from all over the world."

The building occupied by Kraftbräu was constructed in the 1880s and spent most of its life as a warehouse before it went vacant and was turned into a microbrewery. The brewing equipment was cobbled together out of dairy tanks, and the taproom is best described as minimally refurbished. The brick walls are painted white, the floors are made of wood, and small tables are scattered about. The ceiling is high, green, and made of wood, and the lighting fixtures are the type you're likely to find in old public schools.

In one corner is an L-shaped bar that Jim and his friends fashioned out of a display case from a men's clothing store. Behind it is a chalkboard listing what's on tap and how much it costs. (At Kraftbräu, beers with higher alcoholic content tend to carry a bigger price tag.) The backbar was part of a seventy-five-year-old Frigidaire refrigerator. It no longer keeps things cool but did make a good backbar.

From there, it gets weirder. The most noticeable piece of decor is an old moose head. It was donated by the landlord after his wife told him to get rid of it. Then there's the elevator. Jim said it's one of the oldest working Otis elevators in the area, but it can't be used because of safety regulations. But that didn't stop a building inspector who, after a pint too many, started playing with the elevator. We hope he got home safely.

Beers brewed: The menu beers are light lager, German pilsner, Bohemian pilsner, pale ale, and doppelbock, but Kraftbräu brews a wide variety of others. Seasonals include Maibock in the spring, Hefeweizen and altbier in the summer, Oktoberfest in the fall, and winter alt and a high-gravity Yule lager alt in the winter. Specialty beers include doppelbock, amber ale, imperial IPA, and Irish stout. Kraftbräu also makes wine, cider in the fall, and root beer and ginger ale.

Our Picks: All the beer we've sampled at Kraftbräu was brewed by a previous brewer. We were unable to try any on our site visit, so we are not picking any favorites.

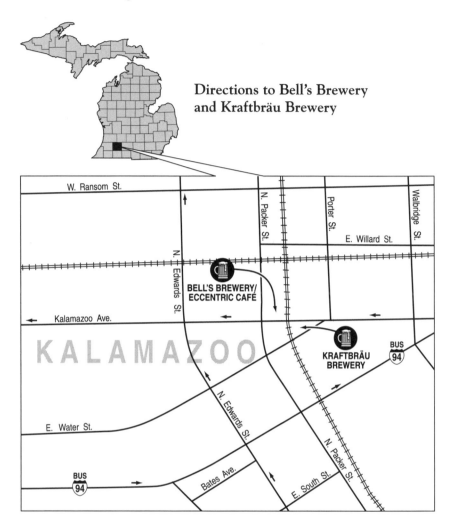

Directions to Bell's Brewery and Kraftbräu Brewery

Kraftbräu doesn't follow the crowd in another respect. Unlike most small breweries, it's a lager house. Jim, who started homebrewing in the early nineties, was influenced by classic Continental styles. His biggest seller, and what he says is "the one our customers miss the most when it isn't on," is a Czech-style pilsner made with an extended two-hour boil using Saaz hops. Although lagers dominate, Jim and Andre brew an occasional ale, and in the fall, they make cider using local apples.

Almost all of Kraftbräu's production is sold on the premises, so you'll have to make the trip to Kalamazoo to taste it. And if you've come that far to try the local brew, chances are you'll stay around to sample the local music as well.

Class of license: Microbrewery.

Opened: September 1996.

Owners-brewers: Jim Quinn and Andre Ellison.

System: 10-barrel Kraftbräu. Capacity is 940 barrels.

Production: 470 barrels in 2004.

Distribution: Available at the brewery only.

Hours: Monday through Saturday, 4 P.M. to 1 A.M.; Sunday, 2 to 10 P.M. (closes later if entertainment is scheduled).

Take-out beer: Growlers and party kegs.

Food: Snack foods only. Customers can bring in their own food.

Extras: Live entertainment is the main attraction here, with bands playing four or more nights per week. On those nights, there's a cover charge after 9 P.M. Other events include poetry slams, "Be in the K.N.O.W." film series, open mike nights, and the holiday Turtleneck and Sweater Party. Smoking in outdoor seating area only.

Happy hour: Daily, 4 to 8 P.M., with reduced pints and growlers.

Parking: Unpaved lots on either side.

Arcadia Brewing Company

103 West Michigan Avenue, Battle Creek, MI 49017
269-963-9520
arcadiabrewingcompany.com

To most Americans, Battle Creek means breakfast cereal, and its most famous resident is Tony the Tiger. That's something to keep in mind when you're looking for the Arcadia Brewing Company. It's on the main street of town, just a few blocks east of Kellogg's Cereal City USA.

The brewery is named for a mythical paradise often the subject of English literature. A perfect name, then, for a brewery that specializes in English-style ales and was founded by a man with deep Scottish roots. His name is Tim Suprise.

Tim is from Kalamazoo—which, by the way, has an Arcadia Creek—and worked as a salesman for a company based in his hometown. He traveled extensively on his job and became a devotee of good beer in general and brewing legend Alan Pugsley's work at the Shipyard Brewery in Portland, Maine. One day Tim went out to Shipyard. That was in 1994.

One thing led to another—the company he worked for was about to reorganize—and Tim entered the brewing business. He bought a brewing system and found a location in downtown Battle Creek, a seventy-five-year-old building formerly used by a Chevrolet dealership, Sears and Roebuck, and an insurance company.

Tim's wife, Mardy, insisted that they offer food in the taproom, which would bring in revenue while the brewery got established. Smart move, as it turned out. The restaurant, called TC's Wood-Fired Fare, is fitted out with a wood-burning oven imported from Naples, Italy, and a southern-style barbecue pit from a Georgia-based manufacturer. Their aromas permeate every corner of the open-designed restaurant area.

With the bottom line a major concern, Tim kept costs down by recycling. The tables inside the restaurant were made from old doors, and the benches are hand-me-downs from the county courthouse. But the deluxe, turn-of-the century wooden bar in back has the most intriguing history. It once belonged to the 21 Club, organized by twenty-one veterans who returned home to Battle Creek after World War II. The Greatest Generation was fond of its beer.

Beers brewed: Arcadia currently brews Angler's Ale, Nut Brown Ale, India Pale Ale, London Porter, Starboard Stout, Whitsun, Amber Ale, Imperial Stout, Special Reserve, and Scotch Ale. It is about to introduce a high-gravity series. The taproom also has two cask ales, along with experimental seasonal beers.

Awards won: 2002 WBC Silver, Strong Scotch-Ale.

Our Picks: Trying Arcadia ales on draft, rather than out of bottles, gave us a new perspective. Maryanne's top choice turned out to be Whitsun Ale, an unfiltered wheat ale. The secret ingredient is Michigan honey. Paul has been a fan of Arcadia's ESB for years. It's been replaced by Amber Ale, but he tasted the two together and found them very similar. So Amber Ale it is. We think you'll enjoy whatever you try.

Arcadia's slogan is "Brewed in the British Tradition." Flags from the British Isles hang proudly from the ceiling, and the beer styles run heavily toward British classics. Which is perfectly logical. The brewing system was built by England's Peter Austin and Partners and is similar to the one at Shipyard. It's visible to both customers and curious passers-by.

Tim gave us a guided tour and explained what makes the Peter Austin system distinctive: English malt, which he invited us to taste. A proprietary strain of yeast from the Ringwood microbrewery in England. A hop percolator, or in British English, a hopback, which brews the hops and also acts as a filter. Open fermenters. A manual cycle for the brewhouse, which makes the brewmaster's touch all the more important. And finally, spent grains, which have to be shoveled out by hand. A labor-intensive process but worth it.

Directions to Arcadia Brewing Company

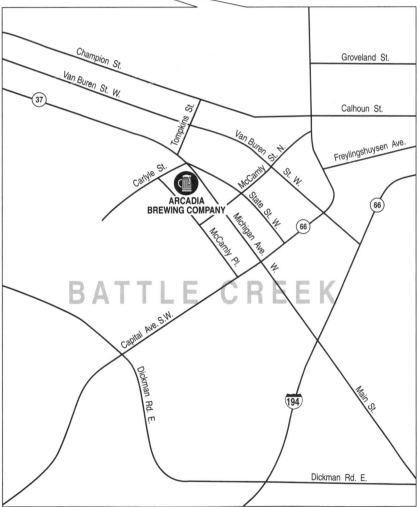

Back inside the bar, Tim offered us a sampler of his beer. We were already familiar with some, especially Battle Creek Reserve, a summer seasonal; IPA, the brewery's flagship beer and biggest seller; and London Porter, which has been promoted to year-round status. Tim said that he's joining the high-gravity movement, and Arcadia will soon roll out four-packs of its Brew Crew Select Series: a double IPA, a bourbon barrel porter, an old ale, and a hazelnut brown ale. He also showed us the new packaging, with more distinctive Celtic-style script. "Brewers need to be about something," Tim told us.

Arcadia's beers are no strangers to beer judges, who have awarded them numerous medals. But Tim told us that his most treasured award was the one his cask-conditioned ESB won at the Traditional Beer Festival in Scotland. Arcadia is all about brewing traditional beers for a new generation. And perhaps the brewery is starting a new Battle Creek tradition in its own right.

Class of license: Microbrewery.
Opened: September 1996.
Owners: Mardy and Tim Suprise.
Brewers: Michael Wachowski, brewer and production leader; Bryan Wiggs and Jack Lamb, brewers; Brian Phelps, cellerman.
System: 25-barrel Peter Austin. Capacity is 7,500 barrels per year. The brewhouse is sized for eventual production of 15,000 barrels per year.
Production: 4,206 barrels in 2004; 4,800 to 4,900 barrels estimated for 2005.
Distribution: Throughout Illinois, Indiana, Ohio, and Wisconsin as well as Michigan.
Hours: Monday through Thursday, 11 A.M. to 10 P.M.; Friday, 11 A.M. to midnight; Saturday, noon to midnight. Closed Sunday.
Tours: Saturdays, noon to 3 P.M., and by appointment.
Take-out beer: Bottles, growlers, quarter and half barrels.
Food: Southern barbecue and wood-fired pizzas and entrees are the signature items. The menu also includes Tex-Mex items, British pub favorites, and some vegetarian dishes.
Extras: Monthly Meet Your Local Brewer night, with someone from the brewing team on hand. Special events include an annual "blues, brews, and barbecue" celebration, a St. Patrick's Day celebration that starts with breakfast, and a Scottish-themed anniversary celebration complete with bagpipers and haggis. Outdoor patio. Darts, pool, and shuffleboard. Ale cheese for sale.

Mug club: Membership is $40 for the first year, $20 a year afterward. Benefits include mugs for the price of pints and discounts on mugs three nights a week.

Parking: Metered lot across the street and behind the brewery, as well as meters on nearby streets.

Dark Horse Brewing Company

511 South Kalamazoo Street, Marshall, MI 49068
269-781-9940
www.darkhorsebrewery.com

DARK HORSE BREWING CO.

Marshall's claim to fame is its preserved nineteenth-century homes, and its trademark is the fountain in the center of town. If you head south from the fountain and drive half a mile, you'll find Wacky Willy's Party Store. That's one of the Morse family businesses. The other one, the Dark Horse Brewing Company, is next door.

Step inside and you'll be transported to the Upper Peninsula. That's because Aaron Morse, the owner and brewer, studied art design—and in his spare time, learned homebrewing—at Northern Michigan University. After he graduated, he and his parents turned a bar in town into a brewpub. Soon afterward, they decided they'd have more success running a microbrewery. As for the name Dark Horse, it was suggested by Aaron's mother. It just seemed to fit, he said.

"Eclectic" is the watchword for this taproom, starting with the building it occupies. It's housed just about everything in its seventy-five-year history: a fueling that sold coal, a grooming salon for pets, an outdoor-sports equipment store, a supplier of movie sets, and a travel agency.

A stone-topped bar dominates the taproom. It was built by Aaron and his friends, who also created the artwork on display. On the walls and ceil-

Beers brewed: The menu beers are Amber Ale; Crooked Tree IPA, Dark Horse's best-selling beer; Raspberry Ale; and Reserve Special Black Bier Ale. Seasonals include a Belgian trippel, a double IPA, a barleywine in the fall. We also sampled a brown beer and an apricot IPA. Dark Horse brews a series of five stouts, the names of which are plays on numbers: Oatmeal Stout, Stout Too, Tres Blueberry Stout, Smoked Fore, and 750 ml (a fifth, get it?) Imperial Stout.

ings, you'll find kitsch from the worlds of entertainment and pop culture. For entertainment, there's
a pool table, a CD boom box, and an electronic
trivia game.

Our Pick: Reserve Special Black Bier Ale, a big and chewy, roasty and chocolaty beer that doesn't fit neatly into style pigeonholes. It's one of the best black beers we've had outside Bavaria.

Aaron told us that his ambition was to open a
small cozy place where people from all walks of life
could fit in. And they do. Dark Horse's customers
range from businessmen to shop owners. Judging from the rows of mugs
hanging on the walls—some eight hundred in all—it seems that everyone in Marshall belongs to the mug club.

In the summer, the fun moves out to Aaron's beer garden. Its centerpiece is an engine from the Harley-Davidson he used to ride. Maybe
that stint in the Upper Peninsula has made him impervious to the cold,
because he hosts a chili cookoff in February. Other beer garden events
include an opening-day party in May; a crawfish boil in June, the year's
biggest event; and an end-of-the-season party, with chicken wings and
live music, in September.

We sat down with Aaron in the taproom's "Elvis corner," which set
the mood for our conversation. He told us that he'd had no formal
training but apprenticed under Matt Allen and "read and read and
read." His first inspiration was Bell's beers, because they were different,
"not just another IPA." Now he counts Dogfish Head, a brewery in Mil-
ton, Delaware, as his chief influence.

According to Aaron, his "goofy personality" is reflected in the beer
he brews. For example, he once made a beer with Michigan peaches,
using the second runnings from a batch of barleywine. But he's dead
serious: His beers are good enough to have won multiple awards at the
state level. They're also good enough to get local drinkers—who are
firmly in the macrobrew camp, or so they thought—to go straight from
national-brand lagers to Crooked Tree IPA, the brewery's number-one
seller, and advance from there to his more exotic brews.

Aaron also has big plans. He's gotten his hands on some bourbon
barrels and is about to branch out into lambics, and he plans to use
those hops growing in back of the brewery in a batch of harvest ale.
He's also going to put those extra fermentation tanks to work and
expand his capacity. Before long, Dark Horse will be joining the thor-
oughbreds of Michigan brewing.

Class of license: Microbrewery.
Opened: Opened as a brewpub October 1997 but has been a microbrewery since September 2000.

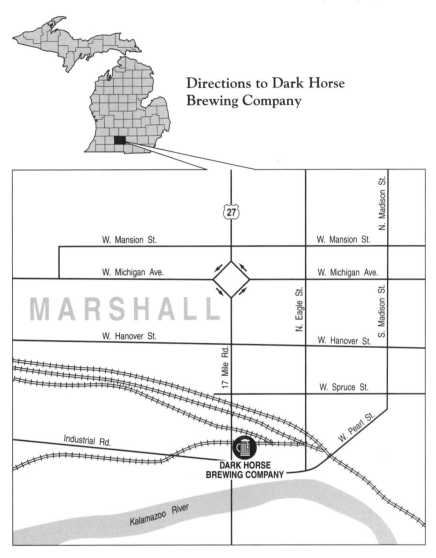

Directions to Dark Horse Brewing Company

Owner: Aaron Morse.

Brewers: Aaron Morse and Trent Thurston.

System: 7- or 10-barrel JV Northwest system. Capacity is about 1,500 barrels.

Production: 850 barrels in 2004; 1,200 barrels estimated for 2005.

Distribution: Most of Michigan, especially Detroit and Ann Arbor, and parts of Indiana.

Hours: Monday through Thursday, 3 to 11 P.M.; Friday and Saturday, 3 P.M. to midnight; Sunday, noon to 8 P.M.

Tours: Yes, if time permits. Call in advance.

Take-out beer: Six-packs, growlers, and kegs.

Food: Simple fare, including sandwiches, pizza, and snacks. When the spirit moves him, Aaron makes pretzels out of the spent grain.

Extras: Live entertainment and a variety of special events. The most unusual was a brewer's dinner served in the dark so that people wouldn't make snap judgments about the beer and food based on their appearance. Open mike on Fridays. Cigars available.

Mug club: Probably the biggest in the state. More than seven hundred ceramic mugs were handmade by an artist friend of Aaron's who lives in the Upper Peninsula.

Parking: Unpaved lot outside.

Michigan Products

When most people think of Michigan, cars or the "Big Three" auto companies generally pop into their minds. That's fair, since the auto industry is a large factor in the state's economy. But we'd be remiss if we didn't point out some of the other wonderful things that we make, raise, and grow here as well.

Chances are good that you, or the little ones in your life, start the day with another famous Michigan product, Kellogg's cereal. Battle Creek is considered the breakfast food center of the world. In 1894, two brothers named Kellogg began experimenting with flaked cereal. Legend has it that it was an accidental creation, but you can learn the story for yourself at Kellogg's Cereal City USA.

Take a good look at that chair you're sitting in or the nearest table. There's a good chance that it was made in Grand Rapids, a city with a long, rich furniture design and manufacturing history. Area firms make everything from the finest sofas to the most beautiful cabinets to that office chair everyone covets—Steelcase.

The western part of the state along Lake Michigan and inward about 30 miles is one of the most famous and prosperous fruit-growing regions in the country. The sandy acid soil, high water table, and relatively mild climate are ideal. Michigan is the number-one cherry producer in the country. Its farmers grow about 75 percent of the tart cherries in the country and about 20 percent of the sweet cherries. Michigan farmers also harvest about one-third of the cultivated blueberries in America.

Eaten any potato chips lately? Michigan leads the nation in production of round white potatoes. More than 2.1 million acres of soybeans are planted here each year, and the crop has been steadily increasing over the last several years. Next time you eat a vegetable burger or tofu, remember Michigan's farmers. Ditto for beans. Our state is the number-two producer of dry edible beans, almost half of which are navy beans. Now you can think of more than Congress when you eat a bowl of Senate Bean Soup.

Michigan has its own signature entries in the carbonated-beverage category: Vernor's ginger ale and Faygo pop. A Detroit pharmacist, James

Vernor, concocted a beverage made of nineteen different ingredients, including ginger and vanilla. He stored a batch in an oak cask in his pharmacy just before he left for military duty in the Civil War. When he returned home and opened his brew, he was pleasantly surprised at the transformation. For years, the only place that sold it was the fountain at his downtown Detroit pharmacy. It became so popular, however, that by the turn of the century, it was being sold in New York and Ohio too. The Vernor family sold the rights, but the product is still marketed nationally.

In 1907, two brothers, bakers by trade, who had recently immigrated from Russia, began selling three fruit-flavored beverages that were based on their cake-frosting recipes. The Feigenson Brothers Bottling Works of Detroit started referring to their product as "pop," for the sound made when opening the bottle. In 1921, they changed the brand name to Faygo because the company name was too long to put on a bottle. Today they make more than forty flavors, including the original three—fruit punch, grape, and strawberry. In the 1960s, strawberry was officially renamed Redpop.

Paczkis weren't invented here, but people line up in the middle of the night at Hamtramck bakeries in order to get their Fat Tuesday fix. Without a doubt, Paczki Day is now a Detroit tradition. Paczkis (pronounced "poonch-keys") are jam-filled yeast doughnuts. It's an old Polish custom to make a big batch and share them with your neighbors the day before Lent begins. If you've never eaten one, stop by a real Polish bakery, and try one or two or . . . One may be all you should eat, but they're too good to have just one. Besides, it's all in the spirit of Fat Tuesday. We recommend raspberry filling.

The pasty is another famous Michigan food that most people associate with the Upper Peninsula and immigrants, but it's actually readily available all over the state. What is it? A pot pie without the pot. A calzone with meat and vegetable filling. To make one, start with a tender dough rolled into a circle, and fill one side of it with beef, pork, carrots, onions, potatoes, and rutabagas. Seal and crimp the edges, slit the top in several spots, and bake.

Pasties made their way to the Upper Peninsula by way of Cornwall, England, brought over by Cornish settlers who came to work in the copper mines. They were a very popular food for lunch, because the entire meal was in one pocket of dough and could be eaten without utensils. Simply start at the corner and work your way down. They stay warm for a very long time—an ideal food for miners.

Michigan also has more than six hundred licensed and privately owned white-tailed deer and elk facilities. Yes, you can still bag your own during deer season, but nonhunters and restaurants create quite a demand. Venison and elk frequently appear on the menu here. And now you know where it comes from.

Whether you make a day trip to Mackinac Island or stay overnight, you have to bring home some fudge—fresh cream, butter, chocolate, and nuts mixed together by hand on a thick marble slab. This style of fudge melts in your mouth. It's the best in the world. Honest.

The West Coast

Here's a factoid that might win you a bet: Michigan has more miles of shoreline than any other state except Alaska. And here's another: The state has more registered watercraft than Florida, some nine hundred thousand in all. All that shoreline means the potential for mishaps on the water, which is why more than a hundred lighthouses were built on Michigan's Great Lakes shoreline. Many of them are open to the public, and people plan vacations around seeing as many of these lighthouses as they can. We have to admit—that's no stranger than our having visited all the state's breweries.

Michigan's west coast takes in ten breweries and a lot of shoreline. Lake Michigan itself is more than 300 miles long, and that doesn't count the many bays and harbors. The extreme southern reaches are dotted with little resort towns that for years have drawn vacationers from Chicago as well as local day-trippers. Hang-gliding from the dunes overlooking Lake Michigan has become a popular activity. To the north are Benton Harbor, the home of Whirlpool Corporation, and South Haven, a tourist town surrounded by farmland. The Saugatuck-Douglas area is known for bed-and-breakfasts, antique shops, and an artists' colony.

The next stop north is Holland, which was originally settled by immigrants from the Netherlands. Its municipal symbol is De Zwaan, a two hundred-plus-year-old working windmill, the last one the Dutch government allowed to leave the country. The city also has a wooden shoe factory, a tulip garden, and a Dutch Village. And every spring, Holland invites the world to its Tulip Time celebration. Despite its strong Calvinist leanings, Holland is the birthplace of two breweries: Roffey's Brewing Company, which is no longer among us, and New Holland Brewing Company, now one of Michigan's largest.

Grand Haven is a resort and boating community at the mouth of the Grand River. It's also one of the few places where beach sand "sings" when you walk over it. Another claim to fame is that it was America's first community to offer wireless Internet access on a citywide basis. Nearby is Muskegon, once known as the "Lumber Queen to the World" and now the largest city on the west coast. Its leading attractions are Michigan's Adventure, the state's largest amusement park, and the perch, salmon, and walleye that live in the lake and river.

Ludington is a former lumber town now known for fishing—salmon fishing in particular. It's also where the SS *Badger* (www.ssbadger.com) boards passengers and their vehicles and ferries them across Lake Michigan to Manitowoc, Wisconsin. To the north are Manistee, known for its Victorian-era downtown buildings and said to be where Father Jacques Marquette died, and Mears, the only place in the East where people can drive vehicles on sand dunes.

Farther north is the resort country of northwest Michigan. Well-heeled vacationers from the Detroit area, as well as from Chicago, have been coming here for well over a century; some built expensive summer homes. Visitors to the area also included Christians who stayed at church-run facilities. More recently, thousands of Michiganders have put up cottages on the area's lakes or bought waterfront condominiums, and entrepreneurs have built golf and ski resorts for those who can escape for only a short time.

The region's hub is Traverse City, a lumber village turned the cherry capital of America. Seventy-five percent of the nation's tart cherries—some 250 million pounds—are grown in the area. In July, Traverse City hosts the National Cherry Festival (www.cherryfestival.org), with parades, fireworks, entertainment, and plenty of activities for kids. Also notable is the Arts Festival (www.interlochen.org/arts_festival) sponsored by the Interlochen Arts Academy. As the area's permanent population has grown, the festival has expanded and now offers a year-round schedule of events.

Many visitors make Traverse City their base for scenic road trips. One of the most popular destinations is Leelanau County, whose biggest natural attraction is the Sleeping Bear Dunes National Seashore (www.nps.gov/slbe). Sand-covered cliffs rise more than 400 feet above the surface of Lake Michigan. The trip down is fast, but the climb back up is, shall we say, a challenge. Glen Lake, which is within the national seashore, is considered one of the most beautiful in the world. The Leelanau Peninsula is also a winegrowing region (www.lpwines.com).

Dividing Grand Traverse Bay is the Old Mission Peninsula, whose microclimate lends itself to growing fruit, wine grapes in particular. The peninsula has its own wine trail (www.wineriesofoldmission.com). Before you leave the Traverse Bay area, you'll probably hear that it is on the same latitude as France's Bordeaux region, and that you're halfway between the equator and the North Pole.

U.S. Route 31 from Traverse City to Petoskey is one of the state's best-known scenic drives. The route passes through Charlevoix, a favorite of yachters and a departure point for Beaver Island, in the middle of Lake Michigan. The Petoskey area is the setting of several of Ernest Hemingway's Nick Adams stories and is where you'll find Petoskey stones, the state stone of Michigan, and rockhounds looking for them. From there, the road leads north to Bay View and Harbor Springs. Nearby is M-119, the "Tunnel of Trees."

Convention and Visitors Bureaus
Holland: www.holland.org
Ludington Area: www.ludingtoncvb.com
Saugatuck-Douglas: www.saugatuck.com
South Haven: www.bythebigbluewater.com
Traverse City: www.mytraversecity.com

Recommended Beer Bars
Holland
Butch's Dry Dock, 44 East Eighth Street, 616-396-8227, www.butchs
.net. Bar and liquor store with more than two hundred bottled beers.

Ludington
Michael's Bar and Grill, 129 West Ludington Avenue, 231-845-7411.
Good bottled-beer selection.

St. Joseph
Schu's Grill and Bar, 501 Pleasant Street, 269-983-7248, www.schus
.com. Offers a view of Lake Michigan and a decent selection of locally brewed beer.

Traverse City
More local places than beer sites, but two recommended establishments are **Poppycock's,** 128 East Front Street, 231-941-7632; and **Union Street Station,** 117 South Union Street, 231-941-1930, www.unionstreet station.net.

Union Pier
Red Arrow Road House, 15710 Red Arrow Highway, 269-469-3939, www.redarrowroadhouse.com. Classic roadside restaurant.

The Livery

190 Fifth Street, Benton Harbor, MI 49022
269-925-8760
www.liverybrew.com

THE LIVERY

Hand-Forged MicroBrews

"Urban pioneers" is a good way to describe Steve Berthel and his business partner, Leslie Pickell, who own The Livery. They've made a big bet that Benton Harbor, one of the state's most downtrodden communities, is staging a comeback.

Once upon a time, Benton Harbor was prosperous. Deluxe hotels and the homes of lumber barons once stood there. In recent decades, the city went into a tailspin; today it has a reputation for poverty and racial unrest. But Steve and Leslie saw past the urban ugliness and noted that Benton Harbor had more available lakefront land than anywhere else on Lake Michigan's east shore. That, they concluded, would one day spur the city's turnaround.

They bought a building that was constructed a century earlier for the Palace Livery and originally held horses but had stood empty since the eighties. It's located in Benton Harbor's arts district, an area that's being repopulated by artists and artisans. City officials, realizing a brewpub's potential to revive the area, worked with them. The Livery held its grand opening celebration the weekend after Labor Day 2005.

This is a dream come true for both partners. Leslie is a music fan who travels around the country listening to the performers she loves. And Steve was the head brewer at Kraftbräu Brewery, where he also helped book entertainment. Steve had just reached a milestone birthday (we promised not to tell which) and decided it was time to write a new chapter in his life. "Function in disaster, finish in style," Steve told us. It's a philosophy that guides him whether he's racing his bicycle or running a business.

We got together with Steve inside the taproom on The Livery's lower level. He told us that he's been a woodworker for years, specializing in the

Beers brewed: The twelve beers on tap are LawnMower Lager, Oktoberfest Lager, Bungtown Export Lager, Hefe Weizen, Paris-Roubaix Pale Ale, Synapse ESB, McGilligans IPA, Thoms Special IPA, Cousin Jax Double IPA, English Ruby Red Ale, Yorkshire Brown Ale, and Irish Stout. Seasonals include Bigford Brothers Kilt Tilter; Maillot Jaune, a bière de garde; Telewhacker; the Liverator, a doppelbock; and Wheat Trippelbock. The Livery serves beers in appropriate glassware.

refurbishment of Victorian buildings, and he'd done much of the work of building the brewpub. The L-shaped wooden bar, and the stools where we sat, were made from secondhand wood. And while we're talking about wood, if you look closely at the posts in the taproom, you'll see the cribbing marks courtesy of the horses in the original livery.

He took us upstairs and showed us more of his handiwork: the stage and the sound booths. Part of Steve's dream was to build a first-class entertainment venue. His is the only brewpub in Michigan with both a stage and a mezzanine. It has a state-of-the-art sound system and has already showcased national acts. And in the middle of all this is the elevator once used to raise and lower horses.

In building The Livery, Steve got assistance from his fellow artists, along with friends and neighbors who helped get it ready. One designed the brewpub's logo, another fashioned the tap handles, and yet another is contributing sculptures. A rotating display of artists' works hangs here, and a photo gallery is upstairs. He's repaid them by naming beers after them.

On to the beer. Steve caught the brewing bug when a fellow bicycle racer introduced him to homebrewing. His first batch was an amber ale made with New Mexican chiles, a sign that he had a knack for brewing. Steve progressed to all-grain brewing and eventually went professional, spending eight years at Kraftbräu before striking out on his own. His skills as a handyman made his dream a reality. He cobbled together the brewing system at a cost of only $60,000. The fermenters are English grundys from Cameron and Tettington.

With a recipe book full of seventy styles, Steve aims to give customers a more diverse selection than most brewpubs. He offers twelve beers on tap, including two to four lagers, and not just the usual suspects. His beer lineup spans the spectrum from pale ales to high-gravity styles, which he plans to sell in bottles. He uses generous amounts of Continental malt, which he believes is worth it: He told us that customers deserve to taste the flavors those malts impart.

Steve is full of ideas that will make The Livery a destination: open mike and karaoke, a deli and café, oak-aged beers. In the short time it's been open, it has attracted a mixture of beer geeks, young people in search of nightlife, and curious locals. That's just the beginning. Steve is sure that Benton Harbor's worst days are over. As he put it, "It's not like turning on a switch but not like turning around the Titanic either."

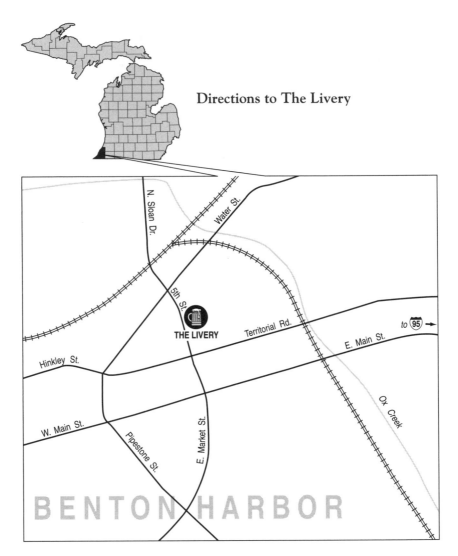

Directions to The Livery

Class of license: Microbrewery.

Opened: August 2005.

Owners: Steve Berthel and Leslie Pickell.

Brewer: Steve Berthel.

System: 9-barrel Berthel.

Production: Projected to be 350 barrels per year.

Distribution: Presently on-premises only.

Hours: Monday through Thursday, 4 to 10 P.M.; Friday, 4 P.M. to midnight; Saturday, 2 P.M. to 1 A.M.; Sunday, 2 to 7 P.M.

Tours: Yes, by appointment.

Take-out beer: Growlers and Cornelius kegs. The Livery expects to sell bottles of high-gravity beers.

Food: Plans were in the works to open a full coffee bar and a vegetarian-friendly deli that serves breakfast items, soups, salads, sandwiches, and desserts.

Extras: Small interior courtyard. Live entertainment; check the website for details. Free wireless Internet access. The Livery is also licensed as a small winery.

Happy hour: Monday through Saturday, 4 to 7 P.M.

Mug club: The Livery is in the process of starting a club. Steve plans to tend bar for members twice a month and give them first crack at newly released beers and beer-appreciation events.

Parking: Lot behind the brewery and on nearby streets.

Saugatuck Brewing Company

6785 Enterprise Drive, Unit #6, Douglas, MI
269-857-7222
www.saugatuckbrewing.com

Saugatuck Brewing Company is a small brewery with a familiar name and big ambitions. Saugatuck is a Lake Michigan resort town known for its shops and galleries, bed-and-breakfasts, and beaches. It's a name that sells itself around here, and more than a million potential customers live within an hour's drive.

The big ambitions come from owner Barry Johnson, who recently launched a second career as a brewer. During the years he traveled the world as a sales representative, he logged, by his estimate, a million air miles. He didn't realize it at first, but he was educating himself about the beers of the world.

A heavy travel schedule is tough on anyone, and it's even tougher if you have a family and you're active in the community (Johnson has served as mayor pro tem, been a Scout leader, and helped direct an area foundation). He decided to get off the corporate treadmill and go into business for himself and give something back to Saugatuck. At the age of fifty-two, Barry took a substantial pay cut and went back to school,

first at the Siebel Institute and then at the Doer-
man Academy in Bavaria. All according to plan.
He points out that a brewery can turn out good
beer and still fail because of bad management. And
he's determined not to let that happen.

There's another part of the Saugatuck Brewery
story, and it begins at the other end of the state.
Back in Michigan, Barry became acquainted with
the brewing community. One person he got to know
was Sandy Harville, who owned a brew-on-premises
operation in Eastpointe. When Harville decided to
concentrate on winemaking, Barry bought the BOP
equipment—after getting some hands-on training.

Beers brewed: Clipson
Sawmill Ale, Derek the Red,
Half Wit Belgian Ale, Hilltop
Helles, Main Street Wheat,
and Singapore IPA.

Our Picks: We got to sample
the beer at the Michigan Brewers Guild's summer festival.
Maryanne's pick was the Hilltop Helles; Paul's was the Singapore IPA. Both were on the
hoppy side, but not overly so.

Saugatuck Brewing—which, by the way, is in the adjacent town of
Douglas—is one of three brew-on-premises operations in Michigan.
BOP customers can choose from more than seventy beer styles that
approximate name-brand beers, and anyone who can follow a recipe
can make beer. It takes two to four weeks to brew a batch, depending
on the style; the yield from a batch is six cases of 22-ounce bomber bottles. Barry hopes that some will graduate to all-grain brewing and introduce their friends to good beer. He's also reaching out to the local
homebrew community.

Saugatuck Brewing also brews its own branded beers. Johnson started
with a six-beer rotation, with names that evoke the region's history and
labels that will carry photographs collected by the town's historical society. News of his beer spread quickly through the area. In fact, when we
dropped by, Barry had no beer to offer because "the locals found us and
drank us dry."

The day we visited, Barry was putting the finishing touches on his
brewery. The tasting room was somewhat spartan, with several round
tables and a small bar. On top of the bar were containers of malt and a
stuffed yeast cell, both of which Barry uses to educate his customers
about beer and introduce them to better ones. His longer-range plans
include more formal beer education, which he dubbed the "Douglas
Brewing Academy."

The current microbrewery and BOP are the first phase of Barry's
strategy. Once he gets his distribution straightened out, he'll be upgrading to a larger system and stepping up production in a bigger location
near his current facility.

Saugatuck Brewing Company, one of the state's newest, is about to
invade the west Michigan beer market. We see three good reasons why

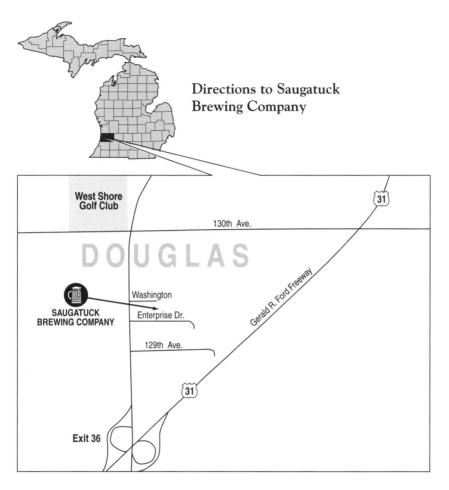

Directions to Saugatuck Brewing Company

it ought to succeed: It's got a seasoned general, a solid plan of attack, and a growing army of beer-loving recruits.

Class of license: Microbrewery.

Opened: June 2005.

Owner-brewer: Barry Johnson.

System: 3.5-barrel Brew Store system for BOP operations; specifically, five 15-gallon kettles and one 31-gallon kettle.

Production and distribution: The brewery is in the process of building a distributor network.

Hours: Tasting room open Tuesday through Saturday, 3 to 7 P.M. Call ahead to arrange to brew your own.

Tours: Yes, call ahead.

Take-out beer: Six-packs, growlers, and kegs.

Food: None. This is a brewery with a tasting room rather than a bar or restaurant.
Parking: In the industrial park. Unit #6 is in the corner. In the summer, potted plants guard the entrance.
Directions: The industrial park is across the street from the Blue Star Antique Store on the Blue Star Memorial Highway. By the time you read this, the brewery should have signage out.

New Holland Brewing Company

Fairbanks Avenue Production Facility
205 Fairbanks Avenue, Holland, MI 49423

Restaurant and Pub
66 Eighth Street, Holland, MI 49423
616-355-6422
www.newhollandbrew.com

The folks at New Holland Brewing believe that craft brewing is an artistic pursuit. Their logo speaks volumes: "Art in Fermented Form." They're genuine, and they're on a steady course, making good, reliable, balanced beer.

New Holland is a story of two childhood friends, Brett Vander Kamp and Jason Spaulding, who roomed together at Hope College, a small liberal-arts school in Holland. Jason studied physical therapy, and Brett studied geology. After graduation, Brett headed to Colorado, where he realized the potential of craft beer.

So in 1996, Brett came back to Michigan and teamed up with Jason again. They pursued their dream of brewing beer in the unlikeliest of places. The city of Holland is a staunch Dutch Reformed community, and Ottawa County even bans the sale of alcohol on Sunday. Most people contemplating a brewery would stop right there.

But young people have the gifts of optimism and determination, not to mention a different perspective. Brett and Jason reasoned that the area was starving for new business; besides, a new bar hadn't opened in Holland for years. Yes, money was an obstacle, but Brett and Jason said to themselves, "This is America. Let's do it."

Lo and behold, they did. It turned out that as conservative as Holland was, starting up a brewery there was very easy. By June 1997, they were open for business, brewing beer in an old factory they'd converted to a brewhouse. They opened a small taproom, and before long, word spread about New Holland Brewing's liquid gold. It gained a following, not just in the Holland area, but across the state.

In September 2002, John Haggerty came on board as head brewer. John, who's originally from Indiana, had spent time out west, where he joined the brewing community at the Big Time Brewery and Alehouse in Seattle. As craft brewing moved east, John moved with it, first to Madison, Wisconsin, and later to the Minnesota Brewing Company. He further rounded his skills by attending brewing school in Berlin. Having been part of large-scale brewing, John wanted to work at a smaller operation where he could have an influence over what was brewed. He and New Holland are a perfect match.

The slow, steady growth that Brett and Jason enjoyed so far was about to explode. In December 2002, they opened a second facility in downtown Holland. They acquired space that was once a J. C. Penney store and later a hardware store, and they opened a brewery, taproom, and restaurant there. Recently, they've added a two-barrel distillery that passers-by can see through the window.

Meanwhile, John Haggerty has been busy expanding New Holland's offerings. The brewery now turns out four year-round beers, four seasonal beers, and a rotating series of four high-gravity beers. But the brewing fun really begins with the ten to twelve experimental beers, plus the ones they brew for special occasions such as Holland's annual Tulip Festival and Autumn Festival.

Beers brewed: The menu beers are Full Circle, a single-malt beer; Sundog, an amber ale; Paleooza, an American pale ale; and Mad Hatter, an India pale ale. The seasonals are Red Tulip, a deep ruby red ale; Zoomer Wit, a summer white beer; Ichabod, a pumpkin ale; and the Poet, a stout. The high-gravity series consists of Black Tulip, a golden trippel; Phi; Pilgrim's Dole, a wheatwine; and Dragon's Milk, an oak-aged strong ale. Experimental and specialty beers are on tap at the Eighth Street facility.

Awards won: 2000 WBC Silver, American-Style Pale Ale; 2000 GABF Silver, American-Style Pale Ale; 2001 GABF Bronze, American-Style IPA; 2002 WBC Silver, Belgian-Style Triple; 2002 GABF Bronze, Wood- and Barrel-Aged; 2004 WBC Gold, American-Style Pale Ale.

Our Picks: We think you'll enjoy anything that New Holland offers, but Paul raved about Phi, a hard-to-describe beer that he thought was somewhat like a Saison and somewhat like a Belgian trippel. Maryanne picked the Raspberry Black, a specialty beer available only at the Eighth Street location—which is the charm of a microbrewery taproom.

New Holland was one of Michigan's first breweries to join both the barrel-aging and high-gravity brewing trends. Sitting in storage are more than fifty bourbon barrels filled with beer in various stages of fermentation. The plan is to develop a library of beers that customers can someday enjoy while comparing the same label across multiple vintages.

One of the most interesting beers brewed by New Holland is Phi, which is part of its high-gravity series. Phi is a ratio discovered by ancient scholars. It can be derived through a series of numbers discovered in the twelfth century by Leonardo Fibonacci. Each number in the series is the sum of the two before it: 1, 2, 3, 5, 8, 13, 21, 34, 55, 89. You get the idea.

Phi is found everywhere, from proportions used in architecture to the structure of the DNA molecule. Investors have even used it to unlock market trends. Brett, Jason, and John recognized the intriguing natural—if not divine—balance this ratio represents. With brewers' eyes, they built a recipe for a perfectly proportioned, well-balanced beer in the same spirit.

The recipe for Phi is developed by pulling numbers out of Fibonacci's series and using them as the basis for ingredient ratios. Each year, the beer will use the same yeast and be brewed with the same gravity and number of international bittering units (IBUs)—always based on the phi ratio. We were told that "the flavor and the color will change annually, demonstrating that consistency and balance do not require a single answer." By the way, Phi checks in at 9 percent ABV. We did say "high gravity," didn't we?

Now that it's firmly established, we expect even more interesting things to come out of New Holland. For one thing, plans are to apply the brewer's unique perspective to distilling. Imagine the possibilities—and the fun—of tasting a style of beer, then tasting that same beer distilled as a spirit. Stay tuned for more art in fermented form.

Class of license: Microbrewery in both locations.
Opened: Fairbanks Avenue facility, June 1997. Eighth Street facility, December 2002.
Owners: Brett VanderKamp and Jason Spaulding.
Brewer: John Haggerty.
System: At the Fairbanks Avenue facility, 30-barrel Sprinkmann. At the Eighth Street facility, 10-barrel Vendome. Total capacity is 10,000 barrels.
Production: About 5,000 barrels in 2004; about 6,000 barrels in 2005.
Distribution: Michigan, Illinois, Indiana, Ohio, Pennsylvania, South Carolina, and Wisconsin

Hours: The Eighth Street facility is open Monday through Thursday, 11 A.M. to midnight; Friday and Saturday, 11 A.M. to 2 A.M. Closed Sunday. Currently, the Fairbanks Avenue facility is not open to the public.

Tours: Yes, by appointment at the Eighth Street facility.

Take-out beer: Growlers and 12-ounce bottles.

Food: Family-oriented fare, featuring pizza and sandwiches. The menu recommends food-and-beer pairings.

Extras: Annual Mad Hatter Celebration in June. New Holland also has a small winery license and distills spirits on site. Game room. Facilities for large groups. Open mike night on Monday. Live music on Friday.

Happy hour: Rotating beer and drink specials Tuesday through Saturday. Check website for specifics.

Parking: Some metered street parking in front. Large public lot behind the restaurant.

Via Maria Trattoria

13 West Seventh Street, Holland, MI 49423
616-494-0016

Holland, Michigan, is in the heart of the state's Dutch country. How Dutch is it? The town symbol is a two hundred-year-old windmill brought here from the Netherlands. But tucked inside the brick buildings of Holland's tidy downtown is a little piece of Italy called the Via Maria Trattoria.

Via Maria's creators turned an old warehouse into the re-creation of a street in a Tuscan neighborhood, a place where "Maria," a housewife, would do her shopping for family dinner. It has trees and plants decorated with white Christmas lights, a small fountain, and small café-style tables scattered about. And because the entire complex is indoors, Maria and her neighbors stay warm and dry when the weather turns blustery.

Beers brewed: 9°, a trippel; Glacier ESB; Via Maria Dave, a California common; Il Sinistro, a Belgian strong pale ale; D'Ambra; and D'Oro.

Our Picks: Maryanne chose D'Oro, one of the flagship beers. It's a golden ale with a hint of honey in the aroma. Paul chose 9°, a Belgian abbey-style ale brewed with Trappist yeast.

Directions to New Holland
Brewing Company and
Via Maria Trattoria

We came in through the back entrance, passing a large wooden patio that becomes the main attraction on long summer evenings. The moment we stepped inside, we were welcomed by the aroma of good things baking inside the wood-fired oven. In the tradition of Italian cafés, Via Maria opens at 7 A.M. and sells breads, pastries, and coffee; later in the day, people drop in for a beer or a glass of wine. There's a full-service restaurant, and the head chefs play the role of Maria, shopping for whatever is in season and incorporating that into their dishes.

We know what you're thinking: beer in an Italian restaurant? But we've been to the wine countries of Europe and have enjoyed good beer, especially on warm days like the one on which we visited. And we weren't disappointed. We sat down with the brewer, Andrew Van Til, inside the Da Vinci Taverna and enjoyed a sampler of his beer. The tavern, which had a small three-sided bar, several tables, and wine glasses on an overhead shelf, was reminiscent of taverns we've been to in Italy. With one exception: the glassed-in brewing equipment that stood guard over the bar.

Van Til grew up in Lansing and currently commutes from Grand Rapids. He discovered good beer during a semester abroad in Spain. It didn't take him long to find the local establishments, where he drank the classic beers of Europe—he lists Belgium as his primary influence—and also discovered the pleasures of café culture. When he got back home, Van Til took up homebrewing and made his own for three years before he went professional.

The brewpub has six beers—five year-rounders and a seasonal—in the lineup. All of them are served out of tanks rather than kegged. The two flagship beers are D'Oro, a golden ale, and D'Ambra, an amber ale. Van Til says that the owners, the mother-son team of Sharon Haan and Scott Campbell, have given him free rein in brewing: They don't want a cookie-cutter or focus-group approach to brewing. He tends bar on Tuesdays, where he receives feedback from customers and gets to talk beer with them.

Via Maria isn't the first venture to brew at this site. Two brewpubs, Backstreet Brewing Company and Black River Brewery, both tried and failed here since 1997. Haan and Campbell hope that the third time is a charm. They're building a following in the Holland area and evidently are gaining a reputation farther afield. While we were there, two visitors wielding a regional "brewspaper" sat at the bar and carried on a lively discussion of the house beers. That's what we like to see.

Class of license: Brewpub.
Opened: September 2001.
Owners: Sharon Haan and Scott Campbell.
Brewer: Andrew Van Til.
System: 10-barrel JV Northwest. Capacity is 900 barrels.
Production: 300 barrels in 2004.
Hours: Monday through Thursday, 7 A.M. to 10 P.M.; Friday and Saturday, 7 A.M. to 11 P.M.
Tours: Call ahead to find out if the brewer will be in.
Take-out beer: Growlers, 5-gallon kegs, and quarter and half barrels by arrangement.
Food: Italian, with house beers used in some menu items.
Extras: Complete bar service. An assortment of baked goods for sale inside the complex. Singer-keyboardist performs on Friday and Saturday evenings, live music some other evenings.
Parking: Some spaces behind the south entrance in back, several municipal lots within walking distance.

Old Boys' Brewhouse

971 West Savidge Road, Spring Lake, MI 49456
616-850-9950
www.old-boys.net

Dogs are man's best friend, and people have honored them in unusual ways. But naming a brewpub for a dog? We'd never heard of that before we visited Old Boys' Brewhouse. It's named for a chocolate Labrador retriever, Brutus the Snake Malone, better known as "Old Boy." He was a kind and gentle companion who could even catch his own fish.

Old Boy did his fishing in Spring Lake, and his namesake brewpub is on the shores of that lake. The area was once known for its therapeutic hot springs. They're no longer in use, and today's visitors tend to be boaters. Some find their way here from Lake Michigan, a couple miles to the west via a channel. If your craft is big enough, you can tie up at the dock and walk to the large patio that overlooks the channel.

If you arrive by car, as most customers do, a grain silo serves as a handy landmark. The building that houses Old Boys' used to be an industrial structure. After the owners refurbished it, they opened it as a microbrewery. They soon discovered that some old salts preferred whiskey to beer and decided to go the brewpub route so they could offer full bar service.

As you enter, you'll see the brewing operation to your left. Go straight ahead, and you'll find yourself inside the lived-in main barroom. It's a convivial place, with high wooden ceilings and uncarpeted floors, stainless steel serving tanks looming over the bar, and banners advertising the many community events that Old Boys' takes part in. For entertainment, there's pool, electronic games, and plenty of television monitors.

Take a closer look, and you'll discover what sets Old Boys' apart: It's decorated in what's best described as Canine Contemporary. Pictures of dogs and dozens of dog-related items, many of them contributed by customers, hang on the walls. Doggie

Beers brewed: The six menu beers are Conner's Kölsch, Waterdog Wheat, Oktoberfest American Red, English Brown Ale, and Olly's Oatmeal Stout. Specialties include ESB, Dog Sitter Dubbel, and strong pale ale. There are also four fruit-based drinks.

Our Pick: Our favorite was the Dog Sitter Dubbel. We recommend that you ask what seasonals or specials are available.

treats are for sale near the entrance. And then there's Woofstock: an annual three-day event featuring agility demonstrations, talks by breeders and trainers, and even doggie yoga and massage.

As for two-legged customers, they tend to be thirty and older, with a strong contingent of locals and families. Old Boys' has an unusual way of honoring regulars: Their names go on the high-backed wooden chairs. The owner told us there are no fixed criteria for becoming a regular. We suspect it's when the other regulars decide you're one of them, which sounds fair enough to us.

Some might find the noise in the barroom a bit much, but things are quieter in the dining room next door. Old Boys' food menu runs toward pub and family favorites, and with the lake nearby, the specialties of the house—marked by paw prints—include seafood dishes.

The brewing side of Old Boys' is in the hands of David Bayes, who's been here for much of its history. Bayes graduated with a degree in creative writing from nearby Grand Valley State, studied at the Siebel Institute, and homebrewed for several years before turning professional. Prior to coming here, he brewed at Great Baraboo and told us that his stint there influenced his beers.

David offers six menu beers; he said that his Kölsch and American wheat beer are the most popular. Asked what styles he prefers, he told us, "I just like to mix it up." His beers go into a number of menu items, including the crust for build-your-own pizzas.

Old Boys' is a casual west Michigan hangout. It's the kind of place where members of the bar staff wear T-shirts from past Woofstocks and don't mind if you've brought the kids—it's one of Michigan's most kid-friendly brewpubs—or whether you've arrived by land or by sea. Or, we suspect, if you happen to be a cat fancier.

Class of license: Brewpub.
Opened: October 1997.
Owner: Melissa Brolick.
Brewer: David Bayes.
System: 10-barrel DME. Capacity is about 600 barrels.
Production: 300 barrels in 2004.
Hours: Monday through Thursday, 11 A.M. to 11 P.M.; Friday and Saturday, 11 A.M. to midnight; summer Sundays, noon to 9 P.M. County blue laws forbid beer sales by the glass on Sunday, but liquor by the glass is okay. Go figure.
Tours: Yes, call ahead.
Take-out beer: Growlers, 5-gallon Cornelius kegs, and half barrels.

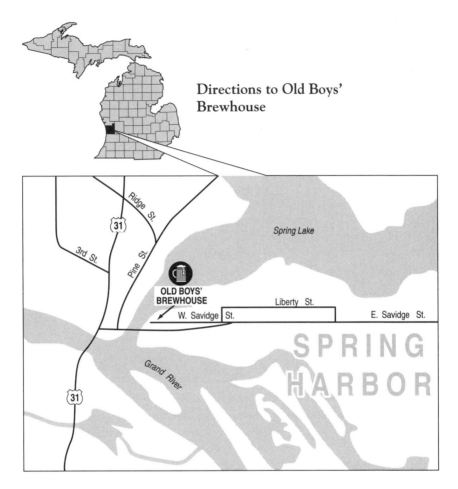

Directions to Old Boys' Brewhouse

Food: Pub menu for all ages. House beers are used in some menu items.

Extras: Full bar service. Guest beers. Kid-friendly, with events for children, a special menu for "the underdogs," and house-brewed root beer and ginger ale. Large waterfront patio in back. Live entertainment Thursday through Saturday, open mike Wednesday. Annual events include an Oktoberfest celebration and the annual Woofstock for dogs. Docking facility for large boats nearby. Keno and pull tabs.

Mug club: Yes. There's even a reserved parking space for the mug holder of the month.

Parking: Lot on the premises.

Directions: If you're headed east on M-104, make a left turn as soon as you cross the bridge, get on the service drive, and you'll see the brewery's logo and a grain silo ahead of you.

Jamesport Brewing Company

410 South James Street, Ludington, MI, 49431
231-845-2522
www.jamesportbrewingco.com

In the heyday of west Michigan's logging trade, ferries carried passengers—cars hadn't been invented yet—around the Great Lakes. Those days live on in Ludington. The steam-powered SS *Badger* plies the route across Lake Michigan.

Two blocks from the ferry dock is the Jamesport Center, a pastel-colored, late-Victorian six-storefront complex that dates back to 1890. It housed a saloon and hotel that catered to Great Lakes sailors, and legend has it that a brothel operated there. It housed everything from a butcher shop to a state liquor store to the local headquarters of the National Maritime Union.

Recently, Kathy MacLean and her partners took over two and a half of its six stalls—the other major tenant is an antiques store—and shipped in a brewing system from a brewpub in Miami Beach. They brought in Michael LaCroix, the brewer at the now-defunct Lighthouse Brewing Company up the coast in Manistee, as a consultant. LaCroix's recipes are the basis of those used today.

On a July day, we shared a table with Kathy, who told us about the brewpub. It took her two years to make the dream a reality—not unusual given the red tape associated with restoring a historic structure and getting into the liquor business. She and her partners have furnished it with a tasteful mixture of nostalgia and soft colors. Their guiding philosophy was "handcraft everything you can."

The barroom has a wooden bar, high wooden tables opposite, brick walls painted over in pastel colors, vintage brewing photos and old beer trays, and our favorite item, an old carnival coin-toss table in the corner. Next to the barroom is a cozy backroom with booths and even a snug with curtains. There's a wooden deck out back, from which

Beers brewed: The menu beers are Altbier, Dry Stout, English Mild, and ESB. Seasonals include Dortmunder, Weizenbock, Apricot Wheat, Smoky Porter, Mocha Java Porter, Kolsch, Amber Steam Style, Hefeweizen, Nitro Stout, Red's Black Cherry Porter, and Scottish Strong.

Our Picks: Paul, who has lately taken a fancy to British bitters, thought the ESB was the best. Maryanne's pick was the German-style Hefeweizen, with enough wheat malt to make a statement.

we could see the water. Kathy told us that, unfortunately, a condo development was about to block the view.

Jamesport's owners travel a great deal, and the food and beer they find on the road often inspire what's on the menu back in Ludington. Not long ago, for instance, one fell in love with Alaskan Smoked Porter while out west. "Any place that makes beer from scratch is going to make food from scratch," Kathy told us. Glancing at the food menu, we noticed that it appealed to a wide variety of tastes and certainly hasn't forgotten dessert lovers.

We were soon joined by the brewer, a west Michigan native named Tom Buchanan. He drove a truck for twenty-three years, then suffered a neck injury and was told to find another line of work. That line of work turned out to be brewing. Tired of bland mainstream beer, Tom and a friend took up homebrewing. When Jamesport Brewing opened, he worked as an assistant to the brewer. He moved up to the top job when winter set in and the brewer decided that he'd be happier back home in Arizona.

Ludington is Budweiser country, so Buchanan decided to start by focusing on traditional ales. But he received a pleasant surprise: His customers' tastes have ranged beyond transitional craft beers; in fact, altbier is the number-one seller. In keeping with the owners' desire to use local products, he's brewed a black cherry porter with local cherries crushed by a friend of the owners. Buchanan does his brewing downstairs, out of sight of his customers, although you might catch a glimpse of him through a small window on the barroom floor.

Kathy says that Jamesport Brewing gets its share of ferry passengers. But even if you're not crossing the lake, the SS *Badger* is still your friend. Follow the signs to the ferry dock and keep a weather eye out for a pastel-colored building. It'll be on your starboard side.

Class of license: Brewpub.
Opened: March 2000.
Owner: SJS Ventures; Kathy MacLean, general manager.
Brewer: Tom Buchanan.
System: 3-barrel New World. Capacity is 400 barrels.
Production: 360 barrels in 2004.
Hours: In the summer, Sunday through Thursday, 11:30 A.M. to 11 P.M.;
　　Friday and Saturday, 11:30 A.M. to midnight. In the winter, Sunday
　　through Thursday, 11:30 to 10 P.M.; Friday and Saturday, 11:30 A.M.
　　to midnight. The seasons are determined by the ferry schedule.
Tours: Yes, ask whether someone is available.

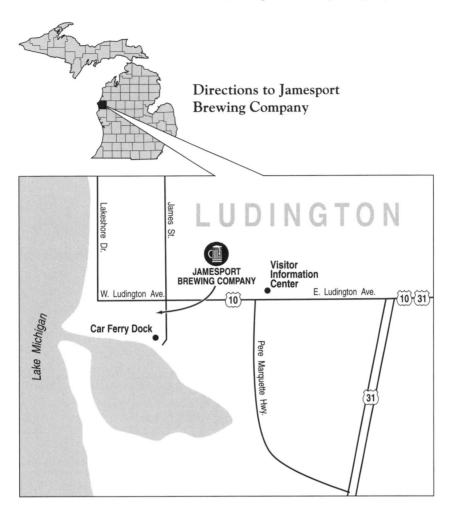

Directions to Jamesport Brewing Company

Take-out beer: Growlers.

Food: All-American pub favorites and a few British items. There are entrees as well, with the emphasis on beef.

Extras: Several brewer's dinners every year. Guest taps with beer from other Michigan microbreweries. This is the only brewpub we've been to that offers a fishing vest with its logo on it.

Parking: Available on James Street and in the lots in back and across the street.

North Peak Brewing Company

400 West Front Street, Traverse City, MI 49484
231-941-7325
www.michiganmenu.com/northpeak.html

North Peak was one of the first restaurants to locate west of downtown Traverse City. Well, not all that far west; you can walk between it and Mackinaw Brewing, the city's other brewpub. The building was constructed in 1900 for a candy factory, and industry observers considered it a large-scale operation for those days. Later, clocks and auto parts were built here, before it was given a new lease on life as a brewpub.

The stainless steel brewery stands guard near the entrance, behind glass and partially below ground level. A short flight of stairs leads up to the hostess stand and, to the right, the O-shaped blond wood bar. Beyond that is a spacious dining area, brightened with large windows, tan brick walls, and European beer posters.

To the left of the hostess stand is a waiting area furnished with sofas and tables and decorated with works from some of the area's many artists. It was there that we caught up with Mary Pat Compagnari, the general manager, while Tim Perry, the brewer, finished up in the brewery. Mary Pat told us that North Peak aims to be known more as a gathering place than a watering hole. It has a strong following among downtown office workers. What she laughingly called "a suits' happy hour" has been voted the best in town.

Schelde establishments don't take food for granted. Wood-fired entrees and pizza dominate the menu; other popular items include hanger steaks, cherry chicken salad, and ale soup. North Peak beers are used as sundae toppings and go into the barbecue sauce and cheddar soup, and pizza crust is made with spent grain. In the off-season, there are beer-and-dinner specials.

Beers brewed: There are eight beers on tap. The five menu beers are Northern Light, North Peak Pale Ale, Steelhead Red, Mission Point Porter, and Shirley's Irish Stout, which is nitro-dispensed. Two rotating taps have a wide variety of seasonals and specialties, including a cherry wheat beer with locally made cherry juice brewed for the National Cherry Festival. The eighth tap is a cask selection. Half-pints are available at lunch. North Peak also brews root beer.

Tim's story was worth waiting to hear. To put it mildly, his brewing career has covered a lot of ground. It began at the Frankenmuth Brewery during the late seventies and continued at Bell's when that brewery truly was a micro. Tim moved to Park City, Utah—to ski, not to brew—then to Maui, where he did brew. His next stop was Pagosa Springs, Colorado, where he found out that some places have even worse weather than Michigan. He arrived in Traverse City in September 2004.

Our Picks: From day one, Schelde brewpubs have turned out reliable pale ales. North Peak Pale Ale is a very hoppy but smooth-drinking American pale ale. Maryanne also found another dry Irish stout to praise—namely, Shirley's Irish Stout.

Tim is a stickler for detail, has very definite opinions about the brewing industry, and brews with a strong sense of adventure. North Peak's owners have given him two taps to play with, and in his short time there, he's brewed some very unusual beer. When we were there, he offered us a Mellow Light and a Summer Cerveza, both made using flaked maize. He said that he was aging a batch of oak-aged Irish red ale and brewing a pilsner flavored with chili peppers. What about the future? He hinted at ginseng ale, a double oatmeal chocolate cream stout, and a single-malt Scotch ale, along with more conventional beers such as doppelbock and an old English ale.

A word about Schelde Enterprises. Even Michigan beer geeks might not know who Howard Schelde is. But they should. He's been the driving force behind no fewer than five Michigan brewpubs.

His story began when he and another restaurateur, Robert Kowaleski, bought a Mr. Steak franchise in Traverse City. From there, Schelde Enterprises moved into upscale restaurants, and it is now considered one of the nation's top multiconcept restaurant companies. The company takes pains to avoid being a restaurant chain and tries hard to make its establishments both first-class operations and good neighbors.

Some have described Schelde brewpubs as "restaurants that happen to brew beer." In our opinion, that's a bad rap. We've been going to them for years and watched them turn out a solid, and improving, selection of beers.

Schelde was among the first to hop on board when Michigan legalized brewpubs, opening Grand Rapids Brewing and Bonfire Bistro in Northville. Schelde Enterprises also manages three other brewpubs that are owned by an investment group headed by Jon Carlson. It's a winning proposition for both parties, as well as the customers.

We've chosen to add this info here because it's where we met Howard Schelde and had the opportunity to chat with him and briefly discuss his restaurant ventures, in particular the brewpubs he owns or

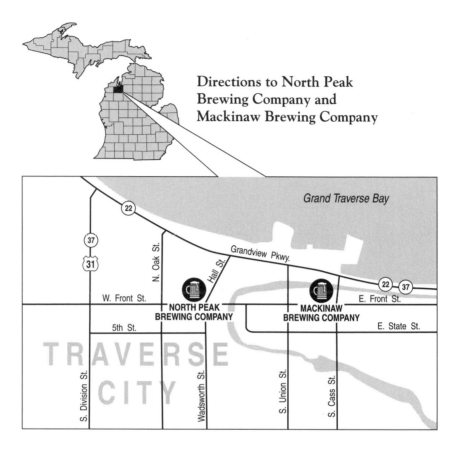

**Directions to North Peak
Brewing Company and
Mackinaw Brewing Company**

manages. We were amazed not only at how much he knew about each location, but also by how much he is still involved, despite being semi-retired. We were honored to be introduced to him.

Class of license: Brewpub.
Opened: September 1997.
Owner: NPBC, Inc., managed by Schelde Enterprises, Inc.
Brewer: Tim Perry.
System: 10-barrel Global.
Production: 664 barrels in 2004.
Hours: Monday through Thursday, 11 A.M. to 10 P.M.; Friday and Saturday, 11 A.M. to 11 P.M.; Sunday, noon to 10 P.M. Closes later from Memorial Day to Labor Day.
Tours: Yes, call ahead. By appointment only on weekends.
Take-out beer: Growlers, quarter and half barrels.
Food: Signature wood-fired pizzas, a variety of sandwiches and entrees.

Extras: Live entertainment outdoors, Tuesday through Thursday, Memorial Day to Labor Day. Magician on Sunday.

Happy hour: Daily, 3 to 6 P.M., with discounted pints. In addition, one beer a day is specially priced. Buy five growlers and get the sixth for $1.

Mug club: Lifetime membership is $50. Benefits include a logo hat and pint glass, reduced-price pints and growlers, half-price admission at special events, and a personal tour of the brewery.

Parking: Lot adjacent to the building. North Peak shares it with other tenants, so be considerate.

Mackinaw Brewing Company

161 East Front Street, Traverse City, MI 49684
231-933-1100
www.mackinawbrewing.com

All right, class. Today's lesson is about Michigan geography. The Mackinac Bridge connects the state's two peninsulas. The town at the southern end of the bridge is called Mackinaw City. And both are more than 100 miles from downtown Traverse City, where Mackinaw Brewing Company is located.

So how did this brewpub get its name? Rod Langbo, the owner, told us that the brewpub's founder was fond of the Great Lakes in general and Mackinaw City in particular. He furnished its interior with models of Great Lakes ships and pictures of the workers building the Mackinac Bridge. When the founder moved on, Langbo, who was the chef and general manager, took over. He's kept the decor as is but plans to add memorabilia from Traverse City.

Mackinaw Brewing is located inside a cream brick structure called the Beadle Building. Built in 1892, it began life as a harness shop for horses. Later on, it was a drugstore and a Big Boy restaurant. It was remodeled to accommodate a brewpub, and part

Beers brewed: The menu beers are Beadle's Best Bitter, Belgian Whitecap, G. T. Golden, Harvest Moon Oatmeal Stout, Peninsula Pale Ale, Red 8 Ale, and "The Bridge" Nut Brown Ale. The eighth tap is the "brewmaster's choice," and the ninth is a rotating seasonal beer.

of the renovation involved exposing the brick. If you look up the stairwell, you'll see brick that was stained by a fire during the 1980s. And while you're looking around, check out the back patio. It offers a view of Grand Traverse Bay.

The brewpub is on the first floor and shares an entrance with offices upstairs. As you enter, you'll see an area for those waiting for a table and a merchandise area just inside. The barroom in front combines the Victorian era and the twenty-first century. It has tile floors, exposed cream brick walls, tin ceilings, and an array of television screens. The bar is topped with granite, and above it is a blackboard listing what's on tap. Behind the bar are brass plaques and liquor bottles.

Farther back is a dining area with red-brown wooden tables and green walls. That was where we chatted with Rod Langbo and Mike Dwyer, the brewer. Rod described Mackinaw as a family restaurant as much as a brewpub. He's a barbecue fan, who installed the first Southern Pride smoker in Traverse City. The kitchen staff smokes what he calls "primal" cuts of meat for twelve hours or more and pulls them by hand. Langbo also told us, "Nothing matches our barbecue like a pint of bitter."

The brewpub staff are one big family and tend to stay around for years. Mike, who grew up in Traverse City, has been here since the day the place opened. He learned his trade via homebrewing and lots of reading, and he got used to the sometimes temperamental Peter Austin system with help from the original head brewer. Mike said that he's had his moments with the system; he confessed to a love-hate relationship with the Ringwood yeast and said that it gets cramped downstairs where the open fermenters are located.

Mike told us that he's given a fair amount of latitude in brewing. Although he offers safe choices such as a golden ale and a red ale, his menu beers also include more distinctive English styles. He has two additional taps that he can use to indulge his creativity. One is the "brewmaster's choice"; the other is a rotating seasonal, where he said he gets to brew "something for me." On our visit, Mike offered us Summer Love, an American-style wheat that's become a Memorial Day to late-September staple.

If you have a taste for both beer and adventure, think about coming up in the dead of winter. With the tourists gone, you'll have the city to yourself. And you'll get to see what Mike Dwyer can do when he has time to push the boundaries of the brewing system.

Class of license: Brewpub.

Opened: June 1997.

Owners: Rod and Lisa Langbo.

Brewer: Mike Dwyer.

System: 7-barrel Peter Austin. Capacity is about 600 barrels.

Production: 500 barrels in 2004.

Hours: Daily, 11 A.M. to 1 A.M.

Tours: Yes, call ahead.

Take-out beer: Growlers and kegs.

Food: Smoked meat and fish are the signature dishes here. Other menu items include whitefish, perch, and walleye; soups and salads; and burgers. The house beer goes into a number of them.

Extras: Cigar smoking allowed in the bar area until 10 P.M. Occasional live entertainment. Outdoor patio. A public beach and a marina are blocks away.

Mug club: The five hundred members, most of them locals, keep Mackinaw Brewing running during the slow months. Lifetime membership is $50. Benefits include a free hat or T-shirt, 10 percent discount on all purchases, an engraved brass plate on display in the brewery, a free birthday dinner, and an invitation to special events such as experimental beer tastings.

Parking: Municipal lot in back of the brewpub, other lots within walking distance, some street parking. Free after 6 P.M. and all day Sunday. Parking can be a headache in the summer.

Traverse Brewing Company

11550 South U.S. 31, Wiliamsburg, MI 49690
231-264-9343

Many Michigan breweries are family operations. But at Traverse Brewing Company, brewing also runs in the family. Owner John Archiable's grandfather brewed in Germany before coming to America, and his father brewed on the sneak when he was in college. John Neidermaier, the brewer, also carries on a family tradition. His grandfather, who came from Poland to Michigan, brewed until Prohibition.

Over a sampler of beers, John Archiable told us the Traverse Brewing story. It goes back to his student days at Ohio University. John owned a food co-op in Athens and took up homebrewing, like his father did as a student at the University of Cincinnati. He found his way to northern Michigan because the polluted air in his hometown of Cincinnati was affecting his health.

It's easy to understand why anyone would pick the Traverse City area, with an abundance of lakes, beautiful skies, and a friendly community. John made a point of mentioning how close-knit he and the other brewers in the area have become. "We want to help each other," he said, which is the unofficial slogan of Michigan's brewing community.

They located the brewery inside a pole barn, a common form of construction in this part of Michigan. It was formerly used as a repair shop, a boat showroom, and a tile company. Because Traverse Brewing is a microbrewery, it's free to offer a modest taproom instead of the upscale restaurant operations found in downtown Traverse City.

Much of what you see was the work of local craftspeople. The L-shaped, blond wood bar was fashioned by a woodworker; a regular built a sound system featuring woofers made out of beer barrels; and the ornamental grass, which resembles barley and wheat, was put in by a nurseryman who uses spent grain from the brewery as compost. The bar seats half a dozen or so. Nearby is a blackboard listing the beer specials. There are some wooden tables, works by local artists on the walls, and a collection of handmade mugs. By design, there is no television here. This is a place to relax, converse, and leave the world's troubles outside.

Through a window, you can see the brewery, and yes, it's a Peter Austin system. John said he bought it as part of an attractive package deal that also included on-the-job training. He learned brewing under Alan Pugsley and apprenticed in Milwaukee and Ottawa. There's also a Dunmore bottling line back there. It was made in the 1950s, and John described it as being as labor-intensive as the contraption that Laverne and Shirley worked on. Speaking of labor, John says that regulars occasionally pitch in with the bottling and packaging operations.

Beers brewed: The menu beers are Manitou Amber Ale, Old Mission Lighthouse Ale, Sleeping Bear Brown Ale, TBC Shandy, TBC Stout, and Torch Lake Light Ale. Seasonals include Prospero IPA, Voss Wend Wheat, Pearl's Pale Ale, Power Island Porter, and Batch 500, a wheat and rye ale. The taproom also offers two cask ales and a constantly changing selection of specialty beers. Traverse Brewing brings out special beers for the National Cherry Festival and Elk Harbor's annual Harbor Days celebration.

Our Picks: Maryanne got reacquainted with Sleeping Bear Brown Ale, which she found sweeter and maltier than most English brown ales. Paul's choice was the Old Mission Lighthouse Ale, a well-made American pale ale.

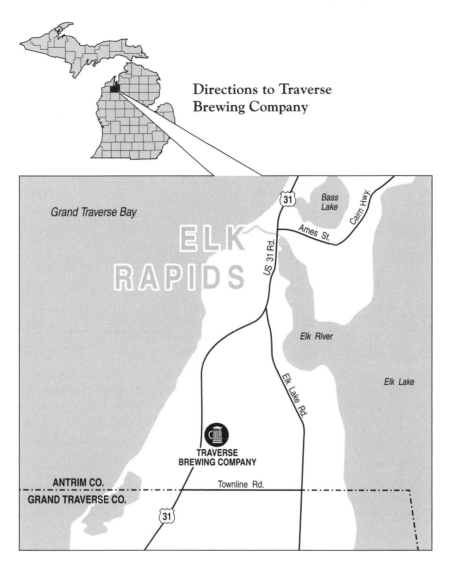

Directions to Traverse Brewing Company

Grand Traverse Bay

ELK RAPIDS

Bass Lake

Cairn Hwy.

Ames St.

US 31 Rd.

Elk River

Elk Lake Rd.

Elk Lake

TRAVERSE BREWING COMPANY

ANTRIM CO.

GRAND TRAVERSE CO.

Townline Rd.

John said that his ambition is to make "good local beer and enough of it to cover the entire state." His year-round beers and seasonals are bottled and distributed statewide, but you have to visit the taproom to try his unusual styles. On the day we visited, the blackboard next to the bar advertised Fire-Roasted Sweet Corn Cream Ale, Rye IPA, Kölsch, and Cherry Beer made with "cherries from across the street."

Because of its location—smack in the middle of northwest Michigan's tourist attractions—Traverse Brewing does a highly seasonal business, ranging from four batches a month in the dead of winter to sixteen to twenty during the summer. John hopes to smooth out production when his fellow brewery shareholders renovate a medical equipment plant that will offer him additional cold storage as well. He's also thinking of adding wine and hard cider to his product line and making his taproom more like a British pub.

And did we mention Traverse Brewing's "beer garden"? It's a circle of chairs with a fire pit in the middle. On cold winter nights—northern Michigan offers plenty of those—John starts a big, roaring fire for the customers. Take that, Jack Frost.

Class of license: Microbrewery.

Opened: January 1996.

Owner: John Archiable.

Brewer: John Neidermaier, head brewer; Steve Ison and John Holtz, assistant brewers.

System: 14-barrel Peter Austin. Capacity is somewhere between 3,360 and 4,000 barrels.

Production: 1,048 barrels in 2004.

Distribution: Available in bottles throughout Michigan and on draft in select locations in the Traverse City area. The brewery makes contract beers for local restaurants and resorts.

Hours: Monday through Friday, 11 A.M. to 8 P.M.; Saturday, noon to 8 P.M. Closed Sunday.

Tours: Monday through Friday, just ask. Groups wishing to tour the brewery should call ahead.

Food: Candy and snacks only.

Extras: Occasional live entertainment. Classic rock played on vinyl every third Wednesday. No television here; that's by design.

Mug club: The taproom's mug collection is growing, but there aren't enough for a mug club—at least, not yet.

Parking: Unpaved lot in front.

Directions: Don't let the post office address fool you. Williamsburg is east of Traverse City, but if you head in that direction, you'll be going the wrong way. The brewery is actually located on U.S. 31 several miles south of Elk Rapids. "If you find yourself in Elk Rapids, you've gone too far," John told us.

Short's Brewing Company

121 North Bridge Street, Bellaire, MI 49615
231-533-6622
www.shortsbrewing.com

One thing is for certain: Joe Short is ambitious. He's twenty-seven years old, has owned a brewery that bears his name for two years, and recently acquired the assets of another nearby brewery that threw in the towel. After "ambitious," the next adjective that describes the brewery is "eclectic."

Before opening SBC, as he refers to it, Joe brewed at the nearby Traverse Brewing Company. John Archiable, the owner there, has great respect for his brewing ability. John laughs about how he calls Joe "the kid," and Joe calls him "old man."

After a yearlong renovation project, not to mention having to address objections raised by a local church to his brewery's getting a license, Joe opened for business. His brewery is inside a 130-year-old building in downtown Bellaire whose most recent occupant was a hardware store. If you look closely at the south side of that cream-colored building, you can still see faded letters spelling "Hardware."

Bellaire has seen better days. Its most prominent business in recent years was Schuss Mountain–Shanty Creek Resort, a ski resort and golf mecca. Unfortunately, a bank has taken over the sprawling complex after its former management failed to come up with enough cash to stave off foreclosure. Residents hope that the resort can survive; the business helps keep the town afloat during the slow winter months.

Back to the brewery. The taproom decor is best described as part garage sale and part junkyard. A collection of old bicycles hangs from the ceiling. As for the furniture, when the brewery opened, Joe

Beers brewed: The menu beers are Huma-Lupa-Licious, an India pale ale; Nicie Spicie; Pandemonium Pale Ale; Pontius Road Pilsner; the Bellaire Brown; the Chocolate Wheat; the Local's Lager; the Soft Parade, which the brewery describes as a fruit rye ale; and the Village Reserve. Seasonals include Autumn Ale, an amber ale; Cup A Joe, described as a coffee creme stout; Funkin Punkin; Razzberry Flanders, a brown beer with fruit; Rocky Top Black Cherry Porter, made with locally grown cherries; Smoked Apple Ale; and Wintertime Wit.

Our Pick: Both of us chose the Huma-Lupa-Licious, where hops actually belong. As we said, Joe Short is a hophead, so it figures that he'd name one of his beers after the hop flower, *Humulus lupulus.*

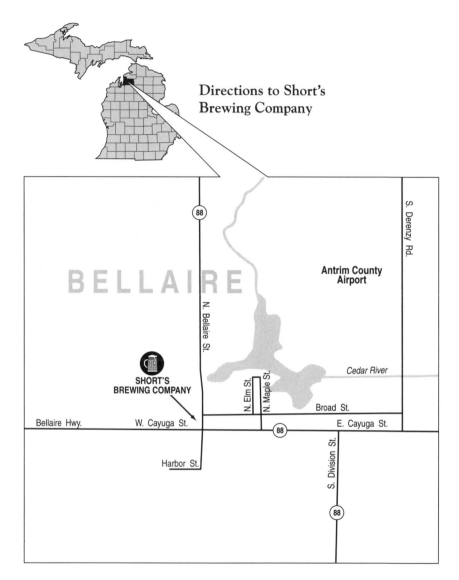

asked his friends to bring an item or two to help decorate it. The signature pieces are old red car seats. The bar is made of wood and seats about ten. A green chalkboard behind the bar lists what's on tap.

The brewery is visible behind glass doors at the rear of the taproom, along with stacks of bagged grains. Next door, in a space almost as large as the taproom, is an entertainment venue, complete with stage. SBC offers regular live entertainment in the evening. Speaking of artistic types, a fellow by the name of Josh Jones turns out the mugs for SBC's mug club in a corner of the building that's been fashioned into a pottery shed. Josh is also in charge of making the deli-style food served here.

As for the beer, another adjective comes to mind: "hophead." Joe likes hops. Lots of them. If you like your beer hopped up to the extreme levels of the Pacific Northwest, you've just died and gone to heaven. If you don't, consider yourself warned: Even the fruit beers at Short's are rich in IBUs.

Class of license: Microbrewery.
Opened: April 2004.
Owner-brewer: Joe Short.
System: 7-barrel Pub Brewing system.
Production: N/A.
Distribution: Currently, select tap accounts in northwest Michigan.
Hours: Monday through Thursday, 11 A.M. to midnight; Friday and Saturday, 11 A.M. to 2 A.M.; Sunday, noon to 11 P.M. Closed on Thursdays during the winter.
Food: A deli menu featuring pub appetizers, soup of the day, sandwiches on ciabatta bread, and pizzas.
Extras: Live jazz on Sundays. Open mike night on Tuesday. Free wireless Internet access. Smoke-free premises.
Happy hour: On Mondays, combination discount on a pizza and a pitcher of beer. On Tuesdays, discounted growler refills. On Wednesday, discounted pints all day.
Mug club: Benefits include cover-free admission; discounts on beer, food, merchandise, take-out beer, and ticketed entertainment; and a discount at the Bellaire Bed and Breakfast.
Parking: Street parking in the vicinity and lot in back.

A word about . . .

Michigan's Craft Beer Movement

Long after brewpubs and microbreweries had become a familiar part of the landscape in the Northwest and New England, they remained a novelty to those who lived in Michigan. During the eighties, when we hit the road for business or pleasure, we made a point of visiting them. Once we got home, reality set in: We made do with imported beer and wondered how long it would take the craft-beer wave to reach our shores. We also took up homebrewing, learned the basics, and deepened our appreciation for beer. And Maryanne discovered something: The same techniques she learned in canning food applied to brewing beer.

It's hard to identify when Michigan's beer scene hit bottom, but the closing of the Stroh brewery in Detroit in 1985 had an enormous symbolic impact on the state. Many Stroh drinkers felt betrayed, especially because the beer was still being brewed out of state, and swore off the brand. After Stroh shut down, there were only three breweries left in the state: G. Heileman Brewing Company, Geyer Brothers Brewery, and Kalamazoo Brewing Company. They represented the past and the future of Michigan brewing.

The Heileman facility was the largest of the three. It opened in 1899 as the Frankenmuth Brewing Company; was taken over by the Carling Brewing Company, which later merged with the National Brewing Company; and finally was bought by Heileman, which went on a buying spree in an unsuccessful effort to compete with Anheuser-Busch, Miller, and Coors. The brewery closed for good in 1991.

Geyer Brothers had been family-owned since 1874, but outside investors gained a controlling interest in the late 1960s. Like many other American breweries, it was struggling, and it would soon come under new ownership and be given a new name: the Frankenmuth Brewing Company (brewery names have a way of getting recycled).

Kalamazoo Brewing Company was the smallest of the three, founded by Larry Bell. His was a typical microbrewery story. Bell, the owner of a homebrew shop, fashioned a brewing system from industrial soup pots and operated out of a plumbing supply company in downtown Kalamazoo. Actually, Kalamazoo Brewing wasn't the state's first modern craft brewery. That distinction belongs to the Real Ale Brewery, which opened in Chelsea in 1982 but closed soon afterward.

For most of the eighties, Michigan craft beer could be summed up in one word: Bell's. Though it produced less than 1,000 barrels per year, Kalamazoo Brewing's Bell's brand won first a regional, then a national following with distinctive beers that included several stouts and Third Coast Ale, one of America's first barleywines. On the other side of the state, Frankenmuth Brewing was also breaking the light-lager mold: One of its offerings was Old Detroit Amber Ale. Even its lagers were, in today's terms, handcrafted; they were also hoppier, and contained a better grade of malt, than national-brand products.

There were also stirrings in Detroit. The owners of the Traffic Jam and Snug in Detroit wanted to brew their own beer but ran into a problem: Michigan's three-tier distribution system barred breweries from selling directly to customers or operating a licensed restaurant. In the end, they resorted to Plan B: Tom Burns, the restaurant's attorney, traded in his briefcase for brewer's boots, becoming the owner of Detroit and Mackinac Brewery across the street.

Detroit and Mackinac opened in 1992. But there was a sad ending to the story. Having realized his dream of becoming a brewer, Burns discovered that he had cancer; he passed away in 1994. A year later, a member of Burns's staff revived the brewery under a new name, Motor City Brewing Works. It remains in business under that name.

Those breweries soon had company. The state's first ten microbreweries also included Frankenmuth Brewing Company, Duster's Microbrewery and Restaurant in Lawton, Big Buck Brewery and Steakhouse #1 in Gaylord, King Brewing Company in Pontiac, Boyne River Brewery in Boyne City, Traverse Brewing Company in Williamsburg, Kraftbräu Brewery in Kalamazoo, and Arcadia Brewing Company in Battle Creek. Of the ten, only Boyne River has closed for good. All things considered, that's an amazing record for survival.

When it comes to brewpubs, Michigan came late to the party but has made up for lost time. It wasn't until 1992 that brewpubs of any sort were legal, and the original legislation was so restrictive that few establishments opened. Traffic Jam and Snug won brewpub license number one. License number two went to Grand Rapids Brewing Company, and a debate simmers about which is really number one. Grand Rapids' supporters point out that beer has been brewed there continuously since December 1993, while Traffic Jam and Snug, until 2004, bought its wort elsewhere and fermented it on the premises. But hey, let's not quibble. Both turn out great beer.

A more permissive law passed in 1994 led to a flurry of brewpub openings in the next two years. Rounding out the first ten brewpubs were Wiltse's Brew Pub in Oscoda, Hereford and Hops Restaurant and Brewpub #1 in Escanaba, Arbor Brewing Company in Ann Arbor, Great Baraboo Brewing Company in Clinton Township, O'Mara's Restaurant in Berkley, Grizzly Peak Brewing Company in Ann Arbor, Lake Superior Brewing Company in Grand Marais, and Royal Oak Brewery. Nine of those ten are still in business.

Michigan's political and economic climates haven't been kind to the state's brewing community. The state's laws are considered more restrictive than most, and the economy has been in the doldrums in recent years. National trends also hit the state, especially the craft-brewing industry shakeout of the late nineties. Several breweries, including Roffey Brewing Company of Holland, Robert Thomas Brewing Company of Grand Rapids, and Lighthouse Brewing Company in Manistee, couldn't survive despite brewing good beer.

But on the positive side, Michigan has had a higher survival rate for brewers than the national average. And the survivors have grown and prospered. Bell's Brewery—that's its new name—is on track to brewing 70,000 barrels in 2006 and is poised for further growth. Founders Brewing Company of Grand Rapids has an expansion on the drawing board, and New Holland Brewing Company of Holland is stepping up production. In southeast Michigan, Kuhnhenn Brewing Company and Dragonmead Microbrewery in Warren and Atwater Block Brewery in Detroit are expanding their distribution.

Now that the last of Michigan's old-guard breweries have closed down, all of Michigan's breweries can be classified as craft breweries. In 2004, their total production was 72,370 barrels. Bell's produced 47,370 barrels, or about 65 percent of the state's craft-brew production.

In both 2004 and 2005, more breweries opened than closed. As a result, the total brewery count, which fluctuated somewhere in the sixties for years, stood at seventy-two at the end of 2005—the highest it has been in the craft-brew era. Michigan ranks sixth nationally in the number of breweries. That total could grow in 2006, with several more brewpubs set to open their doors.

Michigan breweries are also starting to get noticed outside the state's borders. Five of them—Big Rock Chop House, Jolly Pumpkin Artisan Ales, Redwood Lodge Brewing Company, Rochester Mills Beer Company, and Royal Oak Brewery—took home medals from the 2005 Great American Beer Festival. That's up from three medals the year before. And the new owners of Atwater Block have brought back several beers that won GABF medals during the nineties. For Michigan beer lovers, the pint glass is half full, not half empty. On second thought, it's more than half full.

Northeast Michigan

I n some parts of Michigan, breweries fit neatly into a region, like those of the Upper Peninsula. Others didn't. We racked our brains over what to call the region where eight breweries are scattered over an area extending from Port Huron to Mackinac City and westward from the lakeshore to the middle of the state. What we're describing really includes several regions. The Bluewater region surrounds one of the three international crossings connecting Michigan and Ontario: the Bluewater Bridge between Port Huron and Sarnia. Fort Gratiot Lighthouse is part of Port Huron's official logo, and the city is in the process of buying it from the Coast Guard and restoring it as a tourist attraction. In July, Port Huron becomes a dateline on the nation's sports pages when more than 250 crews of boaters take on the elements, and one another, in the Port Huron to Mackinac Race. The race itself is a Michigan tradition, and so is Boat Night, the round of parties the night before.

To the north of Port Huron is the Thumb. How did it get that name? Hold the palm of your right hand in front of you, and—voila!—you're looking at a map of Michigan's Lower Peninsula. The part of your hand that corresponds to your thumb is . . . okay, you get it. The Thumb is an area where dry beans, soybeans, sugar beets, and grains grow.

West of the Thumb is the beer capital of the region: Frankenmuth. The name means "Courage of the Franconians" in English and commemorates settlers from that region of Germany who arrived here in 1845. German was widely spoken until well into the twentieth century. It didn't take long for brewing to get under way; the Cass River Brewery opened in 1862 and is today the site of the Frankenmuth Brewery, a top-class brewpub. German heritage lives on throughout Frankenmuth in a number of ways. Family-style chicken dinners, once a meal for traveling salesmen, attracted day-trippers and have now become an institution. Today the Frankenmuth Bavarian Inn Restaurant and Zehnder's of

Frankenmuth are among the state's top tourist destinations, and according to Andy Rathaus of Sullivan's, both have good beer selections as well. When I-75 drew traffic away from Frankenmuth, the town reinvented itself as a Bavarian-themed community and staged festivals to bring visitors back. It's also the home of Bronner's Christmas Wonderland (25 Christmas Lane, 989-652-9931, www.bronners.com) and two festivals in which beer plays a prominent part: the World Expo of Beer and Oktoberfest (888-FUN-TOWN, www.frankenmuthfestivals.com).

I-75 isn't far away from Frankenmuth, and the route north goes through the Tri-Cities of Flint, Saginaw, and Bay City. Parts of this area have struggled lately as auto companies have gone global and restructured their operations at home. Flint was once the state's largest company town—as in General Motors—and is the birthplace of the modern labor movement. In 1937, an auto plant was the site of a forty-four-day sit-down strike that ended up with GM signing its first collective-bargaining agreement with the United Auto Workers union. Bay City is still a busy port, from which farm products and manufactured goods are shipped to the rest of the world. But most Americans know it as the hometown of Madonna.

North of the Tri-Cities, I-75 splits with U.S. Route 23, which hugs the Sunrise Coast along Lake Huron. This relatively unspoiled area attracts boaters, water-sports enthusiasts, and those lucky enough to own cottages on the Lake Huron shore. Oscoda is at the mouth of the Au Sable River, which is a favorite of trout fishermen and canoeists alike. Oscoda is also the gateway to the Huron National Forest, where the River Road Scenic Byway winds past some of the Lower Peninsula's most beautiful scenery—including, if you're lucky, a bald eagle or two. Farther north is the paper-milling city of Alpena, where leisure activities include fishing and scuba diving—the waters off the coast are rich in shipwrecks.

If you stay on I-75, you will pass Gaylord, a town best known for its alpine architecture and unusual geographic location—halfway between the equator and the North Pole. The Gaylord area has nearly twenty golf courses, and numerous lakes and streams for boating and fishing. In the winter, the area attracts cross-country skiers and snowmobilers.

Between I-75 and U.S. Route 23 is northeast Michigan, an area so thinly populated that the state has reintroduced a herd of elk. Once upon a time, huge swaths of Michigan were covered with white pines, some of which grew 200 feet tall. But by the end of the nineteenth century, timber companies had cut nearly all of them down—there weren't many environmentalists around to object. The Hartwick Pines State

Park, seven miles northeast of Grayling, is where you'll find the last stand of these pines in the Lower Peninsula. Not far away, near Mio, are the nesting grounds of the Kirtland's warbler, an endangered songbird that some state lawmakers would like to see replace the robin as the state bird.

The Lower Peninsula ends at Mackinaw City, the southern end of the Straits of Mackinac, which was of vital military significance when the Great Lakes region was a war zone. Today Mackinaw City is at the southern end of the Mackinac Bridge, one of Michigan's best-known landmarks. The idea of a bridge spanning the straits had been batted around since before the invention of the automobile, but work didn't start until the fifties. "Big Mac," as it's known, opened on November 1, 1957. At 7,400 feet, it's the longest suspension bridge in the Western Hemisphere—even longer than the Golden Gate Bridge. The annual bridge walk is a Michigan tradition, when thousands of people, led by the governor, walk across the bridge on Labor Day morning.

Recommended Beer Bars
Frankenmuth
Frankenmuth Bavarian Inn, 713 South Main Street, 800-228-2742, www.bavarianinn.com.
Zehnder's of Frankenmuth, 730 South Main Street, 800-863-7999, www.zehnders.com.
Tiffany's Food & Spirits, 656 South Main Street, 989-652-2022. A century-old restaurant that was formerly a hotel, and later a beer garden.

Quay Street Brewing Company

330 Quay Street, Port Huron, MI 48060
810-982-4100
www.quaybrew.com

Even landlubbers get to take part in the Port Huron to Mackinac boat race. Well, sort of. Thousands of revelers join the contestants on Boat Night, the race-eve party on the banks of the Black River. Many wind up at the Quay Street Brewing Company.

We dropped in shortly after the race and talked to Vicki Peterson, one of the owners, and Greg Egan, the brewer. Vicki told us the Quay Street story. She was in the process of selling her restaurant in town when a building on the riverfront went on the market. Built during the 1950s, it was once the site of a state unemployment office and later a cosmetology school. The idea of a brewpub intrigued her because her nephew was brewing his own beer.

The partners renovated the building and created an establishment with a nautical flavor. It's a sunny, family-friendly place with its own mascot, a dog named Buster. His Thumbs Up Root Beer is a hit with the kids. Quay Street attracts a year-round clientele from the Port Huron area, who are joined in the summer by tourists. Boaters, too. Quay Street is the only brewpub in Michigan whose website gives directions by water.

Beers brewed: There are six beers on tap. The menu beers are Blue Water Pale Ale; Michigan Cream Ale, the brewpub's biggest seller; Nuttin' Better Brown Ale; Quay Street Wheat; Raspberry Wheat; and Shillelagh Stout. Specials include Ed's Red, Bohemian Pilsner, Gold, IPA, Scotch Ale, and Porter. Quay Street also brews root beer.

Our Picks: Maryanne loves stout, and the Shillelagh Stout proved to be a winner. Paul's pick was the Blue Water Pale Ale, which reminded him of the ales he had in Britain.

Quay Street's barroom has high ceilings, tile walls, and in the summer, leafy trees outside the windows. For those who like watching the world go by, a row of stools lines the picture window. You literally can become part of the woodwork here. Scattered around it are small metal plaques honoring "Valued Customers," who earn that distinction simply by showing up often enough.

One of the regulars is Brigitte Bardot. She doesn't show up in person, but a huge movie poster of her in her prime hangs above the bar. It was donated by a regular who didn't have room for it in his house. The same customer hosts an annual Bardot celebration and film festival at the brewpub.

Throughout the dining area, you'll find interesting photos—mostly maritime and breweriana—decorating the walls. There's also a "Hall of Fame" above the door to the kitchen, with items contributed by traveling customers. Inside the kitchen, you might find Vicki at work; she's also part of the kitchen staff.

But let's talk about the beer. Greg is another brewer with a background in science—namely, biology—who got into homebrewing when he realized he could make better and cheaper beer than what was on sale. He still works with local homebrewers and is part of the culinary arts program at the local community college.

Greg brews with water from Lake Huron, which, he says, lends itself to light, delicate beer. One such beer is Michigan Cream Ale, named for

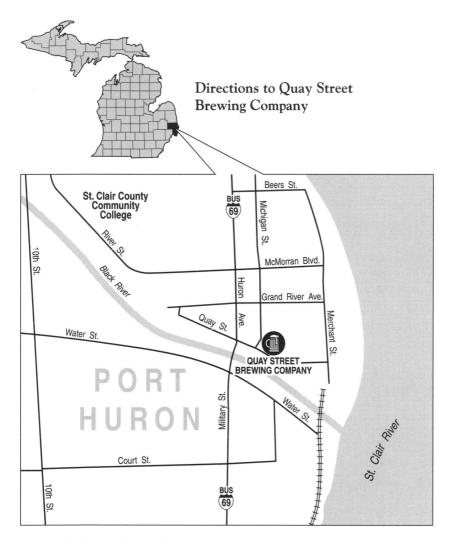

Directions to Quay Street Brewing Company

a pre-Prohibition beer called the Cream of Michigan. Its nearby brewery, C. Kern Brewing Company, touted it as a "health restorative," an advertising no-no nowadays. Greg's brewing is also influenced by Canada. His wife is from the Toronto area, and he frequently hops over the border and tries the beer on the other side.

The brewing equipment, which was shipped here by barge, stands behind glass in the barroom. Greg said that customers like to see him working because it reminds them that the beer is made by human hands. He also told us about the fog. Yes, the fog. The bar area is air-conditioned, but the steam-fired brewery isn't; on hot days, he has to contend with the pea soup.

If you come during the summer when the patio is open, you can get a navigation lesson with your beer. Walk out onto the patio, then turn left. See that body of water in front of you? That's the St. Clair River. Beyond it is Canada.

Class of license: Brewpub.
Opened: July 1997.
Owners: Jeff Knaggs, Ed Peterson, Mike Ziegler, and Victoria Peterson.
Brewer: Greg Egan.
System: 7-barrel DME. Capacity is 800 barrels.
Production: About 400 barrels in 2004.
Hours: Monday through Wednesday, 11:30 A.M. to 11 P.M.; Thursday through Saturday, 11:30 A.M. to 1 A.M.; Sunday, noon to 8 P.M.
Tours: Yes, if Greg is in. The best time to find him is around lunchtime.
Take-out beer: Growlers, 3- and 5-gallon kegs, and half barrels.
Food: Extensive menu, with entrees and family fare as well as pub favorites. Look for seafood dishes and rotating daily specials. The aim is fresh fare at reasonable prices.
Extras: Live entertainment (piano jazz) on Fridays and Saturdays. Children's menu. Docking facility in back.
Parking: Municipal lot across the street, where you can park for three hours for a quarter.

Redwood Lodge Mesquite Grill and Brewpub

5304 Gateway Center, Flint, MI 48507
810-233-8000
www.flintfood.com/rw.htm

It pays to advertise. While driving down U.S. Route 23, we spotted a grain silo and a logo that said, "Brewpub." A brewpub in Flint? Let's check it out. We made tracks for the silo and found Redwood Lodge Mesquite Grill and Brewpub. That was in the days before we took copious notes inside brewpubs. We vowed to come back someday. But one thing after another got in the way, and it was years before we paid a return visit, in connection with this book. We can report that the beer is even better. For that you can thank the brewer, Bill Wamby, who will be with us in a minute.

First, let's talk about Flint. Most Americans' impression of it comes from Michael Moore's documentary *Roger and Me*, which was not in the least flattering. Yes, Flint is suffering, but it's not dead. There are people living in the area who are weathering the economic storm. These are the people George Falaras is attracting to his Blue Collar Gourmet establishments. Redwood Lodge is one of them.

This is very much a high-end steak house, which serves certified Black Angus steaks and exotic wild game; kangaroo medallions were on the menu the day we visited. It has both a mesquite grill and a wood-fired oven, and—here's a nice touch—freshly baked loaves of bread are served to dinner guests.

The interior resembles a gigantic Up North hunting lodge, with blond wood ceilings, game animals and fish mounted on the walls, and lighting fixtures made of antlers. The large dining area is filled with wooden tables, each with a little lamp on top. And in one corner is a mural with deer grazing in a forest scene.

The brewery is in the back. Copper fermentation tanks are mounted behind the bar, and several more to the side stand guard. A "Fresh Beer" sign hangs above one row of tanks, and to the side of the bar are blackboards listing not just what's on tap—but what to expect on tap. There's also a row of banners with the awards that Bill Wamby's house beers have won.

Bill's family moved here from Cleveland when he was a boy. He spent most of his adult life as a chef and got into brewing rather late in life. It all started when he got a homebrew kit for his birthday, and later, won second prize at the Michigan State Fair homebrew competition. For the record, it was a cherry stout.

So at age forty-four, Bill found himself learning a new trade from the bottom up, beginning as a part-timer at the Big Buck Brewery and Steakhouse in Auburn Hills. He was living in the Flint area at the time

Beers brewed: There are twelve beers on draft. The menu beers are American IPA; Brown Porter; Cream Stout; Kölsch; Munich Helles; Pale Ale, an English-style pale ale; Redwood Light, which accounts for one-third of sales; and Russian Imperial Stout. The other four taps are seasonals. There are also two cask ales—one usually a pale ale, and the other a rotating special.

Awards won: 2002 WBC Silver, Sweet Stout; Gold, Old Ale; 2003 GABF Gold, British Stout; 2004 WBC Gold, French-Belgian-Style Saison; 2005 GABF Bronze, American-Style Dark Lager.

Our Picks: Paul chose the American Dark Lager. You can't go wrong with a beer that beat Michelob Amber and took home a medal at the GABF. Maryanne went with the Kölsch Style Ale, a smooth and delicate beer.

and found an opportunity in his backyard: Redwood Lodge was looking for a brewer. That was in 1999. On his watch, he's doubled beer production and earned recognition from his peers.

Bill's a big believer in competitions. He explained that they encourage brewers to take chances and also provide them with feedback. Most important, however, they give the "little guy"—Redwood Lodge, for instance—the chance to compete against, and beat, the big guys.

Bill is also giving back to the brewing community. When he sat down with us, he was wearing a Master Brewers Association of the Americas golf shirt. The MBAA was formed in the nineteenth century, when most of its members, and the owners of the breweries they worked for, were German. Industry consolidation killed most of them, and their organization came close to extinction. Today it's in the hands of craft brewers like Bill.

About Bill's beer. Echoing what he's heard from German and English brewmasters, he emphasizes balance. He credits management for recognizing the importance of the brewing side of the business and giving him the latitude to brew good beer. Having said that, he takes a "don't beat 'em, join 'em" approach to win over macrobrew lovers. Bill hopes to "march the people up the steps," getting them to try, say, a Kölsch or a Helles and later graduate to darker and stronger styles.

The customers are coming to Redwood Lodge. The surrounding area has filled up with office buildings and hotels, bringing in a steady stream of office workers and business travelers. And on occasion, passing beer travelers like us. Don't let the menu prices scare you off. It's close to four major highways and, at a minimum, is a great place to stop for a beer or two and an appetizer. Bill Wamby's beer shouldn't be missed as you travel in this part of Michigan.

As a side note, Flint is starting to attract young people, and public- and private-sector groups hope to get the redevelopment ball rolling with an entertainment and restaurant complex downtown. If all goes well, George Falaras, the main investor, will open a second brewpub there.

Class of license: Brewpub.
Opened: December 1997.
Official corporate name: Redwood Brewing Company. The restaurant is called Redwood Lodge.
Owners: Blue Collar Gourmet Restaurant Group.
Brewers: Bill Wamby, head brewer; Dave Shaw, assistant brewer.
System: 15-barrel DME. Capacity is between 1,400 and 1,500 barrels per year.

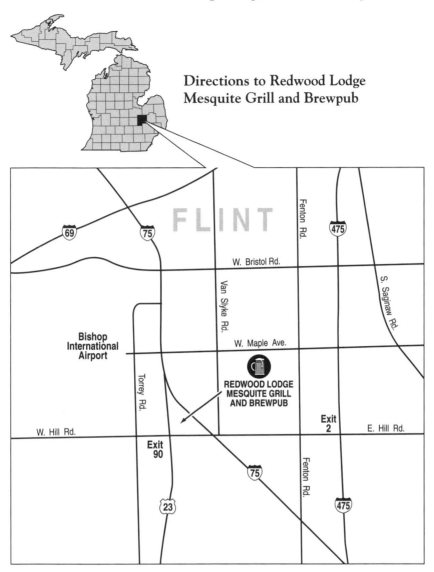

Directions to Redwood Lodge
Mesquite Grill and Brewpub

Production: 1,008 barrels in 2004.

Hours: Monday through Thursday, 11 A.M. to midnight; Friday, 11 A.M. to 1 A.M.; Saturday, noon to 1 A.M.; Sunday, noon to 10 P.M.

Tours: By appointment.

Take-out beer: 22-ounce bottles, growlers, kegs, and half barrels—"just about any container the law allows."

Food: Upscale dining in a casual atmosphere. Featured items include certified Black Angus steaks, wild game, mesquite-grilled meat, and wood-fired pizzas.

Extras: Quarterly brewer's dinners. Live music five nights a week. The Old Sequoia, a room with high-end cigars, Scotches, and wines, is a place for the guys to hang out. Outdoor patio. Redwood Lodge operates a beer tent at the Buick Open, a professional golf tournament held at nearby Warwick Hills Golf and Country Club.

Happy hour: Daily 4 to 6 P.M.

Mug club: Annual membership fee is $45. Benefits include discounts on mugs and beer to go.

Parking: Lot outside.

Area attractions: Warwick Hills is the site of the Buick Open, a stop on the PGA Tour. During the tournament, Redwood Lodge operates a beer tent on the nineteenth hole.

Frankenmuth Brewery

425 South Main Street, Frankenmuth, MI 48734
866-273-9324 (toll-free)
www.frankenmuthbrewery.com

The last of Michigan's pre–craft brew era breweries stood in Frankenmuth until 1996. Unlike most others, it didn't fall victim to economics. A tornado did it in. Shortly before midnight on June 21, the twister picked up the roof of the Frankenmuth Brewery. It took the owners seven years to repair the damage.

Except for that seven-year sabbatical—and of course, Prohibition—beer has been brewed at this location since 1862. The story began with the opening of the Cass River Brewery. Twelve years later, John Geyer bought it. The brewery stayed in the Geyer family until outside investors bought a controlling share in 1968. The last Geyer retired from the business in 1991.

After World War II, America's brewing industry consolidated rapidly, and Michigan was no exception. In 1990, Randall Heine, a Frankenmuth native, bought the brewery and reinvented it as a microbrewery that turned out a line of beers under

Beers brewed: There are nine beers on tap—eight menu beers plus either Oktoberfest or Gold Medal Winter Bock. The menu beers are German-Style Pilsner, Geyer's American Cream Ale, Hefeweizen, Irish Dry Stout, Mel-O-Dry Light Lager, Mitternacht Münchner Dark Lager, Old Detroit Amber Ale, and Pioneer Pale Ale.

the Frankenmuth and Old Detroit labels. When the tornado hit, production had risen to 30,000 barrels, and the beer could be found in twenty-five states.

Today the Frankenmuth Brewery has been reinvented again. The Heine family invested some $10 million to rebuild the huge brick building as a high-end brewpub. It is one of the classiest we've seen in this country. The interior is new and squeaky clean, but if you keep your eyes peeled, you'll find reminders of nearly 150 years of brewing history. Starting with the copper brewkettles guarding the parking lot next to the brewery.

Walking inside, we passed a large merchandise shop that sells everything from T-shirts to souvenir glasses to collectible 5-liter cans. At the entrance to the brewpub itself was a hostess stand fashioned from brewing equipment from the original brewery. Above it was a chandelier that, we later learned, was originally part of the bottling line installed here in 1935. It weighs nearly a ton.

The brewpub has much of the atmosphere of a German beer hall. There are high ceilings, Bavarian blue-and-white banners bearing the brewery's logo and a German eagle, and tables and chairs handmade from teakwood imported from Ireland. At one end of the room was a long wooden bar with rows of tap handles at either side. Above it were double-stacked stainless steel serving tanks, and off to the side was part of a grist hopper that once saw service here.

We found a table near the bar, not far from a happy group of diners who occasionally broke into song, and waited for Curt Hecht to finish his brewing chores. Curt isn't just the brewer, he's also a link between Frankenmuth's brewing past and present. On the basis of experience, he's the dean of Michigan brewers, having worked for three different owners at this location over a twenty-seven-year period.

Curt was born and raised in Frankenmuth. His brewing career began when that of the last of the Geyer brothers, Walter, ended. Walter took him under his wing and taught him how to brew. "Brewing" meant making beer in the exacting German style, which meant observing the Reinheitsgebot, or Bavarian Purity Law of 1516. Curt contends that the brewery was making "handcrafted" beers even before that term entered the language.

After an unofficial three-year apprenticeship, Walter showed up one day with his fishing tackle, said that he was retiring, and told Curt,

Awards won: 1989 GABF Silver, Bock Beer; 1990 GABF Silver, European Dark; 1991 GABF Gold, Bock; 1992 GABF Gold, Bock.

Our Picks: Maryanne's choice was Geyer's American Cream Ale, a style she's seen a fair amount of in the Northeast and Canada. This was a good example of the style. Paul thought of picking the cream ale but went instead with the Pioneer Pale Ale, more in the West Coast tradition than a German classic.

"You're now the brewer." Since then, Curt's worked with five different German brewmasters who've taught him the business and engineering aspects of brewing. As a result, he believes very strongly that a brewmaster must be technically proficient.

The brewing system at Frankenmuth certainly isn't for amateurs. After the tornado, Newlands Systems fashioned it using surviving portions of the old 100-barrel system imported from Germany, including a control panel that would delight a NASA engineer. The operation is so automated that Curt can control the brewing process by pushing buttons. And if Michigan ever loosens its distribution laws, Curt could turn out much, much more than he does now.

Curt then gave us the "insider's" tour of the brewery, starting with the sparkling-clean brewhouse with blue tile walls and brown tile floors and a bottling line brought here from Germany. He led us through the brewery's many backrooms, including an old racking room the Geyers once used to store hops. He was careful to show us the brickwork from the original brewery and showed us a bar built to resemble the one at the Geyer brothers' pre-Prohibition bar across the street.

Back at the bar, Curt shared a sampler with us. Most of his beers are German-style lagers, but he's added some ales to the lineup. The names are drawn from the brewery's rich history. Mel-O-Dry was a name used by the original Frankenmuth brewery, along with the dachshund logo; the American Cream Ale bears the Geyer name; and Old Detroit Amber Ale is the revival of a beer that had a following in Michigan during the eighties. As for the German beers, Frankenmuth won medals at the Great American Beer Festival for dark lager and bock in pretornado days.

Curt left us with the impression that the Frankenmuth Brewery is in good hands. He said that the Heines are thinking long-term—as in the year 2062. The family hopes that Frankenmuth's residents will gather in Heritage Park across the river and toast two hundred years of brewing with Frankenmuth's true-to-style German beer.

Class of license: Brewpub.
Opened: June 2003.
Owners: Brewery Development, Inc.
Brewer: Curt Hecht.
System: 20-barrel Newlands. Capacity is about 5,000 barrels.
Production: 800 barrels in 2004.
Hours: Sunday through Thursday, 11 A.M. to 11 P.M.; Friday and Saturday, 11 A.M. to 2 A.M.

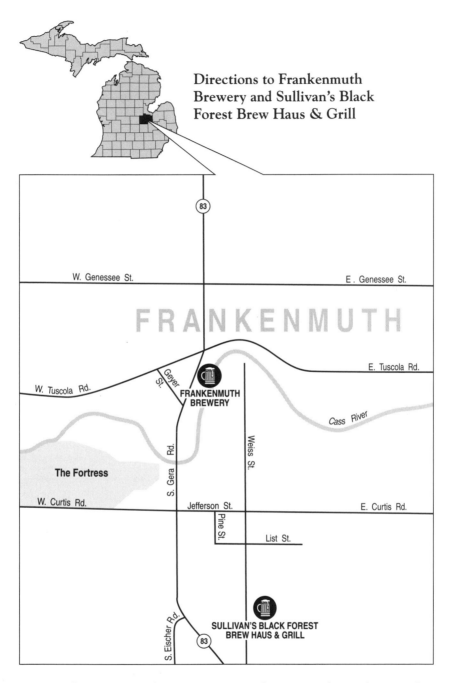

Directions to Frankenmuth
Brewery and Sullivan's Black
Forest Brew Haus & Grill

Tours: Thirty-minute brewery tours on the quarter hour, from 1:15 to
6:15 P.M. The cost is $4, which includes a sampling of beer in the
private tasting room. Call ahead to make sure tours are offered.

Take-out beer: Bottles, growlers, and kegs to go. A couple of beers are available in 5-liter cans.

Food: An extensive menu offering a wide variety. It includes German favorites such as sauerbraten, braised pork shanks, and weiner schnitzel.

Extras: This four-story complex features a number of bars and three outdoor patios, one of which overlooks the Cass River and Heritage Park. Live entertainment Thursday through Sunday during the summer. After-work deck party Thursdays during the summer. Private banquet rooms.

Happy hour: Monday through Friday, 4 to 6 P.M. Also, a burger and beer special all day Tuesday.

Parking: Small lot on the premises. Additional parking a block to the west.

Sullivan's Black Forest Brew Haus and Grill

281 Heinlein Strasse, Frankenmuth, MI 48734
800-890-6877
www.blackforestbrewhaus.net

They come from hundreds of miles away to shop at Bronner's, the gigantic Christmas store in Frankenmuth. How gigantic is Bronner's? We're talking 350 fully decorated Christmas trees, tens of thousands of ornaments, and an electric bill of 900 bucks a day. That's a lot of ho-ho-ho.

Across the street from Bronner's is a building that looks like a Bavarian ski lodge. That's Sullivan's Black Forest Brew Haus. Its German accent is unmistakable from the moment you walk in: You're greeted by a piano and the lyrics to the German sing-along tune "Ist Das Nicht Ein Schnitzelbank?"

You'll also soon realize that you're inside a brewpub. There's a fishbowl-style brewery with stainless steel tanks directly in front of you. To your right is a cooler with growlers of beer and a few old wooden casks above it. The brewery dominates the bar area. Above it is a row of growlers, some contributed by traveling employees, others sold by brewpubs elsewhere and swapped out for Black Forest growlers. On the walls, you'll find breweriana from the old Frankenmuth Brewery, along with old photos of Frankenmuth.

A few moments after we arrived, brewer Andy Rathaus emerged from the fishbowl and showed us around before leading us upstairs to the banquet room. It was clean and modern, with Old World lamps and heavy wooden beams giving it a Bavarian ambience. Catered affairs, we were told, are an important part of Black Forest's business.

Black Forest began life as a restaurant called The Matterhorn. It went through a series of owners—one of which put in a brewery—before Sullivan Marketing took it over several years ago. The Sullivan people, who have been in the restaurant and catering business for decades, brought a sense of stability, which shored up business for both the food and brewing operations. Frankenmuth is a tourist town, but locals are the key to success.

Andy is originally from Sonoma, in California's wine country, and went to college at Chico State, the home of Sierra Nevada. So it follows that he's familiar with both the grain and the grape. He worked for a winemaker in California but didn't brew until his wife's employer transferred her to Michigan. Andy went to work at Redwood Lodge Mesquite Grill and Brewpub, where he learned brewing from the bottom up. For continuing education, he took up homebrewing. His studies paid off: He got the job at Black Forest in late 2004.

Beers brewed: Black Forest offers twelve beers. The menu beers are Amber Waves of Grain, a Vienna-style amber lager; Sherwood's IPA; Sully's Irish Oat Stout; and Woody's Kolsch. Seasonals include Bumble Bee Wheat, Busch Road Brown, Hager's Maple Porter, Honey Hefeweizen, Mai Dunkel, Sam's Pale Ale, and Winter Wit Bier. Specialties include Baltic Porter; Holy Cow!, a milk stout; Imperial Stout; and Smokey and the Bandit Rauchbier. Beer is sold in pitchers, mugs, pints, glasses, and samplers.

Our Picks: Paul couldn't stop raving about the Busch Road Brown, an American brown ale with a malt flavor that wouldn't quit. Maryanne's choice was Sully's Irish Oat Stout, a strong and hoppy rendition of a style that Michigan brewers just might do better than anyone else.

As the name implies, Black Forest specializes in German-style beers. The number-one seller is a lager, and the seasonals include many German classics. But you'll also find English, Belgian, and American styles here. Andy aims to brew beers that are true to style, and he's a bug on detail. If he's brewing a Belgian-style beer, he insists on using Belgian yeast. He's also involved in the area's beer culture, hosting the local homebrew club and arranging educational events for beer lovers.

In our conversations with Michigan brewers, we asked what they did with spent grains. Maryanne just knew there would be an amusing story someplace. She finally hit pay dirt. Andy told us that his were used to make dog biscuits.

Things have been looking up for Black Forest. Zehnder's, which owns a famous German restaurant in town, put up a water park across the street next to Bronner's. But you don't have to be from out of town, have a German lineage, or even celebrate Christmas to have a good time. Just bring an appetite for good beer.

Class of license: Brewpub.
Opened: April 1996.
Owners: Sullivan Marketing, Inc.
Brewer: Andy Rathaus.
System: 10-barrel Pico.
Production: 194 barrels in 2004; 400+ barrels estimated for 2005.
Hours: Daily, 11:30 A.M. to 10:30 P.M.
Tours: Yes, by appointment.
Take-out beer: Growlers. They'll fill your Cornelius kegs. There are plans to add 22-ounce bottles.
Food: The atmosphere is German, but the food is American. The signature dish is Sullivan's fish and chips, which are famous around here. Other items include barbecue, deep-dish pizzas, char-grilled burgers, and sandwiches.
Extras: Special events, such as the annual St. Patrick's Day party and Oktoberfest. The Beer Appreciators Society meets once a month to munch on hors d'oeuvres, hear an educational talk, and try four samples of the feature beer style along with a free pint. Keith Boesnecker entertains Thursday through Sunday evenings, and Matchbox Mike performs on Friday and Saturday nights.
Happy hour: Monday through Friday, 4 to 7 P.M., with discounted pints. Discounts on growler refills Tuesday and Wednesday.
Mug club: Membership is $25 a year.
Parking: Lot outside. (See map on page 201.)

Sanford Lake Bar and Grill

3770 Bailey Street, Sanford, MI 48657
989-687-5620

Sanford Lake
Bar & Grill
...and brewpub

The most unusual part of our travels was how many times we heard the phrase "Welcome to the smallest brewery in the state." One brewer who said that was Dick Corbat, who showed us his homemade system. It was cobbled together from two half barrels, a bottle of oxygen from a hospital supply store, and a gas burner—think turkey fryer. The heat exchanger is an ice chest with a pump. It looks like something from a Food Network competition. The brewery is actually in a pole barn. To get to the brewing equipment, you get a good look at Dick's car collection, which includes an early sixties Impala convertible.

As you might have guessed, there's a story behind Dick's brewery at the Sanford Lake Bar and Grill. After Dick and his wife, Sharlyn, bought the bar in 1987, he started brewing with what he called a "glorified homebrew kit." He dreamed of eventually establishing a microbrewery on the premises when the state's brewing laws began to change. But the Environmental Protection Agency told him no, unless he hooked it up to the city sewer system—a proposition that didn't make financial sense. But Dick was determined to brew, even on a small scale. With a walk-in cooler to keep his kegs cold and a walk-in refrigerator to keep his equipment sterile, he brews surprisingly good beer.

Sanford Lake isn't a brewpub so much as a lakeside bar and grill from yesteryear. It's the kind of place you might remember your parents, or grandparents, taking you to on a lazy summer Sunday. The bar is located inside a building that's been here since at least the 1930s. It began life as a dance hall, part of a resort called Francis Grove Beach. Over the years, it went through a series of owners, closed down, and then reopened as a bar.

The interior is dark and cozy. It's decorated with everything from fiddles to saddles, old gas pumps, a couple of traffic signals, baseball caps, and

Beers brewed: Corbat's Porter; Sharlyn's Red Crown Ale; and Barking Spider Beer, which Sunday-night regulars call "Duff Beer" for obvious reasons.

Our Picks: Yes, these are extract beers, but we're sure Dick's house beers would win a head-to-head taste test against the national brands. Paul gave the nod to the Corbat's Porter, a lighter version of the style. Maryanne's choice was the Red Crown Ale, a perfectly good American amber.

breweriana. There are some dartboards in the back, and the hardest-working popcorn machine we've ever seen—250 pounds get popped every month. The furniture is low-maintenance: wooden tables and metal and plastic chairs. It's a place where you can bring the kids and not feel guilty about it.

Dick offers three regular beers: a lager, an amber, and a porter. He admits that they're entry-level beers, an accommodation of his regulars' taste for national-brand beers—the biggies still account for the huge majority of beer sales. Given his druthers, Dick would brew ales and challenge his customers with offbeat styles. On occasion, he does throw a German ale or a Belgian abbey-style beer, along with a cherry or raspberry rye beer, into the mix just to see what happens.

Geeks may be aghast, but Dick's most famous beer was called Flat and Skunky. He even had a label made for it. It's too bad he couldn't find us a label; we would have pestered our publisher to put it on the cover.

The homes on Sanford Lake's shores are inhabited by residents, not summer tourists, which means the bar attracts a year-round clientele. Dick and Sharlyn give them plenty of excuses to party: Super Bowl Sunday, Valentine's Day, and St. Patrick's Day, and we're only into March. Sunday is the biggest day here, with NASCAR in the summer and Lions football in the fall.

Dick makes sure his customers are well fed. The menu offers Beer Can Chicken, pizza, hamburgers, a good selection of appetizers, and generous pub-style dinners. But the specialties of the house are two Michigan classics: fried lake perch and walleye. They're served every night of the week. Dick proudly offered us a couple of pieces, and we understand why they're so popular.

Good food, cold beer, and old-fashioned hospitality are on the menu at Sanford Lake. With the homogenization of our culture and the intrusion of chain restaurants, places like this are disappearing. Enjoy them while you can.

Class of license: Brewpub.
Opened: The first batch of beer was served in 1994.
Owners: Dick and Sharlyn Corbat.
Brewer: Dick Corbat.
System: Half-barrel Corbat. "I sell all the beer I want to make," Dick told us.
Production: About 50 barrels a year.
Hours: Tuesday through Thursday, 4 P.M. to 1 A.M.; Friday and Saturday, 11:30 A.M. to 2 A.M.; Sunday, noon to midnight. Closed Monday.

Directions to Sanford
Lake Bar & Grill

Tours: Yes, ask ahead.

Take-out beer: Once in a while, Dick bottles his beer in 7-ounce bottles and sells it by the six-pack.

Food: Family fare. Fried perch is the feature item; if you're not sure you like perch, theirs might change your mind. Also on the menu: pizza, hamburgers, and all the pub-grub appetizers you expect. Pub-style dinners Tuesday through Thursday nights.

Extras: Open year-round. In the back, a play area with horseshoe pits, a lifeguard by the lake in the summer, and a dock in the back for boaters. Children's menu.

Parking: Lot adjacent.

Directions: Sanford Lake Bar and Grill is located on the west side of Sanford Lake. From U.S. Route 10, take the West River Road exit and go north about 2 miles; you'll see the marquee for the bar on your right. Turn right, and the bar is 100 yards ahead.

Mountain Town Station

508 West Broadway, Mount Pleasant, MI 48858
989-775-2337
www.mountaintown.com

Mount Pleasant is the tribal home of the Chippewa Indians. Today it is the home of Central Michigan University, which has adopted the Chippewa as their school symbol (the Chippewa tribe has no issue with the university using its name as their symbol), and more recently, the tribe's sprawling Soaring Eagle Casino. It's also the home of a brewer with an unusual story to tell. He's Wendell Banks, an organic farmer by trade. And he's the brewer at Mountain Town Station in Mount Pleasant.

But we're getting ahead of ourselves. First let's talk about Mountain Town Station. Once upon a time, the Ann Arbor Railroad served Mount Pleasant, and the train station was a few blocks west of downtown. In 1995, a group of investors restored the station, building a brewpub and steak house inside. In doing so, they managed to preserve much of the old station.

The bar area is dimly lit, and the music from the jukebox isn't so loud as to drown out conversation. The bar itself seats about a dozen, and it has a locomotive bell on top. Overhead are white Christmas lights, and breweriana and vintage photos are scattered about. The copper-lined brewery is opposite the bar, behind windows decorated with growlers, bottles, and cans, and even a model train overhead.

The interior of the dining room resembles a hunting lodge as much as a train station. A large stone fireplace and generous amounts of dark wood are in keeping with a restaurant whose signature dishes are steak and prime rib, with a selection of wine to accompany them. The restaurant caters largely to a forty-and-over crowd, some of whom, we suspect, are celebrating a run of luck at the casino.

There's also an outdoor patio, which is next to the railroad tracks and Mountain Town's other claim

Beers brewed: There are eight beers on tap. The menu beers are Broadway Ultra Lite, Cow Catcher Red, Gambler's Golden Ale, Hobo's Breath Brown, Iron Horse India Pale Ale, Railyard Raspberry Wheat, and Steam Engine Stout. When we visited, the seasonal was Chip River Weizen, an unfiltered version. Expect to see Belgian ales on the menu soon.

Our Pick: Iron Horse IPA was the best of the beers we sampled here. Some brewers get carried away with their hops when they brew this style, but Wendell knows when to "say when" with them.

to fame. On weekends, it runs a dinner train, which includes a two-and-a-half-hour ride through the countryside, a four-course meal, and if you wish, the house beers.

But back to Wendell. He got into brewing via a friend who home-brewed, and he discovered that if you can follow directions, you can brew decent beer. He started professionally in 2000, when he learned that the brewer at Mountain Town Station had quit. His "résumé" was a feature written about him in a local "brewspaper." Wendell got off to a roaring start. His first batch of beer was Kölsch. "I happened to nail it," he said. "It was one of the most popular batches ever at Mountain Town Station."

When he isn't brewing, Wendell is organizing an effort to grow barley and malt in mid-Michigan. He's gotten grants from the federal and state governments and helped organize a farmers' co-op. Currently, several hundred acres of barley are under cultivation in the Mount Pleasant area. Some of the malt from that barley finds its way to Mountain Town Station, earning the brewpub our gold medal for using Michigan products in beer.

Wendell says that Mountain Town's owners give him room to experiment with his beer. For him, the brewery serves as a laboratory. He also has definite opinions about style guidelines. They're fine up to a point—they tell customers what to expect—but he thinks beer geeks have gotten carried away with them. He said that his red ale is just that, a red ale—not an Irish or an American red ale. As he put it, "I make a different ale every time."

Given the direction in which he's going, it came as no surprise when he told us that he's gotten interested in Belgian-style ales. If everything goes right, they'll be available in bottles at the brewpub. His longer-term ambition is to start a Belgian-style farmhouse brewery in mid-Michigan. When he does, he'll have yet another story to tell.

Class of license: Brewpub.
Opened: October 1996.
Owner: Jim Holton is the principal owner.
Brewer: Wendell Banks.
System: 15-barrel Bohemian.
Production: About 500 barrels a year.
Hours: Monday through Thursday, 4 to 10 P.M.; Friday and Saturday, 11:30 A.M. to 10 P.M.; Sunday, 11.30 A.M. to 9 P.M.
Tours: Yes, if the brewer is in.
Take-out beer: Growlers and quarter and half barrels.

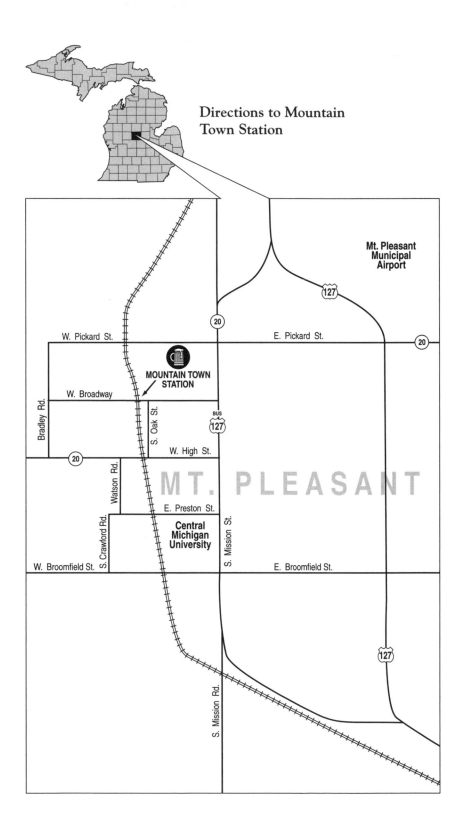

Directions to Mountain Town Station

Food: The accent is on beef. Signature dishes include hand-cut Black Angus steaks and prime rib.

Extras: Weekend dinner trains most of the year. Extensive bottled wine selection. Wireless hot spot. Kid-friendly, with a special menu and crayons. Keno and NTN trivia.

Happy hour: Thursday is Pint Night.

Parking: Large lot adjacent.

Wiltse's Brew Pub and Family Restaurant

5606 F-41, Oscoda, MI 48750
989-739-2231
www.wiltsebrewpub.com

Unless you live in Michigan, you're probably not familiar with the Sunrise Coast. It's the name given to the Lake Huron shoreline. Unlike the state's west coast, it draws hunters, fishers, and retirees rather than well-heeled tourists. This is Paul Bunyan country. In fact, the Michigan legislature recently pooh-poohed other states' claims to the legendary character and declared Oscoda his birthplace.

Oscoda was rocked by the 1993 closing of Wurtsmith Air Force Base, the region's largest employer. Many businesses suffered, but one that has ridden out the storm is Wiltse's Brew Pub and Family Restaurant. It opened in 1982 as a small family establishment, no fancier than a hamburger stand, but its owners have expanded it through good times and bad.

Owner Dean Wiltse began brewing in December 1994, at first offering extract-only beers. In 1996, he moved up to all-grain, bringing in a 4-barrel Pico system fashioned by a Detroit-area homebrewer, along with one 10-barrel and two 5-barrel fermenting tanks. He also recruited Steve Moore to take over the brewing duties. When Steve isn't brewing, he's the general manager of the restaurant. He grew up in Southern California but found his way to northern Michigan courtesy of the

Beers brewed: The four menu beers are Wiltse's Premium Lager, Blue Ox Stout, Paul Bunyan Ale, and Old Au Sable Weizenbier. Oscoda Rare is a rotating seasonal brewer's choice. The house-brewed root beer is popular with kids.

Air Force. He flew B-52s in Vietnam and was eventually stationed at Wurtsmith for a number of years.

Steve got into brewing when he took a home-brewing course at the local community college. That was about the time that Dean needed an extra pair of hands at his brewery. Steve prefers hoppy beers, such as India pale ale, and beers that are generously flavored. But because this is what he calls "Joe Six-Pack country," he's had to ease his customers into craft beers. His efforts have paid off. The house beers, which once accounted for a quarter of his beer sales, now account for three-quarters.

Our Picks: Paul chose the Blue Ox Stout, which Moore described as a hybrid stout. Maryanne chose the lager and proclaimed it the best "transition" house beer she'd tasted in her Michigan travels.

The year-round beers, with names inspired by the Paul Bunyan legend, are a lager, a stout, an amber ale, and a weizenbier. The fifth tap offers Steve a chance to brew what he likes to drink; his Oscoda Rare series has included Oktoberfest, doppelbock, several Belgians, and a Kölsch. He told us that he puts spent grain from the brewing process to an unusual use: It's fed to the local deer.

Wiltse's consists of a banquet facility, which does a brisk business in weddings and meetings of civic organizations; a family dining room; and a bar area. It's a laid-back and friendly place, where people of all ages feel at home. The trappings are best described as a mix of nostalgia, local color, and breweriana—chosen by Dean Wiltse himself. As you enter, you see hop bines growing, so you know right away that you'll find something good inside. The brewing system is part of the decor; you can see it from the bar, as well as through an eight-sided glass window at one end of the dining room. Steve hangs a sign outside the brewery telling customers what he's brewing.

The bar area is warm and welcoming. The U-shaped bar is custom-made from solid oak; above it hang beer glasses and German-style half-liter mugs for members of the mug club. One wall of the bar is dedicated to photos of the B-52—look for the picture of a dashing young Steve Moore—and other Air Force planes.

Wiltse's atmosphere is straight out of *Cheers*. It's a place where the staff really do know the regulars' names. And the friendly treatment extends to visitors to Oscoda as well. While we were sampling the house beers, a customer dropped in, took down his ceramic mug, ordered a Kölsch, and started talking beer. As for the beer, it was excellent: a Sunrise Coast attraction in itself.

Class of license: Brewpub.
Opened: December 1994.
Owners: Dean and Debbie Wiltse.

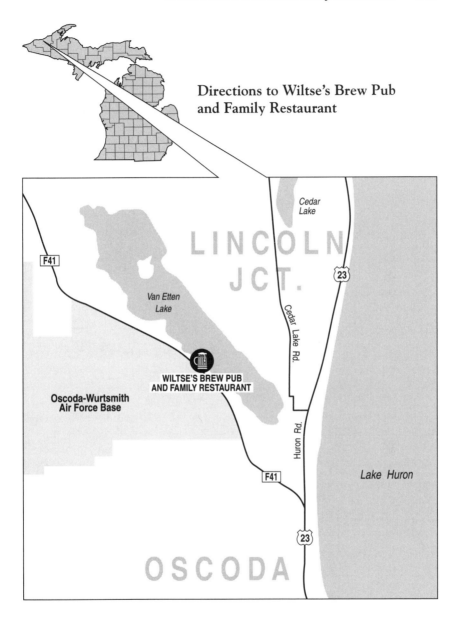

Directions to Wiltse's Brew Pub
and Family Restaurant

Brewer: Steve Moore.

System: 4-barrel Pico prototype.

Production: 160 barrels in 2004, which is close to capacity.

Hours: In the summer, 8 A.M. to 11 P.M.; the rest of the year, 10 A.M. to 11 P.M. May close earlier on slow evenings.

Tours: By request.

Take-out beer: Growlers.

Food: Family fare, pub food, and some Tex-Mex items. Children's menu. House beers are used in fish batter and soups; sometimes there's an "aleburger" on the menu.

Extras: Guest taps include Michigan micros. Banquet facilities. Family- and kid-friendly. Occasional live entertainment.

Mug club: Yes.

Parking: Unpaved lot on the premises.

Big Buck Brewery and Steakhouse #1

550 South Wisconsin Avenue, Gaylord, MI 49735
989-732-5781
bigbuck.com

You weren't hallucinating. That was an oversize beer bottle—47 1/2 feet tall, to be exact—that you saw along I-75. It isn't just a beacon to passing travelers. It's also a working silo, capable of holding 30 tons of grain. And it's the symbol of the Big Buck Brewery and Steakhouse.

In April 2005, Big Buck celebrated its tenth anniversary. But not before it went on a trip to financial hell and back. After the Gaylord location opened amid much fanfare, which included a blessing by the local Catholic bishop, its owners put together an ambitious business plan. They aimed to open Big Buck restaurants across the country, just as Old Chicago and Rock Bottom had done. In 1996, they took Big Buck public. Even though it never turned a profit, its shares traded as high as $50 apiece.

Big Buck also opened locations in Auburn Hills and Grand Rapids, Michigan, and Grapevine, Texas. Then the bubble burst. Big Buck shares sank to less than a dollar, and the Nasdaq exchange was forced to delist them. Meanwhile, the company approached Wayne County's employee pension fund for a loan. The pension fund, apparently believing

Beers brewed: The eight menu beers are Antler Ale; Big Buck Beer, the flagship beer; Black River Stout; Buck Naked; Doc's ESB; Fighting 11th IPA; Raspberry Wheat; and IPA (India Pale Ale). There is also a rotating seasonal beer. Additionally, Big Buck brews soda for this location and the one in Auburn Hills.

that Big Buck would open a brewpub in Detroit, lent it millions of dollars, much of which it never saw again.

As the money ran out, Big Buck went into survival mode. It brought in new management, took itself private, and filed for Chapter 11 protection. Under the bankruptcy court's protection, it restructured its debts and got expenses under control. Big Buck emerged from bankruptcy in mid-2005, shortly before we visited, and is on its way back. In fact, CEO Mark Provenzano told a Gaylord newspaper that he's looking at new locations. As he put it, "You grow, sell, or die."

Our Picks: We found all of Mike's beers good. Paul particularly enjoyed the ESB, which is also the favorite among mug club members. Maryanne was torn between the ESB and the Fighting 11th IPA.

The owners sank more than $4 million into this brewpub, and much of that money went into the artwork. The first thing you see—after the beer bottle—are the glass and wood doors with deer etched on them. Take a look around and you'll see carved wood trim on the bar and even nature-themed drawings on the floor. It's the work of local artists.

Big Buck's interior, which encompasses both a bar and a dining area, is best described as part hunting lodge; part German beer hall, though it's brighter and newer than those in the Old Country; and part cathedral. The fermentation tanks are mounted on an altarlike structure behind glass windows at the end of the building. Those tanks will quickly grab your attention, even if you're not a beer enthusiast.

Like a hunting lodge, Big Buck has a steeply angled wooden loft ceiling. There's wood everywhere: The floors, tables, and chairs are made out of it, and even the overhead lamps are fashioned out of wooden half barrels. It's offset by stone pillars and metal beams. Throughout the dining area, you'll find mounted animal heads—mostly deer—and a huge bison head oversees the brewing operation.

Also on display are snowshoes, a toboggan, and other sporting equipment, reminders that you're Up North. Then there are the antlers. Thousands of them, left behind by mule deer that live in northern Michigan. They've been fashioned into furniture and decorations. The chandelier over the bar is made of deer antlers, and so are the lamps above the tables.

Mike Eme is the brewer here. He was a firefighter in Fort Wayne, Indiana, and took up brewing after he retired. The Fighting 11th India Pale Ale honors his old firehouse—and his favorite beer style. In developing beers, Mike emphasizes mouthfeel, telling us, "I want it to stick to the roof of their mouth like a jar of peanut butter." An easygoing guy, Mike doesn't mind working in what brewers call a fishbowl. "It's

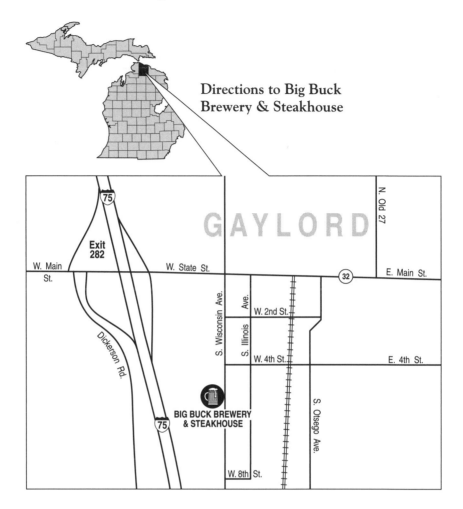

fun to see people looking inside like it's a store window at Christmas," he said.

Antler Ale, the "transitional beer," is a big seller, but Mike has managed to work bigger beers into the lineup. He brews a high-gravity ale for the holidays and has recently branched out into Belgian-style beers. For some reason, customers get attached to a particular style and remain fiercely loyal to it. Mike said that the Raspberry Wheat has a cult following, and if the ESB runs out, "I get calls at home."

Big Buck is making an effort to integrate the beer and food. Every week, Mike pairs dinner specials with his beers, and the house beers go into the Beer Cheese Soup, fish batter, sausages, and other items. And how's this for an unusual beer-and-food pairing: fried Oreos and stout.

Speaking of food, Big Buck has gone "back to the basics," emphasizing meat and potatoes. Even the original recipe for mashed potatoes is back on the menu.

At Big Buck, the clientele ranges from the ultracasual to the ultra-rich and from hard-core outdoorsmen to jacket-and-tie types. But they all have one thing in common: They've been lured here by that big bottle and what it represents.

Class of license: Brewpub.
Opened: April 1995.
Owners: Publicly held until 2004, now privately held.
Brewer: Mike Eme, head brewer; Don James, assistant brewer.
System: 20-barrel JV Northwest. Capacity is 20,000 barrels.
Production: 1,500 barrels in 2004.
Hours: Monday through Thursday, 11 A.M. to 11 P.M.; Friday and Saturday, 11 A.M. to midnight; Sunday, 11 A.M. to 10 P.M.
Tours: Yes, just ask.
Take-out beer: Growlers, party pigs, and kegs.
Food: Casual dining, with an emphasis on steak, prime rib, walleye, and perch. Unusual items include venison beer sausage and venison Reubens.
Extras: "Little Buck" menu for children. Free wireless Internet access. Live entertainment most Saturdays and Sundays.
Happy hour: Monday through Friday, 4 to 6 P.M. Also, discounts on pints of Buck Naked Light and Big Buck on Thursday nights and on growler refills Tuesday through Thursday.
Mug club: Yes, with two levels of membership. The most important benefit is a mug of beer for the price of a pint.
Parking: Large lot outside.

A word about . . .

Festivals

All year long, there's a festival going on somewhere in Michigan. Communities large and small celebrate something that makes them special: a historic event, a local product, or just the changing of the seasons. Here's a sampler of events from the Michigan calendar.

Winter

In early January, the auto industry unveils its newest models at the annual International Auto Show. It attracts auto journalists, celebrities, and hundreds of thousands of auto buffs.

Ice sculptors converge on Plymouth for the annual Ice Spectacular in late January. If the weather cooperates, their artwork stays on display for days afterward.

For more than fifty years, Houghton Lake has reveled in winter, celebrating the sport of ice fishing at Tip-Up Town, USA, in early January.

Spring

In late March, the boys' state basketball champions are crowned at the Breslin Center in East Lansing. A number of players who starred in this tournament—most notably Magic Johnson—went on to greater fame and fortune.

The Detroit Tigers have struggled for years, but opening day in early April is still a beloved rite of spring for baseball fans.

Holland celebrates its Dutch culture and the blooming of thousands of tulip bulbs with the Tulip Time celebration in early May.

Summer

June brings fifteen-hour-long days, which strawberry plants love. Belleville hosts the National Strawberry Festival in late June.

The United States and Canada hold a unique joint celebration of their national birthdays at the International Freedom Festival in Detroit and Windsor, Ontario, in late June and early July. The festival fireworks draw hundreds of thousands to both sides of the river.

Traverse City–area residents call their part of the world the "Cherry Republic" and celebrate in style at the National Cherry Festival in early July.

218

In mid-July, Port Huron hosts the start of the Port Huron to Mackinac boat race and the Boat Night party the night before the race. Competitors have included Walt Disney, Ted Turner, and Gordon Lightfoot.

Locals dread them, but art fans and people-watchers love them. We're talking about the art fairs in downtown Ann Arbor in late July.

South Haven, in the heart of Michigan's blueberry-growing region, puts on the National Blueberry Festival in early August.

Woodward Avenue from Ferndale to Pontiac turns into a miles-long classic car show in the Woodward Dream Cruise in late August.

Labor Day is the unofficial end of summer in Michigan. It's also the day that the governor leads a throng of pedestrians on the annual walk across the Mackinac Bridge.

Fall

In early September, Marshall rolls out the welcome mat for architecture fans and history buffs with its Historic Homes Tour. At about the same time, Paw Paw throws its doors open for the Wine and Harvest Festival.

We're about talking furry animals, not the fraternal organization: In late September, the Elk Fest is celebrated in the northeast Michigan town of Atlanta.

The annual Backyard Brawl, the football game between the University of Michigan and Michigan State University, is a movable feast. The 2006 contest took place in early October.

In mid-November, half a million hunters mobilize for the opening day of deer season, almost a religion in many Michigan households.

Thanksgiving Day means it's time for two Detroit traditions: America's Thanksgiving Day Parade downtown and a Detroit Lions home game at Ford Field.

Beer Events

Beer fans? You haven't been forgotten. The biggest beer event is the Michigan Brewers Guild's Summer Beer Festival, held in Ypsilanti in late July. It draws more than five thousand people. And we do mean biggest: It features some of the biggest beers you'll find at a tasting event.

Other festivals where you'll find Michigan beer include the World Expo of Beer in Frankenmuth in late May, the Festival of the Sun in Lansing in late June, and Hopps of Fun in Mackinaw City in early September.

Oh, we almost forgot. Like it or not, you'll probably get to take part in the Orange Barrel Festival, held on highways throughout the state. It's Michiganders' least favorite festival by a wide margin.

The Upper Peninsula

Michigan's Upper Peninsula (U.P.) is a state of mind. And, if some "Yoopers," as they're called, have their way, it would be a separate state. Many feel neglected by the politicians in far-away Lansing, so much so that there was a tongue-in-cheek effort to make the U.P. the fifty-first state, called Superiorland.

The U.P. was somewhat of an afterthought. In the 1830s, Michigan finally attracted enough settlers to qualify for statehood. But Congress first had to resolve a dispute between Michigan and Ohio over the "Toledo strip." It did so by awarding the strip to Ohio and giving Michigan the vast Upper Peninsula as a consolation prize. That decision didn't console many Michiganders, who found little use for an even colder, more remote piece of land.

Their attitude changed several years later when the state geologist confirmed that there were huge amounts of native copper in the Keweenaw Peninsula. America's first mining rush was under way. The copper rush, complete with prospectors scrambling to stake their claims ahead of the others, generated far more revenue than the California gold rush. Copper mining also populated the U.P. with immigrants from Scandinavia and Britain, who had a lasting influence on the region's culture.

Iron ore was discovered next, and it generated even more revenue than the copper. Eventually mines were opened in other parts of the world, and production slowed to a trickle. Former boomtowns shrank to a fraction of their population, and tourism replaced mining as a source of revenue.

One of the state's biggest tourist destinations is technically in the U.P. It's Mackinac Island, where Michigan governors have residences, cars are banned, day-trippers buy fudge to take home, and the very rich—not to mention five U.S. presidents—have stayed at the elegant

Grand Hotel. The romantic movie *Somewhere in Time* was filmed at the hotel, along with Esther Williams's *This Time for Keeps*.

On the Upper Peninsula side of I-75 is St. Ignace, from where you can catch a ferry to the island. Or you can continue north to Sault Sainte Marie, the oldest settlement in the state, established by French missionaries in the seventeenth century. Because the St. Mary's River drops 21 feet between Lake Superior and Lake Huron, engineers had to dig a canal around it. The result was the Soo Locks, an engineering marvel. With the opening of the St. Lawrence Seaway, the locks carry quite a bit of international traffic, and they've been called "the Panama Canal of the North."

West of the Soo is the town of Paradise. Keep going west from there and you'll reach Tahquamenon Falls, the second-largest waterfall east of the Mississippi, and even farther west, the Pictured Rocks National Seashore, where cliffs rise as much as 200 feet above Lake Superior. North of Paradise is Whitefish Point, "the Graveyard of the Great Lakes." It was off Whitefish Point that the *Edmund Fitzgerald*, whose sinking singer Gordon Lightfoot made famous, went down in a storm. The Great Lakes Shipwreck Museum (18335 North Whitefish Point Road, 888-492-3747, www.shipwreckmuseum.com) commemorates many other ships that have been lost in Lake Superior.

The Upper Peninsula's largest city is Marquette. "Largest" is relative; its population is only twenty thousand. Like many cities left behind by the mining companies, its downtown is rich in historic buildings. The city is also the home of a U.S. Olympic training center and Northern Michigan University, whose football team plays in "Da Yooper Dome," which is made of wood.

Iron mining once made Neagunee one of the richest cities in Michigan. The Michigan Iron Industry Museum (www.michigan.gov/hal/0,1607,7-160-17447_18595_18611-54393—,00.html) tells the story of the mining and smelting industry and how it gave rise to the port cities of the Great Lakes. Ishpeming was another city the iron mines put on the map. It's considered the birthplace of ski jumping in the United States and is the home of the National Ski Hall of Fame (www.skihall.com).

Farther south is Escanaba, which locals jokingly call the "Banana Belt" because the waters of Green Bay shield the area from the worst of winter's blasts. Paper, lumber, and especially shipping are key industries. Escanaba is the only ore port remaining on Lake Michigan. Nearby is Gladstone, where the Upper Peninsula State Fair—yes, we have two in Michigan—takes place in mid-August.

The Keweenaw Peninsula was neglected for most of the twentieth century, but in the 1970s, efforts began to preserve the area's copper-mining heritage. The Keweenaw National Historical Park (25970 Red Jacket Road, 906-337-3168), in conjunction with eighteen cooperating sites, commemorate the heritage of copper mining. The area is also the state's snow capital; it's not unusual for 25 feet of the white stuff to fall here. Houghton is best known for Michigan Technological University, a perennial power in college hockey. Speaking of hockey, Dee Stadium near the waterfront in downtown Houghton is the birthplace of the professional sport. The first organized pro league (www.cchockeyhistory.org) played here in 1904. Houghton is also the mainland headquarters of Isle Royale National Park in Lake Superior. Isle Royale is the most remote park in the entire system.

There's no getting around it: The western U.P. is remote. It's in a different time zone from the rest of the state, the Green Bay Packers and Milwaukee Brewers are the home teams, and people go to the Twin Cities to shop. So it's only natural that you'll find Michigan's largest state park—the vast Porcupine Mountains Wilderness State Park, a haven for hikers and winter-sports enthusiasts.

Casinos are one more Upper Peninsula attraction. The Ojibwa, also called the Chippewa, were among the first to take advantage of the legalization of tribal gaming. You'll find five Kewadin casinos (www.kewadin .com), the Bay Mills casino in Brimley (www.4baymills .com), and the Chip-In casino in Harris (www.chipincasino.com).

Although the Upper Peninsula has only 3 percent of Michigan's population, it's the home of nine of the state's seventy-two breweries. That's amazing enough, but even more so, in an industry where start-ups often don't make it, no U.P. brewery has closed its doors. Let's hope that trend continues.

Convention and Visitors Bureaus
Keweenaw County: www.keweenaw.info
Marquette County: www.marquettecountry.org

Recommended Beer Bars
Hancock
North Shore Grill n' Pub, 2131 Jasberg Street, 906-482-4678. Good tap selection.

Red Jacket Brewing Company/ Michigan House Café and Brewpub

300 Sixth Street, Calumet, MI 48060
906-337-1910
michiganhousecafe.com

Years before the California gold rush, people flocked to the Keweenaw Peninsula hoping to make a fortune in mining. They were looking for copper, not gold, and eventually found billions of dollars' worth of the metal.

In 1905, the town of Red Jacket, now part of Calumet, was so wealthy that five trains a day from Chicago stopped here. A brewer named Joseph Bosch, seeing an opportunity to attract business travelers, built a twenty-one-room hotel inside the Michigan House Building. It also offered a deluxe watering hole with a huge stand-up mahogany bar and a men's smoking room complete with a ticker tape machine.

As the mines played out, Calumet gradually became a near ghost town. After World War II, the Michigan House's hotel rooms were converted into apartments. The building eventually was abandoned and stood empty for fifteen years, when the bank said "enough." Then Tim and Sue Bies arrived—just in the nick of time.

The Bieses were looking to buy a bar in the Upper Peninsula and found the building with a foreclosure notice tacked on the door. Once the Bieses decided to buy it, they said, "everything seemed to fall into place." Of course, when you've been in the beer distribution business and have experience in local government, as Tim had in Alpena, things tend to go more smoothly.

The Bieses gradually restored the Michigan House to its original elegance and added touches that honor both the building and the town. A plaque commemorates "Big Annie" Clemenc, who led copper miners through the streets of town during the strike of 1913. Another pays homage to

Beers brewed: Oatmeal Espress. It's a dry stout, made with thirteen double shots of espresso in every batch and enough oat flakes to give it that oatmeal flavor. Tim's thinking of adding a cherry stout for the holidays—he has a tree in back—and might put local thimbleberries in a beer as well.

Our Pick: Oatmeal Espress, unless someone unearths one of Joseph Bosch's pre-Prohibition recipes. Bies hopes that might happen someday.

Joseph Bosch. A Bosch Brewing logo and a huge mural depicting revelers hang above the bar. The decor also includes the original bar, stained glass, old photos and breweriana, and a piano in the corner.

The barroom has some quirky touches as well: an outsize rod and reel overhead, which give a nod to Sue's Hawaiian upbringing; an early version of a snow scoop, a tool much needed around here; and Guinness signs covering vents "that were there for no reason whatsoever."

The dining room also has been restored to its 1905-vintage appearance. There's no smoking anymore—attitudes about that have changed—but the room is now an Internet hot spot. As for the food, Tim said, "We're cooks that brew beer," and he and Sue offer a menu that's a far cry from the meat-and-potatoes fare listed on the yellowed menu that hangs near the bar.

Here's where the brewery comes in. Tim had homebrewed for years, so beer has been a prime attraction since the Michigan House Café opened. Some thirty microbrews—most of them from Michigan—are available, along with a selection of imports.

But Tim wanted to add something special to the beer lineup and decided to brew an oatmeal stout. Why that style? He didn't want to compete against all the good pale ales and India pale ales on the market. Besides, stout is one of his favorite homebrew recipes. Oatmeal Espress has become the Michigan House's signature beer, and it's a good choice for the state's northernmost brewery.

The Michigan House draws families and professional people from the area, as well as tourists—largely from Wisconsin and Minnesota—during the summer. It has also become a draw for artists, who are beginning to trickle into the village. Most customers have a couple of beers, usually with dinner, and then move on—either back home or to one of the many bars nearby.

Most of the copper is gone, but Mother Nature still serves up snow in abundance. It's not unusual for Calumet to get 20 feet of the white stuff a year, and the Michigan House keeps a running total of how much has fallen so far. A few pints of beer have probably been wagered over the final total.

Class of license: Brewpub.
Opened: 1996. Brewing began February 2005.
Owners: Tim and Sue Bies.
Brewer: Tim Bies.
System: Half-barrel Sabco ("Save a Barrel") system.
Production: One half-barrel batch a week. Annual production is 26 barrels.

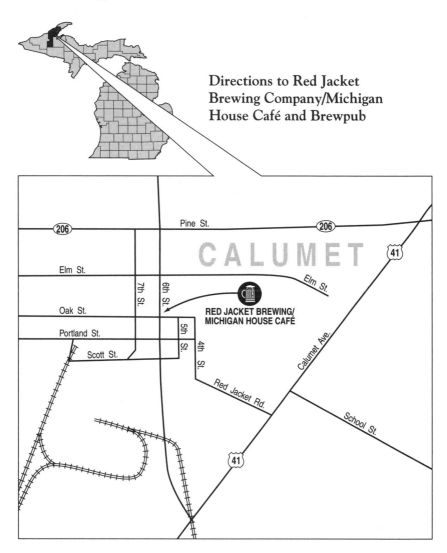

Directions to Red Jacket
Brewing Company/Michigan
House Café and Brewpub

Hours: Closed Wednesday so staff can get ready for the weekend and
  Bies can brew his next batch. Sunday, noon to 9 P.M.; other days,
  11:30 A.M. to 10 P.M.

Tours: Tim told us, "If someone wants a brewery tour, we'll roll it out."

Take-out beer: Sorry, no. Sit-down customers get dibs on the house beer.

Food: The menu features items made with local products, especially
  trout and other fish caught in Lake Superior.

Extras: Two rooms for overnight guests. Internet hot spot.

Parking: Angle parking on nearby streets, free after the meter maid
  leaves for the day. One local told us she calls it a day at 5 P.M.

Directions: Going north on U.S. Route 41, turn left at the light imme-
diately past the tourist office on your right. That puts you on the
Sixth Street extension. It's a little more than half a mile to the
Michigan House.

Keweenaw Brewing Company

408 Sheldon Avenue, Houghton, MI 49931
906-482-5596
www.keweenawbrewing.com

In our travels around the state, we heard both sides of some beery
debates. Do people make too much of style guidelines? Does winning a
competition help business? And does craft beer belong in cans? At
Keweenaw Brewing Company, the answers are all yes.

Keweenaw Brewing may be fairly new on the Michigan brew scene,
but these folks have some definite ideas about beer and the beer business.

First, the owners are Dick Gray and Paul Boissevain. Years ago, they
were students together at Houghton's legendary Michigan Tech. Fast-
forward. Living in Colorado, they were regulars at Denver's Wynkoop
Brewery, where they met Dave Lawrence, who
learned to brew there after transferring from the
kitchen side of the operation.

In 2003, Dick and Paul decided to open a brewery in this cold and out-of-the-way place they once
called home. Houghton was a copper-mining town
in its heyday, and to this day, it is famous for its
resources and environmental studies. They called
Dave and brought him on board. Dave had been
working in Leadville, Colorado, another old mining
town. An outdoor enthusiast himself, he understood
the challenges they faced. He also wanted to be eco-
friendly and help provide the people of Houghton
with a local watering hole.

So the three embarked on renovating a hundred-plus-year-old building the locals referred to as

Beers brewed: The menu
beers are Pick Axe Blonde,
Red Jacket Amber Ale, Mag-
num Pale Ale, and Hilde's
Brown. By the time you read
this, all four should be available in cans. Seasonals
include Coal Porter, Empress
Hefeweizen, Mogiana Malt
(alcohol and caffeine!), RAM
Stout, Kracken Malt Liquor,
and Tower Black Ale, and
these might become year-
rounders as well. Beer is
available in pints, half-pints,
and samplers. Keweenaw also
brews root beer.

the old Country Squire. Years ago, it was a popular men's clothing store in the center of downtown. The trio did most of the work themselves, though they hired local craftsmen for the plumbing and electrical work. They used recycled materials and poured a curved concrete bar. A blackboard salvaged from a local elementary school lists the beers on tap. The walls are a revolving display of local artwork. The result is a frugal, rustic atmosphere with a beer and mining theme.

Our Picks: Having just heard about Dogfish Head Brewing Company's Liquor de Malt, Paul was curious about Kraken Malt Liquor. He found it sweet and smooth, and entirely different from the stuff in 40-ounce bottles. Some brewers go through the motions with their amber ales, but Maryanne thought highly of Red Jacket Amber Ale, which was rich in both malt and color.

As for the beer, Dave brews what he describes as "a new breed of American beer." He does it in a brewery brought here from New Orleans—a temperamental one. "The brewery and I had to go to marriage counseling," he told us. In all-American fashion, he uses "a melting pot of ingredients" in his beer. Malt from several countries, hops and yeast from others. And he doesn't worry about re-creating some other town's water. While Pick Axe Blonde—his first beer to be canned—and Red Jacket Amber are the biggest sellers, Dave is pushing the boundaries with a Hefeweizen made with a yeast strain that only three brewers use, along with fruit beers and some Belgians.

Yes, we said canned. Keweenaw is the only brewery in the state to can its beers as we write this. Since November 2004, Dave has been using a canner from Cask Brewing Systems in Calgary, which processes fifteen cans a minute.

There are good reasons why. Canned beer can go places where bottled beer can't, like hiking trails and beaches. Many believe that cans are easier on the environment. Shipping is easier. And it's affordable, now that a microcanning system is on the market.

The cans are manufactured by Ball—the same company that makes the jars and lids your grandmother uses for preserving fruits and jellies. Once you know that, it's an easy leap to grasp that the cans are actually lined with glass—hence, there is no metallic taste. The can is filled, it gets a shot of carbon dioxide, the lid goes on, and it's sealed. It's efficient because you don't have to stop the line if one breaks, as you have to do with bottles.

The brewery is in the middle of a major expansion. The first phase involved expanding the taproom into space that, ironically, was formerly occupied by a Christian bookstore. By the time you read this, phase two will be complete. There will be a new production facility in South Range, a few miles away, with a 50-barrel JV Northwest brew-

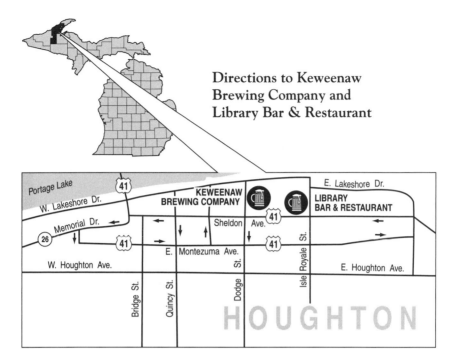

Directions to Keweenaw
Brewing Company and
Library Bar & Restaurant

house. When it's complete, all four current menu beers will be canned, the year-round beer lineup will expand, and the taproom in Houghton will become an experimental facility.

We said earlier that Keweenaw wants to be eco-friendly. Its spent grains are picked up by a local organic farmer. By the time South Range is up and running, Dave expects that the brewery will also recycle the hops and yeast.

Keweenaw Brewing Company's goal is to expand as far as it can without sacrificing quality—namely, the Upper Peninsula, northern Wisconsin, and no farther. That's the best reason I've heard for cultivating friends north of the bridge.

Class of license: Microbrewery, the first and only in the Upper Peninsula.
Opened: April 2004.
Owners: Dick Gray and Paul Boissevain.
Brewer: Dave Lawrence.
System: In Houghton, an 8-barrel Pub Brewing Systems.
Production: 468 barrels in 2004. After expansion, production will be
    considerably higher.
Distribution: The western Upper Peninsula and, by now, northern
    Wisconsin.

Hours: Taproom is open Monday through Wednesday, 3 to 10 P.M.; Thursday through Saturday, 11 A.M. to 11 P.M.; and Sunday, noon to 8 P.M.

Tours: Yes, call ahead.

Take-out beer: Cans, growlers, and quarter and half barrels.

Food: Roasted peanuts, that's it. Customers can bring food in. There's a book with menus from local restaurants if you want to order.

Extras: Nonsmoking seating with a fireplace area. Free wireless Internet access. Rotating displays of works of local artists on the walls. Board games.

Happy hour: Cheap pints mean happy-hour prices all the time.

Parking: Free parking (two hours until 5 P.M., unlimited afterward) on the decks behind Sheldon Avenue. Metered parking on Sheldon Avenue. Those meters are set back from the street for a reason: Houghton averages more than 15 feet of snow per season.

Library Bar and Restaurant

62 North Isle Royale, Houghton, MI 49931
906-487-5882
www.librarybrewpub.com

We have no doubt that many a Michigan Tech student has said to his roommate, "If my dad calls, tell him I'm at the library." And many parents probably never caught on to the fact that the Library was a brewpub in downtown Houghton.

After parking our car in back and climbing up a steep side street—"How did we wind up in Seattle?" we muttered—we walked into the barroom. Classic brewpub interior, we thought, with high ceilings, exposed brick walls, and thick metal beams. At the end of the wooden bar, we found Bob Jackson, the brewer, working on a crossword puzzle under shelves filled with hundreds of old books.

Bob told us that the building dates back to 1898, when it housed an odd couple: cabinetmaking

Beers brewed: The menu beers are Copper Town Ale; Java Stout; Keweenaw Gold, an American-style wheat; Miner's IPA; Rabbit Bay Brown; Shafthouse Dry Stout; and Whiteout Wheat. Seasonals include Belgian Trippel, Library Olde Barley Wine, Pick Axe Porter, Portage Premium Lager, and Rock Harbor Light Ale.

and embalming businesses. In pre-Prohibition days, it became a high-end restaurant called the Board of Trade. That name stuck, but the restaurant became less upscale as mining petered out. In 1967, a Tech student bought the building and reopened it as a bar and restaurant called the Library. He later sold it to the present owners, Jim and Julie Cortright, who kept the name.

Our Picks: Maryanne picked the Belgian Trippel, an abbey-style beer that Bob brought out for our opinion as to whether it was ready. Indeed it was. Paul's top choice was Copper Town Ale, an American pale ale. It was well hopped but didn't go overboard with bitterness.

When state lawmakers legalized brewpubs, the Cortrights took steps to open one. But not before a spectacular fire put their plans on hold. It all but destroyed the building, leaving only a stained-glass window untouched. The window and the original sign outside the Library are all that survived.

The Cortrights rebuilt the building and added a glassed-in dining room that offers a striking view of Portage Lake and the town of Hancock on the opposite shore. Between the barroom and the dining area stands the brewery, where, on winter days, Bob can pause, look out the windows, and watch Mother Nature at her nastiest.

Tech freshmen might be intimidated by Upper Peninsula winters, but they don't faze Bob. He's seen worse, having come here from Duluth. He wound up in Houghton to get his master's in physics. By that time, he'd been "seriously homebrewing" for years, carrying on a family tradition his father started during Prohibition.

In 1998, while studying for his doctorate, Bob learned that the Library was looking for a brewer, and he's been the brewer ever since. Since brewing is only part-time work, he supplements his income by tending bar some nights. "The best feedback about my beer comes from customers who aren't aware who they're talking to," he told us with a laugh.

One of the liveliest debate topics among Michigan brewers involves whether to enter competitions. Bob definitely takes the affirmative. Near the entrance, you'll see the medals he took home from the Michigan Beer Guide Brewers Cup. Bob's beers are largely derived from his homebrew recipes. His preference runs toward summer beers and lighter lagers. Portage Premium Lager is one of his pride-and-joy beers. He brews it during the spring, when the Library is quiet—business is highly seasonal in Houghton—and he has the capacity to ferment a lager. His biggest lament is that he could use another fermenting tank.

Bob also caters to fans of "big beers." He has to: Lots of winter means lots of demand for hearty beers. His offerings include a bock beer, an English-style strong ale, a Scotch ale for Christmas, and a barleywine brewed in half-barrel batches from his homebrewing equipment and laid down for a year. He's currently moving into Belgian-style ales, and fruit beers might be next on his list.

According to Bob, there are some sophisticated beer drinkers in Houghton, thanks to the faculty and students at Tech. Even if you're not the scholarly type, you won't feel out of place. The only required reading at the Library is the menu and the beer card.

Class of license: Brewpub.
Opened: October 1997.
Owner: Jim and Julie Cortright.
Brewer: Bob Jackson.
System: 5-barrel Pico.
Production: 243 barrels in 2004; expected to be the same in 2005.
Hours: Sunday through Thursday, 11:30 A.M. to 10 P.M.; Friday and Saturday, 11:30 A.M. to 11 P.M.
Take-out beer: Growlers, kegs, and quarter and half barrels.
Food: Contemporary and traditional favorites, including signature soups and sandwiches for lunch; Black Angus steaks, pasta, and seafood for dinner; and homemade ice cream.
Extras: Beer dinners and themed tastings. Guest taps include Michigan microbrewed beer. Online "Library Card" entitles students to discounted food. Children's menu.
Happy hour: Monday through Friday, 4 to 7 P.M., with reduced pints.
Parking: Lot in back of bar and other businesses. Free parking for two hours until 5 P.M., unlimited afterward. (See map on page 229.)

Jasper Ridge Brewery and Restaurant

1075 Country Lane, #287, Ishpeming, MI 49849
906-485-6017
www.countryvillageresort.com/html/brewery.html

It's not just another roadside attraction. Country Village, on the north side of U.S. Route 41, is a complex of more than thirty businesses. It began in the late eighties with the Country Inn, a hotel and restaurant, and expanded from there. Today it includes a second hotel, several restaurants, a cineplex and bowling alley, and a discount store.

Country Village is in Ishpeming, in the heart of Upper Peninsula iron-mining country. Since 1996, it's been the home of a brewpub that celebrates the region's mining heritage: the Jasper Ridge Brewery and Restaurant. It's named for Jasper Knob, a nearby rock formation that is the world's largest gemstone. The knob is made of alternating bands of jasper, a semiprecious stone, and hematite, better known as iron ore.

When we walked into Jasper Ridge, one of the first things we saw was a display case filled with minerals from the area. Inside, there's a lounge and a somewhat larger dining room. The lounge was your basic sports bar, but with a twist: The helmets and jerseys were from area high school teams.

This is not a fern bar for yuppies, but a place for locals to hang out. Behind the wood-topped bar are beer mugs and a small blackboard with a list of what's on tap. The tables are topped with Formica, the walls are made of concrete, and the main attraction is a big-screen TV with the game on. But there's no doubt that you've come to a brewpub. The brewery stands between the lounge and dining room, and the passageway between them is decorated with old photos and bottles from long-defunct Upper Peninsula breweries.

Beers brewed: The menu beers are Gallagher's Irish Stout, Jasper Brown Ale, Jasper Lyte Lager, Raspberry Wheat, Red Earth Pale Ale, and Ropes Golden Wheat. Seasonal beers include Black Cherry Ale, Copper Kölsch, Iron Red Ale, and Oktoberfest. There are also a number of specialties, including rye beer, hefeweizen, Java Stout, and last but not least, Blueberry Wheat, with whole blueberries. Jasper Ridge also brews root beer.

Our Picks: Maryanne chose the Red Earth Pale Ale. Pale ales aren't supposed to be red, and this wasn't. They are supposed to be hoppy, and this was. Paul's pick was Gallagher's Stout, which can be found somewhere between sweet and dry stout on the style map. Thumbs up.

People don't need much of an excuse to hold a special event here. There's an Oktoberfest, a Halloween bash, a Seventies Party, a Mardi Gras, and an Island Castaway Party. If someone's celebrating a milestone birthday, the bar staff might make that an event, too. Jasper Ridge draws its share of visitors to iron country and, in the cold of winter, flocks of snowmobilers. Country Village is on a major east-west trail.

Grant Lyke, a native of Newberry, has been in charge of the brewery since the day it opened. He took up homebrewing in the early nineties, and before he knew it, he was in the grip of "a hobby that went crazy." He's promoted several homebrew recipes into the regular lineup and came up with some others after being inspired by trips to the Northwest.

Grant brews a long list of specialty beers, some of them "on a whim," as he put it, and some by popular demand—if enough customers

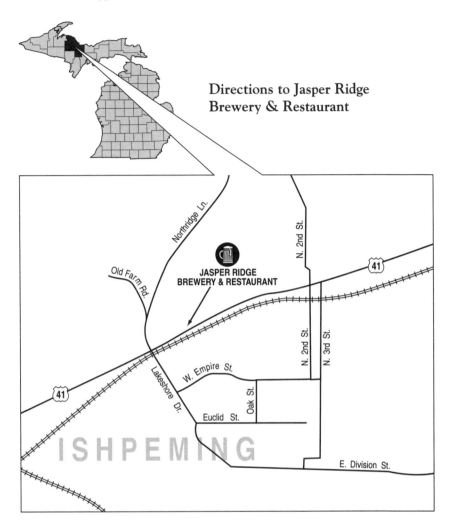

Directions to Jasper Ridge Brewery & Restaurant

suggest something, he'll brew it. Like the brewpub itself, the beer names evoke Ishpeming's mining past. The wheat is named for a gold mine that operated until recently; the pale ale is named for the area's red-colored soil; and Copper Kölsch is, well, self-explanatory.

The regulars tend to be older, but families with children and singles in their twenties like it here as well. If the beer doesn't draw them, the food will. It's American-style family fare with something for most tastes, and the owners rotate the menu in June and December. Jasper Ridge beers go into the batter, Onion Blossoms, Beer Cheese Soup, and Drunken Chicken, sautéed with onions and mushrooms.

This is a brewpub for all seasons—they get all four up there, despite what the wisenheimers downstate claim. Regardless of the time of year, something's happening here at Jasper Ridge, and you'll fit in here in no time.

Class of license: Brewpub.

Opened: October 1996.

Owner: PCBM Management Company.

Brewer: Grant Lyke.

System: 10-barrel Pico.

Production: About 300 barrels in 2004.

Hours: Sunday, 11 A.M. to 11 P.M.; Monday through Saturday, 11 A.M. to midnight.

Tours: Call ahead and ask if Grant is in. You're most likely to find him early in the day.

Take-out beer: Growlers (including plastic ones called "camp jugs"), 5-gallon kegs, and quarter and half barrels.

Food: American-style family fare. Specialties include fajitas, prime rib beef sandwiches, cheese and beer soup, and pizzas. There's a special "Budget Buster" lunch menu.

Extras: Karaoke. Thursday night trivia competitions.

Happy hour: Monday through Friday, 3:30 to 6:30 P.M. Specially priced beers during Red Wings games, NASCAR races, and other sporting events.

Mug club: Lifetime membership is $10, making this the cheapest mug club in the state. Benefits include reduced mugs.

Parking: Lot outside.

Vierling Restaurant/ Marquette Harbor Brewery

119 South Front Street, Marquette, MI 49855
906-228-3533
www.thevierling.com

LOUIS VIERLING
EST. 1883

MARQUETTE
HARBOR
BREWERY &
RESTAURANT

During the late nineteenth century, Marquette was a prosperous port from which iron ore and copper were shipped to the world via the Great Lakes. But as the mines played out, the city sank into the economic doldrums. Eventually things got so bad that local banks were leery of investing their funds downtown.

But newlyweds Terry and Kristi Doyle were willing to take a gamble. They bought the Finlandia Restaurant and restored it to the days of Marquette's mining glory. The days of Louis Vierling's Saloon, to be exact. Later they added a brewpub, and Marquette Harbor Brewery became part of the name as well.

Let's go back in time and meet the Vierlings. Martin Vierling, who moved to Marquette during the Civil War, drifted into the liquor business. He built a saloon where the brewpub now stands and, in 1890, handed the business over to his son, Louis. It offered "an especially agreeable place for gentlemen who desire liquid refreshment of an excellent quality." The saloon also had a "sample room," where escorted women could enjoy a meal or a drink. After Prohibition, the building housed a series of businesses.

In doing the renovations, the Doyles paid close attention to historic detail, installing a hundred-year-old oak bar that came from one of Vierling's rival establishments. They filled the interior with vintage items like photos, stock certificates, city maps, and stained-glass windows. Some were part of the original saloon's decor. Terry pointed to the oil paintings in shadow boxes; those were originals. He also showed us where a photo of Vierling hangs. It's between the doors to the men's and women's rooms.

Beers brewed: The menu beers are Blueberry Wheat, with whole blueberries; Canadian Blonde Ale; Captain Ripley's Red Ale; Honey Wheat; Plank Road Pale Ale, the biggest seller; and Spear's Tug Stout. Seasonals include Scottish Ale, ESB, altbier, Bohemian pilsner, Amber Ale, Nut Brown Ale, Porter, peach, and bock beer. Beer is sold in glasses, pints, mugs, and samplers.

Terry told us that he got interested in beer at an early age. His father was from Dublin, where he worked at the Guinness brewery. As for Terry, he discovered the beers of the British Isles on his holidays from an oil company job in Africa. Thus the Vierling became known for beer, offering a good range of imports. After Michigan amended its liquor laws, Terry decided to open a brewpub. He found a system at a great price, had it shipped to Marquette, and put it to work.

Our Picks: This time, it was Paul's turn to pick a stout. The Spear's Tug Stout was a dry American stout. Chumley told us, "It's hard to mimic Guinness." No need to. This was wonderful. Maryanne had a tough time choosing but ultimately gave the nod to Captain Ripley's Red Ale.

Derek Anderson, who goes by the nickname "Chumley," is in charge of the brewery. Also a Marquette native, he worked at the Vierling for eighteen years, starting in the kitchen. He learned to brew by reading and studying, talking to other brewers, and simply by doing. Chumley's been brewing here since December 1995, except for a stint at the Tahquamenon Falls Brewery and Pub, which had a similar brewing system, when the owner needed an extra pair of hands. That explained why Blueberry Wheat, with whole blueberries, was available here as well as at Tahquamenon Falls. Chumley said it's the number-one seller and added, "I'd be shot if I didn't have it."

Chumley's menu beers offer the Vierling's customers an easy transition from name-brand American and Canadian beer to craft-brewed ales. His seasonal beers are bolder, and you can expect to find several on tap along with the year-rounders. After we sampled his handiwork, Chumley took us to see the brewery. It's in a downstairs corner, and passers-by can look inside and watch him at work. He told us that the area gets uncomfortably hot in the summer, but on snowy days, it provides a warm, welcome refuge from the elements.

When the Doyles bought this property, they discovered that "the cooks have the best view in town." Thanks to their efforts, that view of Lake Superior and Marquette Harbor is now available to their guests, some of whom come with their children and grandchildren. Louis Vierling, smart businessman that he was, must be smiling down at them.

Class of license: Brewpub.
Opened: December 1995.
Owners: Kristi and Terry Doyle.
Brewer: Derek Anderson, who goes by the nickname Chumley.
System: 5-barrel Bohemian Brewery Importers. Capacity is near 400 barrels.
Production: 310 barrels in 2004; 350 to 360 barrels estimated for 2005.

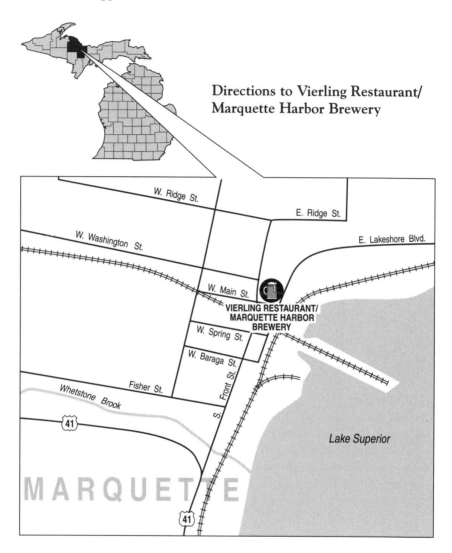

Directions to Vierling Restaurant/ Marquette Harbor Brewery

Hours: Monday through Saturday, 11 A.M. to close. Kitchen is open until 10 P.M. Closed Sunday and major holidays.

Tours: Ask if the brewer is available.

Take-out beer: 1-liter plastic containers, the kind cider or maple syrup is sold in.

Food: The Vierling's fresh, homemade food brings in more revenue than the house beers. Lake Superior whitefish, freshly caught at the local docks, is the signature dish.

Parking: Two hours' free parking on streets and in the municipal lot on the lakefront, a one-block uphill walk away.

Hereford and Hops Restaurant and Brewpub #1

624 Ludington Street, Escanaba, MI 49829
906-789-1945
herefordandhops.com

This one isn't hard to figure out. Hereford is a breed of cattle, and all know what hops are used for. Hereford and Hops is a brewpub that specializes in beef. It's the only brewpub in Michigan where customers can grill their own steaks.

The brewpub occupies the ground floor of a five-story building, originally erected as the Delta Hotel in 1914. It's listed on the National Register of Historic Places. Over the years, this once luxurious hotel fell into decline. It was turned into a home for the elderly run by a religious order and later stood empty for a while. That was when the current owners, Jack and Sharon Mellinger and Don and Rebecca Moody, took it over and renovated it.

Don Moody was a homebrewer, and as soon as Michigan legalized brewpubs, he and his fellow owners decided to build one. The idea of grilled beef comes from the days when the Mellingers raised Herefords and sold the meat to local restaurants. The menu features big cuts of beef, all the way up to 22 ounces, along with prime rib and barbecue. However, Hereford and Hops has recently become more of a bar and restaurant, and the menu goes beyond cuts of beef. While we're talking about food, we'll pass along a rumor—namely, that this building once housed the first Kentucky Fried Chicken franchise ever awarded.

Hereford and Hops consists of several rooms. The dining room is to the left of the entrance and has much of the elegance the Delta Hotel must have had in pre-Prohibition days. The barroom is

Beers brewed: There are eight beers on tap. The menu beers include Hefeweizen; Whitetail Ale, the most popular beer; Cleary Red, the other flagship beer; Black Springs Double Stout; and Raspberry Ale. Specials and seasonals include German weissbier; Redemption IPA; Schwarzbier; a "hoppy rotation" of Redemption IPA, Hop Rocket Ale, and ESB; Oktoberfest; a pumpkin ale made with real pumpkin and spices; Christmas ale, with a different recipe each year; a bridal ale (cherry stout for 2005); Nut Brown Ale; Highlander Ale, a light Scottish ale; Winter Wobble, a high-alcohol English-style brown ale; and a maple bock in spring.

to the right, with the brewing system on display through a window opposite the bar. The wooden backbar is decorated with H&H shirts worn by bar staff (our favorite said "Drink Until You're Finnish") and beer bottles.

From the thirties to the sixties, the hotel housed See Jay's, a popular night spot. Don Moody had pictures of it and relied on them when he renovated the bar area. Much of the decor is from the See Jay's era. There's also some breweriana, including several wooden cases from pre-Prohibition-era Upper Peninsula breweries. A popcorn machine stands near the bar, and a list of what's on tap is on a wooden board mounted underneath a deer head.

Awards won: 2004 WBF Gold, Schwarzbier.

Our Picks: The beer selection was the best we had in the Upper Peninsula. It was a tough choice, but Maryanne went with a German-style weissbier, which had moderate amounts of banana and clove flavor. Paul chose Redemption IPA, which was extra strong and hoppy, crisp, and dry. Everything we sampled was excellent.

The brewer is Mike Sattem, who not only grew up in Escanaba, but also was part of the construction crew that restored the Delta Hotel. When the original brewer left, Mike became his replacement, taking over in August 2003. He told us that he's partial to hoppy beers, pale ales and IPAs, as well as heavy stouts, including double and foreign-style stouts. Mike also brews root beer and cream soda, which we highly recommend.

The house beers go into the batter for fish and chips, the Brewer's Bloomer onion, sauces, and chili. The cedar planks used for smoking fish are soaked in them as well. Mike uses the spent grain to fatten the local deer, but just in case you're wondering, venison isn't on the menu.

As the #1 in the name implies, this is the original Hereford and Hops. There are two others, one in Wausau, Wisconsin, and another near Pittsburgh. Mike emphasized that Hereford and Hops isn't a chain, and the beers are somewhat different here than at the other two locations.

Hereford and Hops is gradually changing its focus, and part of that effort is reflected in heartier, more adventurous beers than the average brewpub offers. The beers are strong enough to ward off the Upper Peninsula winter. Speaking of which, if you show up on the right weekend, you can take part in the annual Jimmy Buffett Bash.

Class of license: Brewpub.
Opened: December 1994.
Owners: Jack and Sharon Mellinger, Don and Rebecca Moody.
Brewer: Mike Sattem.
System: 7-barrel JV Northwest.
Production: 580 barrels in 2004.

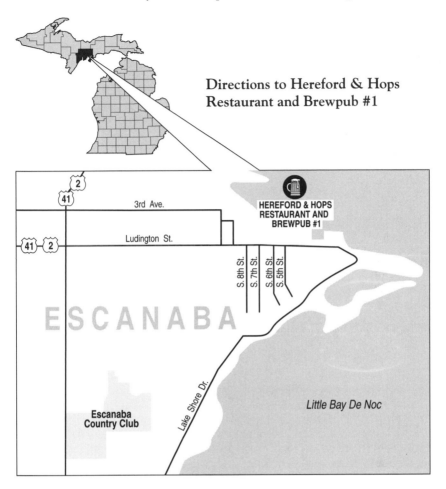

Directions to Hereford & Hops Restaurant and Brewpub #1

Hours: Daily, 11 A.M. to 10 P.M.

Tours: Yes, call ahead.

Take-out beer: Growlers, party pigs, and 22-ounce "bomber" bottles.

Food: The signature items are large cuts of beef that customers grill themselves. Barbecue, chicken and fish dishes, pasta, pizzas, and sandwiches are also on the menu. Much of the food is bought from local sources.

Extras: Friday-night fish fry. Keno and pull tabs. NTN trivia. Occasional pig roasts on the open grills.

Happy hour: Sunday through Friday, 4 to 7 P.M., with reduced pints. Also, reduced pints during Red Wings games.

Mug club: Yes, the onetime membership fee is $25.

Parking: Angle parking on Seventh Street. Parking lot across Seventh Street.

Tahquamenon Falls Brewery and Pub

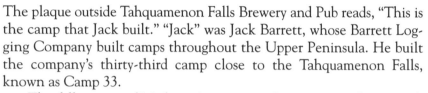

Upper Tahquamenon Falls State Park, Paradise, MI 49768
906-492-3300
www.tahquamenonfallsbrewery.com

The plaque outside Tahquamenon Falls Brewery and Pub reads, "This is the camp that Jack built." "Jack" was Jack Barrett, whose Barrett Logging Company built camps throughout the Upper Peninsula. He built the company's thirty-third camp close to the Tahquamenon Falls, known as Camp 33.

The falls is one of Michigan's top natural attractions, the second-largest waterfall east of the Mississippi. The Tahquamenon River, which plunges over the falls, was made famous in Henry Wadsworth Longfellow's poem *Hiawatha*. According to Native American lore, "Tahquamenon" comes from the river's amber color, the result of tannic acid from the cedar and hemlock swamps that feed it.

Jack dabbled in oil and real estate and was a shrewd businessman to boot. He bought some land near the falls and eventually traded most of it to the state in return for the right to harvest timber elsewhere. More important, he got the state to promise to build a road and parking area next to the land he held on to. There Jack and his wife, Mimi, built a gift shop and a replica of Camp 33.

Jack insisted that the road and parking lot end three-quarters of a mile from the falls in order to preserve the area's pristine beauty and allow visitors to better appreciate the view. After Jack died in 1959, his grandchildren carried on his legacy. Bowing to changing tastes in 1990, they tore down the camp replica and replaced it with a gift shop and concession stand. In 1996, they added a brewpub.

We're pretty sure that Jack would approve of what they've done. The brewpub is inside a northern Michigan chalet that has been described as

Beers brewed: Lark offers four beers on tap from her fifteen-beer rotation. Usually, one of the four is a lager. You're most likely to find Lumberjack Lager and Falls Tannin on the menu. Seasonals and specialties include a dry Irish stout, a raspberry ale, a porter, a pale ale, a peach ale, and a blueberry ale with whole blueberries. This last one was Lark's idea, and it's caught on at other Upper Peninsula brewpubs that have added it to their menus.

"rustic but spacious." It features a floor-to-ceiling fireplace, an essential feature of the logging camps Jack constructed. The ceiling is made of white wood; below it are wooden supports and whirring fans. Decorating the walls are pelts and mounted animal heads: North Woods natives such as timberwolf, black bear, and elk. Visitors can buy tamer versions of these creatures at a gift stand, which also sells brewpub T-shirts reading, "Brewed in the Forest Primeval."

Our Picks: Maryanne's top choice was the Lumberjack Lager, an honest blond-colored lager. Customers agree with her choice: It's the number-one seller. Paul went with the Falls Tannin, an American red ale named for the tannic acid from cedar trees that colors the falls.

The brewery stands on the south end of the building, opposite the fireplace. Stainless steel serving tanks stand guard over the bar; above them are empty bags of malt and a coyote pelt. Brewing operations are in the hands of Lark Carlyle Ludlow, Jack's granddaughter and one of the state's few female brewers. In between onslaughts of tourists—several busloads arrived while we were there—she told us the story of Tahquamenon Falls.

Lark got interested in brewing in the early nineties and decided that a brewery would provide an "added dimension" for park visitors. She said that the idea faced resistance from those who feared traffic and drunkenness, but now she and her staff are considered unofficial ambassadors for the park. Lark brews traditional beer styles and is careful to keep her beer accessible to tourists, who might not be familiar with craft beer. The names of many beers in her constantly changing lineup—fifteen or more in the course of the year—are inspired by the area's wilderness heritage.

The brewpub is part of a complex that also includes a souvenir shop, which burned down in late 2004. Fortunately, the brewpub was spared—fire used to be a major risk to breweries—and the souvenir shop was rebuilt. In the middle of the complex is a fireplace where in winter, those lucky enough to claim one of the high-backed wooden chairs can enjoy the warmth. Beer in hand, too: It's okay to take your drink out there so long as it's in plastic, not glass.

Class of license: Brewpub.
Opened: December 1996.
Owners: Lark Carlyle Ludlow, Barrett Ludlow.
Brewer: Lark Carlyle Ludlow; executive chef David Foster sometimes pitches in.
System: 10-barrel Bohemian.
Production: 800 barrels in 2004; expected to increase slightly in 2005.

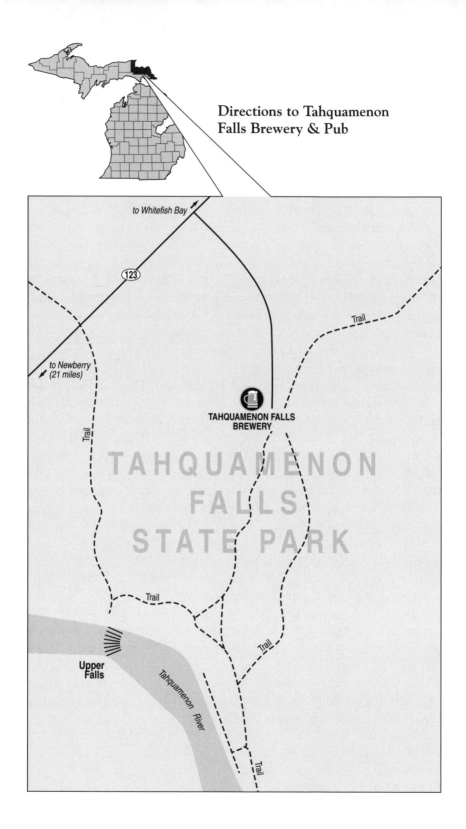

Directions to Tahquamenon Falls Brewery & Pub

to Whitefish Bay

123

to Newberry
(21 miles)

Trail

Trail

TAHQUAMENON FALLS
BREWERY

TAHQUAMENON
FALLS
STATE PARK

Trail

Trail

Upper
Falls

Tahquamenon River

Trail

Hours: Sunday through Friday, 11 A.M. to 8:30 P.M.; Saturday, 11 A.M. to 9 P.M. The brewpub is closed in April, the worst travel month of the year, and again between late October and mid-December.

Tours: No, but Lark will answer your questions about her brewery.

Take-out beer: Growlers.

Food: Hearty fare, especially in the winter, when snowmobilers stop in. Whitefish dinners are the specialty, and the menu also includes Upper Peninsula dishes such as smoked fish dip, wild rice soup, and pasties.

Extras: Occasional live music. Party the weekend before Halloween. Children's menu.

Parking: Lot inside the state park entrance. You'll have to pay $6 to enter the park, but it's worth it. The falls are one of Michigan's top natural attractions.

Directions: The brewery is surrounded by state land, so signage along M-123 is minimal. The park entrance is about 14 miles west of Paradise. Look for a brown sign reading, "Upper Falls, Tahquamenon Falls State Park," and turn there. The park entrance and complex where the brewpub is located are 100 yards south of the highway.

Superior Coast Winery and Brewery

410 Ashmun Street, Sault Sainte Marie, MI 49783
906-635-8463

As owner Susan Merrill puts it, "This is a hobby on steroids." Well, it's actually two hobbies—hers and her husband's—on steroids. Superior Coast Winery and Brewery, the Upper Peninsula's newest brewery and the state's third brew-on-premises operation, is a boutique where customers can make their own wine and beer.

Susan, an interior decorator by trade, found herself in "the Soo" when her husband accepted a position at Lake Superior State University. She wanted to do something different. She loved wine. He loved beer and had homebrewed for years. So it was only natural that she start a business that would educate consumers and help them make their favorite beverages.

Sault Sainte Marie is where Lakes Huron, Michigan, and Superior come together. The Soo is a year-round attraction for visitors, with such sights as the Soo Locks, the busiest in the world; the spectacular beauty of the nearby Agawa Canyon; and more than 1,500 miles of snowmobile trails. But the town also has a hardy year-round population. And there's something about northern winters that inspires homebrewing. That's what members of Alaska's vibrant brewing community said to us when we ventured up there for a barleywine festival.

Merrill knew she had found the perfect location, inside a former Woolworth's store in the heart of downtown. She preserved much of the original woodwork and the floor-to-ceiling mirrors, adding her own fashionable touches such as the trompe l'oeil Tuscan landscape on the wall.

Although Susan was careful to point out that Superior Coast isn't a taproom, customers can taste samples to help them decide what to make. On the beer side, there are thirteen recipes available. Once the customer chooses a recipe, staff explain the brewing process and provide the wherewithal to do everything on the premises. Think of it as homebrewing without the cleanup and carboy storage. Several weeks later, the customer comes back to rack and bottle the beer. Some arrive with friends and make a party of it. In case you're wondering, an average batch yields about sixty-four 12-ounce bottles.

Superior Coast is a perfect opportunity to learn how to homebrew or, if you're already hooked, a good place to do it if you don't have much space at home. Susan told us that many of her customers come in to make a batch or two for a special occasion such as a wedding—do they know they're reviving the ancient English custom of bride ale?—or to mark an anniversary.

By one estimate, about 85 percent of professional brewers start out as homebrewers. Susan's little brewery in the Soo might be the place where Michigan's next brewing star finds his—or her—inspiration.

Beers brewed: Your choice of thirteen ale, porter, and stout recipes.

Our Pick: We visited before the first batches of beer were ready for the tasting room. You'll have to ask for a sample when you get there.

Class of license: Microbrewery.
Opened: August 2005.
Owner: Susan Merrill.
System: Superior Coast Brew on-premises.
Production: N/A.

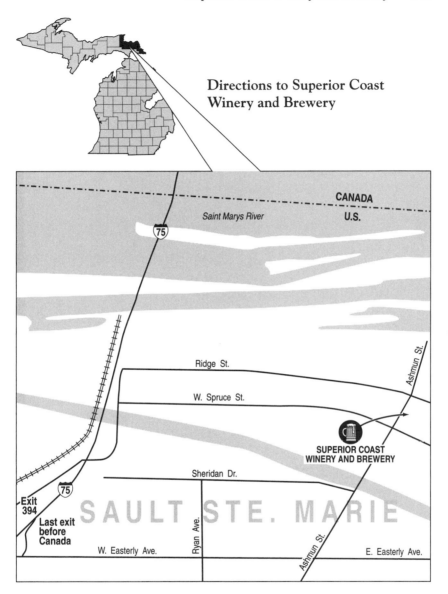

Directions to Superior Coast Winery and Brewery

Hours: Monday, Tuesday, and Thursday through Saturday, 10 A.M. to 6 P.M.; Wednesday, 10 A.M. to 8 P.M. Closed Sunday. Unlike some businesses in Sault Sainte Marie, Superior Coast is open year-round.

Tours: None per se, but customers are welcome to come in, browse, see the fermenting carboys, and sample the eight beers.

Take-out beer: What you brew and bottle.

Food: None.

Parking: Metered on street.

BEERWEBS

The Internet has become a valuable tool for beer enthusiasts, especially those who enjoy beer traveling as much as we do. One of the best websites out there is **BeerAdvocate.com,** a beer community of fifty thousand-plus members, many of whom are both knowledgeable and opinionated. Members review breweries and beer bars as well as individual beers and carry on lively discussions about beer-related topics. Another site we often visit is **RateBeer.com,** which, as the name implies, is somewhat more oriented toward aficionados who like to try new beers and tell the world what they think of them. Like BeerAdvocate, its members rate establishments as well as individual beers.

The Michigan Brewers Guild's website, **www.michiganbrewers guild.org,** provides links to its members (most of the state's brewers belong) and information about the two beer festivals it sponsors. Speaking of festivals, allow us to add a shameless plug for our own site, **Beer Festivals.org,** which offers a comprehensive listing of beer-tasting events around the world, feature articles, and links to good beer sites. And the Michigan Festivals and Events Association's website, **www.michigan fun.us,** lists hundreds of festivals celebrating everything from bologna to blueberries, not to mention beer.

Outdoor recreation is an important part of life in Michigan, and for many, that means hunting and fishing. The Michigan Department of Natural Resources' website, **www.michigan.gov/dnr,** has the information you need about getting a license, hunting and fishing seasons, and other regulations. The DNR site also has information about Michigan's many state parks, forests, and campgrounds. The Michigan Department of Economic Development's website has a travel section, **travel.michigan .org,** with information about a wide range of activities, events, and destinations, and it's worth a virtual visit before you hit the road.

One final word of caution: Michigan is big. With 58,110 square miles of land, 38,575 square miles of Great Lakes waters, and 1,305 square miles of inland waters, it's the nation's eleventh-largest state. Southeast Michigan, where most residents live, is relatively compact (though traffic can be a nightmare), but the rest of the state is a different story altogether. From Detroit to Iron Mountain, at the western end of the Upper Peninsula, it's a 487-mile, eight-hour drive. So give yourself plenty of time to explore Michigan. And watch out for deer: They're a major cause of traffic crashes.

GLOSSARY
OF BREWING TERMS

Adjuncts. Substances other than barley that brewers use to convert starch into sugar during fermentation. They include wheat, which is used by craft brewers to make a variety of styles, and corn and rice, which are not. Beer purists object to the use of corn and rice, which they associate with cheap, mass-produced beer. So did the Germans. Their beer purity law, or Reinheitsgebot, outlawed adjuncts.

Alcohol by volume (ABV), alcohol by weight (ABW). Many Michigan beer drinkers believe, wrongly, that Canadian beer is stronger. One reason for the misconception is that Canadians—and most of the rest of the world—measure the alcoholic strength of beer by volume. Because alcohol weighs about 20 percent less than the same volume of water, the result is different percentages: A beer that's 4.0 percent ABW in the States is 5.0 percent ABV in Canada. Making matters even more confusing is that American craft brewers tend to use ABV rather than ABW to measure the alcoholic strength of their beer.

Ale. Ale is beer that is brewed with top-fermenting yeast and usually fermented at 60 to 75 degrees Fahrenheit, a higher temperature than that at which lager ferments. Ales tend to be fruitier than lagers because of the nature of the yeasts used to brew them. They also tend to mature more quickly, which is one reason why craft brewers decided to brew them—they're less time- and equipment-intensive.

Barley. A grain that has proved especially suitable in making beer. Brewers like barley because it's hardy, it stores well, and its kernels are rich in an enzyme that converts starch into fermentable sugar. Eighty percent of the barley grown in North America is of the six-row variety; the rest is two-row barley. Six-row barley has a coarser flavor and causes cloudiness in beer. For this reason, many American microbrewers prefer two-row barley.

Barrel. In the United States, the official unit of measure for beer volume. A barrel is equivalent to 31 gallons, or roughly 13 3/4 cases of 12-ounce bottles.

Barrel-aged. Used to describe beer that is aged in a wooden barrel so that it can acquire some of the character of what was in the barrel before—typically, bourbon or port wine. Barrel aging has become popular among Michigan brewers, especially those who brew stouts, big beers, and off-the-wall styles.

Beer. A general term that refers to a fermented drink made from grain and seasoned with hops. Beer is divided into two categories: ale, which is by far the older of the two, and lager, which accounts for the vast majority of beer brewed today. Americans, who drink mostly lager, often use "beer" to mean lager, while our ale-drinking British cousins often use "beer" to mean ale.

251

Beer festival. An event where attendees can try beer from multiple brewers at one location. Festivals are held in parks, convention centers, museums—anywhere a crowd can gather. Many festivals are sponsored by brewers' organizations. Michigan's leading festival is the Michigan Brewers Guild's Summer Beer Festival, held annually in Ypsilanti.

Beer geek. A term that seems derogatory but really isn't—that is, if it's used by another beer geek. It refers to a person who takes beer seriously. Very seriously. Many beer geeks are homebrewers and tend to fit a profile: They're mostly male, bright, mechanically inclined, and think that beer is much too important to be a hobby. There's a subtle difference between a beer geek and a beer snob; if you show snobbish tendencies, your fellow beer geeks will let you know.

Big beer. A generic term used to describe beer with a high alcoholic content, generally 8 percent ABV or higher. Big beers are nothing new. Over the years, they've gone by a number of names, including "malt liquor," "old ale," and "strong ale." Brewers in nineteenth-century England brewed strong ales, called barleywines, for holidays and other special occasions. The style has been revived by American craft brewers; Bell's Brewing Company's Third Coast Ale was one of the first. English brewers also made a powerful version of stout for the court of Russia's Catherine the Great, and it came to be known as imperial stout. Today "imperial" is an adjective used to describe a high-alcohol version of a style. One example is "imperial IPA," an extrastrong India pale ale, which was recently added to the list of categories in the Great American Beer Festival competition.

Bitter. An English term for a hoppy ale, usually served on draft. Bitters, in ascending order of alcoholic content, are ordinary bitters, best or special bitters, and extra special bitters. Bitters have long been a familiar product of American craft brewers. They're hoppier than mass-market lagers, but less hoppy than pale ales and India pale ales.

Bottle-conditioning. Adding a small amount of fresh yeast and sugar into the bottle along with the beer. The purpose is to increase the beer's alcohol level, carbonation, or both.

Bottom fermentation. The method of fermentation associated with lagers, in which the by-products of fermentation settle to the bottom. Bottom fermentation takes place at cooler temperatures and generally results in a cleaner, crisper-tasting beer. Bottom-fermented beers need to mature for a longer time before they are ready to drink.

Brewhouse. The part of a brewery where wort is produced and boiled. It is the heart of the brewing operation.

Brewkettle. The vessel in which wort is boiled with hops. Traditional brewkettles were copper, but more recently they have been made out of stainless steel.

Brewpub. A combination bar and restaurant where beer is brewed on the premises. Total beer production is modest; in Michigan, a brewpub is limited to 5,000 barrels a year. The first modern American brewpub was opened by Bert Grant in Yakima, Washington, in 1982. Michigan's first brewpub license was awarded to the Traffic Jam and Snug in Detroit, which opened in 1993. Most breweries in Michigan are licensed in the brewpub category.

Campaign for Real Ale (CAMRA). A British organization formed in the 1970s to fight the disappearance of cask-conditioned ale. It grew to become one of Europe's most successful consumer movements. Today it has more than fifty thousand members, including some in North America. CAMRA sponsors the annual Great British Beer Festival in London, one of the world's biggest and most famous beer festivals.

Cask-conditioned ale. Also known as Real Ale. It refers to beer that undergoes a secondary fermentation in a wooden cask, from which it is dispensed. To start the secondary fermentation, the brewer adds yeast and sugar to the cask before it leaves the brewery. Cask-conditioned beer is dispensed without the use of extraneous carbon dioxide and is drawn from the cask using a handpump.

Celis, Pierre. A milkman from Belgium who decided to revive witbier, a beer made with wheat malt and spiced with coriander and curaçao orange peel. He and a retired brewer produced their own version of witbier and called it Hoegaarden, after Pierre's hometown. Celis sold Hoegaarden to the Belgian brewing giant Interbrew, then moved to the United States, where he produced a line of Belgian-style beers under his own name. He sold that brewery, which eventually was acquired by the Michigan Brewing Company of Webberville.

Contract brewer. A brewery that hires other breweries to brew its beer. One reason for contract brewing is flexibility: The brewery doesn't have to buy a plant and equipment or see them sit idle if production is less than capacity. Contract brewing has been the subject of intense debate. Some look down on contract-brewed beer as soulless and commercial, not true craft beer. Defenders of contract-brewed beer analogize it to a meal cooked by a renowned chef in someone else's kitchen: It's still the handiwork of that chef.

Craft beer. Beer made by a loose alliance of microbreweries, brewpubs, and small regional brewers, who are often referred to as craft brewers. What craft brewers have in common is a dedication to reviving locally brewed beer in a variety of styles, both traditional and innovative. Craft beer accounts for slightly more than 3 percent of the American beer market, but despite its small market share, it has strongly influenced the brewing industry.

Cream ale. An ale once common in Michigan and surrounding regions. It was developed by brewers who tried to brew pilsner-style beers but didn't have the right lager yeast. They substituted ale yeast, then fermented the beer at warm temperatures like an ale and aged it at low temperatures like a lager. The style acquired the name "cream ale." Another ale aged like a lager is Kölsch, a light-colored beer native to Cologne, Germany, and often brewed by American craft brewers.

Draft. Used to describe beer served from a keg and pressured through a tap by carbon dioxide or a mixture of nitrogen and carbon dioxide; or beer served from a cask and dispensed without adding extraneous gases.

Dry-hopping. Adding a few hop cones to a batch of beer after putting it in barrels. Dry-hopping imparts a hoppy aroma to the beer.

Esters. Compounds produced by fermentation that give some beers the aroma of banana, grapefruit, pear, or other fruits. The aromas depend on the strain of yeast used and are more likely to be found in ales than in lagers.

Extract. Malt extract made by mashing malt and then reducing the resulting sweet, unhopped wort to a syrup. It's similar to concentrated wort. Because extract brewing requires less-elaborate equipment and not as much technical expertise, it's popular with beginning homebrewers. Some professional breweries use extract systems, but they're less common than in the early days of craft brewing. Experts insist that extract-brewed beer can't be as good as whole-grain beer, but it is possible to brew a good extract beer.

Extreme beer movement. A movement of craft brewers dedicated to pushing the boundaries of brewing. Jim Koch, the founder of Boston Beer Company, is credited with starting the movement with his Samuel Adams Triple Bock in 1994. Some extreme beers are esoteric varieties, such as Dogfish Head Brewing Company's Midas Touch, a winelike beverage that replicates what King Midas might have enjoyed when he was alive. Others are ultrastrong beers, such as Boston Beer Company's Utopias (2005), an ale with 25 percent ABV—twice that of the average wine.

Fermentation. The process of converting wort into beer by adding—or, in brewing jargon, "pitching"—yeast, which reacts with the sugar in the wort to produce alcohol, carbon dioxide, and by-products.

Firkin. A cask holding 9 imperial gallons (11¼ U.S. gallons) of beer—somewhere between a quarter and a half barrel—and specially designed so that beer can be poured from it either by gravity or through a handpump. The name is so amusing to North Americans that it's often used in pub names.

Gravity. The density of fermentable sugars, relative to water, in a brewing mixture. The sugar-and-water mixture is denser than water alone, and thus its gravity will be higher than 1.0. The higher a beer's original gravity—its gravity when fermentation begins—the stronger the beer is likely to be at the end of the brewing process. Many American craft brewers follow the British custom of listing the original gravity of their beers, along with their percent alcohol by volume (ABV).

Great American Beer Festival (GABF). A beer festival sponsored by the Association of Brewers and held in early fall in Denver. It has been an annual event since 1982. The festival has grown over the years, attracting 29,500 attendees in 2005. The GABF is also a prestigious brewing competition in which Gold, Silver, and Bronze Medals are awarded in sixty-nine categories. In 2005, 466 breweries took part and entered 2,335 beers.

Growler. Before bottled and canned beer was common, customers brought reusable jugs or other containers to taverns and had them refilled there. One commonly used container, shaped like a bucket with a hinged metal lid, came to be known as a "growler." Experts disagree on the term's origin; one often-heard explanation is that air trapped inside the container made a growling sound when it was opened. The term has been part of American English for decades. In the early twentieth century, men sent their children out with an empty growler with the instruction, "Rush the growler." Modern growlers are glass half-gallon jugs that, because of federal and state laws, are required to have a label with the brewery's name and various other information.

Guest beers. Beers served at a brewpub that were brewed elsewhere. Some Michigan brewpubs offer local microbrewed beers along with their own products.

Handpump. A hand-powered pump used to dispense beer from a cask. Either a handpump or a gravity tap is used to dispense cask-conditioned beer.

Hectoliter. A metric measure of brewing capacity: 100 liters, or 26.4 U.S. gallons. Although the United States doesn't use the metric system, the rest of the world does, and some brewing equipment used by American brewers was manufactured overseas.

High-gravity beer. Another way of saying "high-alcohol beer." Beer with a high original gravity is likely to have a high alcoholic content at the end of the brewing process.

Hops. The dried fruit of a climbing vine that, when added to beer, imparts aroma and bitterness. Over the centuries, brewers have used a wide variety of herbs, plants, and other substances to flavor beer. Since the Middle Ages, hops have become the dominant flavoring agent.

House beers. In the case of a brewpub, beers that are brewed there. In the case of a beer bar or a restaurant, beers made especially by a brewery to be served at that establishment.

International Bittering Unit (IBU). A measurement of the level of hops compounds in beer. In general, the greater the number of IBUs, the more bitter the beer tends to taste.

John Barleycorn. An expression many think refers to whiskey. However, the folk song by that name actually describes the process of making beer, beginning with farming and harvesting grain, followed by the steps in the process of brewing it. Although both beer and whiskey share the steps of malting through fermentation, the song makes no mention of distilling—the final step in making hard liquor. Speaking of distilling, some Michigan brewers have branched out into spirits—a logical next step, if you think about it.

Keg. A container in which fresh beer is sold to customers to drink at home. Traditionally, a keg was a half-barrel metal container (or a quarter-barrel container called a "pony keg") in which the beer was kept under pressure until it was "tapped," an art in itself. Nowadays, beer is also sold in smaller, easier-to-use versions of the keg, including cylindrical 5-gallon containers called Cornelius or "corney" kegs, and small, 3-gallon-plus, self-contained dispensing systems called "keggies."

Lauter tun. A large, round, shallow vessel where wort is separated from the mash by draining it through slotted bottom plates, called a "false bottom," into the brewkettle.

Light beer. A term used to describe a beer with 10 to 35 percent fewer calories than regular beer.

Liquor Control Commission (LCC). The state agency responsible for enforcing the Michigan Liquor Control Code, a complex body of law that governs the licensed-beverage industry. The LCC issues licenses and has the power to suspend or revoke them for code violations.

Macrobrew. A derogatory term used by some beer enthusiasts to describe big breweries' products. To some, it connotes bland "industrial beer" that isn't brewed for serious beer drinkers. The major brewers call that characterization unfair and point out that they spend heavily to ensure that their product is fresh, consistent, and pleasing to consumers.

Malt. Barley that has been soaked in cold water, allowed to germinate under cool and moist conditions, and dried in warm air. Malting barley makes it easier for the brewer to convert its starch to fermentable sugar.

Mashing. The process of steeping malt in hot water in order to convert the grain in that malt into fermentable sugars. The mixture of water and grains is called mash.

Mash tun. A large vessel, often made of copper, in which mash is processed.

Menu beers. The beers that a brewery offers year-round. In addition to menu beers, most breweries offer seasonal and specialty beers.

Michigan Beer Guide Brewers Cup. An annual competition sponsored by the *Michigan Beer Guide*. It draws more Michigan participants than the Great American Beer Festival or the World Beer Festival, because its in-state location presents fewer logistical challenges and because some brewers believe that recognition by one's peers is of primary importance.

Michigan Brewers Guild. A trade association formed with the aim of promoting Michigan beer and strengthening the state's brewing industry. Most of the state's brewers belong to it. The guild sponsors the annual Summer Beer Festival and has recently added a Winter Beer Festival featuring big and cask-conditioned beers.

Microbrewery. In Michigan, a brewery that produces thirty thousand barrels or less beer per year. A microbrewery may sell its beer directly to customers at the brewery and, via distributors, to retail outlets.

Neo-Prohibition. What some call the recent trend toward placing greater legal restrictions on alcohol. Although there is no organized movement to make alcohol illegal, critics allege that activist groups are pushing legislation that would discourage social drinking. Some warn that the "Noble Experiment" of Prohibition didn't happen overnight and could happen again.

Oktoberfest. The world's largest beer event, held annually in Munich. It began as a royal wedding celebration in 1810 and gradually became a festival featuring German food, music, and of course, beer. Blob's Park in Jesup, Maryland, takes credit for staging America's first Oktoberfest. That was in 1947. Today hundreds of American communities, not to mention drinking establishments, hold their own versions of Oktoberfest. Interestingly, the Oktoberfest-style beer produced by American craft brewers is no longer served at Munich's Oktoberfest. Instead, you'll find a paler lager called Helles, German for "light-colored."

Pasteurization. A process named for its inventor, Louis Pasteur, the French microbiologist. Pasteurization involves exposing something to high temperatures for a few seconds to kill the microorganisms inside it. In the case of beer, pasteurization keeps it fresh longer. However, critics claim that it robs the beer of its flavor because it has essentially been "cooked."

Pilsner. The world's most popular style of beer, accounting for about 80 percent of beer sold worldwide. "Pilsner" is a German word meaning "from Pilsen," a town in the present-day Czech Republic now known as Plzen. The region surrounding Plzen abounds in aromatic Saaz hops, fields of two-row barley, and very soft water, which proved a winning combination.

Prohibition. The period from 1920 to 1933, when it was illegal to manufacture, sell, or transport alcoholic beverages in the United States. The Eighteenth Amendment banned the sale of "intoxicating liquors"—those containing more than 3.2 percent ABW—and later, Congress passed the Volstead Act, which banned the sale of all alcoholic beverages. Prohibition devastated American brewing and, according to critics, encouraged organized crime and made the nation's drinking problem worse. In April 1933, Congress repealed the Volstead Act, thus relegalizing "3.2 beer." Later that year, the Twenty-first Amendment repealed Prohibition and gave states the power to regulate alcohol.

Regional brewery. A general term referring to a brewery that produces more than a microbrewery but less than a national-brand brewing company. Some regionals, like the Yuengling Brewery of Pottsville, Pennsylvania, are mainstream breweries that managed to survive Prohibition and postwar consolidation. Others, like the Boston Beer Company, started out as microbrewers and continued to grow. Still others, like the Matt Brewing Company of Utica, New York, are traditional breweries that reinvented themselves by switching to craft beer.

Reinheitsgebot. The German beer purity law, which has its roots in a 1516 Bavarian law limiting beer ingredients to barley malt, hops, and water. (It was later amended to allow wheat beer but dictated that those beers be made with at least 50 percent malted wheat and brewed with ale yeast.) The law, which is considered one of Europe's earliest consumer-protection measures, grew into a complicated set of regulations that governed German brewing. Many still consider the Reinheitsgebot the gold standard of brewing, and most German breweries—and many American craft breweries—adhere to it.

Sampler. An assortment of small (3- to 6-ounce) glasses of beer containing different beers produced by a brewery. Samplers allow the customer to get acquainted with the beer selection without the risk of overconsuming. Most Michigan breweries sell samplers. Those that don't will offer a taste if asked.

Seasonal beers. Seasonals are rotating beer styles that are traditional for the time of year—for example, barleywine in the winter, bock beer in the spring, wheat beer in the summer, and Oktoberfest beer in the fall.

Secondary fermentation. The process by which the brewer allows beer to continue fermenting, in either a cask or a bottle, after it leaves the brewery. Beer made in this manner is still a living thing when it reaches the consumer.

Specialty beers. Specialty beers are those that the brewer makes irregularly or only once. They're more likely to be extreme, experimental, or hard-to-find styles.

Steam beer. A distinctly American style of beer revived by Fritz Maytag's Anchor Brewing Company and now imitated by a number of craft breweries. The beer is said to have gotten its name because kegs of it give off a fine mist when tapped. That's because it is highly carbonated, the result of its being brewed with lager yeast but aged at temperatures more like those used for ales. The style is also referred to as California common beer—a term you'll sometimes find on beer menus.

Style guidelines. A set of criteria—including original and final gravity, hop bitterness, and color—that define a category of beer. These are important factors in judging beer in competitions. Style guidelines are the subject of debate within the brewing community. Some insist that beers should be brewed true to style; others reject guidelines as artificial and believe that the most important criterion for beer is that it taste good.

Temperance movement. A grass-roots movement aimed at curbing drunkenness. At first its primary focus was on hard liquor, but it later shifted toward a total ban on alcohol. Before the Civil War, a number of states, including Michigan, had short-lived prohibition laws; enforcement was spotty and the laws were unpopular. But a new prohibitionist movement arose in the late nineteenth century and ultimately succeeded in banning alcohol.

Three-tier system. When Prohibition ended, most states passed laws requiring that those who produced alcohol, those who distributed it, and those who sold it at retail be separate entities. The objects of the three-tier system were to curb abusive practices on the part of manufacturers and to keep underworld figures out of the newly legalized liquor trade. Critics argue that the three-tier system creates an unfair barrier to craft breweries that want to grow. Defenders argue that distributors benefit brewers by relieving them of the chore of transporting and storing beer.

Tied house. A bar owned by a brewery. Before Prohibition, tied houses were common in America. In fact, breweries owned or controlled a majority of the nation's taverns, often under anticompetitive arrangements. Because brewpubs are tied houses by law, states had to amend their laws to allow them to function.

Top fermentation. The method of fermentation associated with ale, in which the by-products of fermentation rise to the top of the vessel. Top fermentation takes place at warmer temperatures and generally results in a fruitier beer. Top-fermented beers require less time to mature than bottom-fermented beers.

Unfiltered beer. Beer that is bottled without strict filtration. The residue that isn't filtered out, such as inactive yeast cells, gives the beer a hazy appearance when poured into a glass. Haziness is a characteristic of some beer styles, such as Belgian witbier.

Vertical tasting. An event that has grown in popularity, in which customers try different vintages of the same beer.

Vintage beer. Though beer is usually best when fresh, some beers take on a more interesting character as they age. Some breweries or beer bars put away part of each year's production, much like wine; the stored beers are often known as "library beers." Commercial examples of vintage beer include Fuller's Vintage Ale and Samuel Adams Triple Bock.

Winter warmer. A general term that describes beer brewed specially for the Christmas season or wintertime in general. Winter warmers, which encompass a number of beer styles, are stronger than year-round beers, usually dark-colored, and often include spices such as nutmeg, cinnamon, and licorice. In brewing winter warmers, brewers aim to produce something different: a beer that changes from year to year and doesn't neatly fit style guidelines.

World Beer Cup (WBC). A prestigious competition held every two years and open to brewers around the world. It has been called brewing's equivalent of the Olympic Games. The 2004 event attracted 393 brewers from forty countries, who competed for medals in eighty-one categories.

Wort. The sugary liquid that results from steeping grain in hot water. It's sometimes referred to as "unfermented beer" because yeast has not yet been added to it.

Yeast. A one-cell organism used to ferment wort into beer. Although humans have brewed beer for thousands of years, they didn't understand the role that yeast played in the brewing process until the nineteenth century, when scientists isolated the yeasts involved. Later, scientists developed specific strains that would impart distinctive flavors associated with certain styles of beer. For example, Peter Austin and Partners of Dorset, England, isolated a strain called Ringwood yeast, which results in beers with a somewhat nutty flavor. A number of Michigan breweries use Peter Austin systems and have permission to use the Ringwood strain.

INDEX

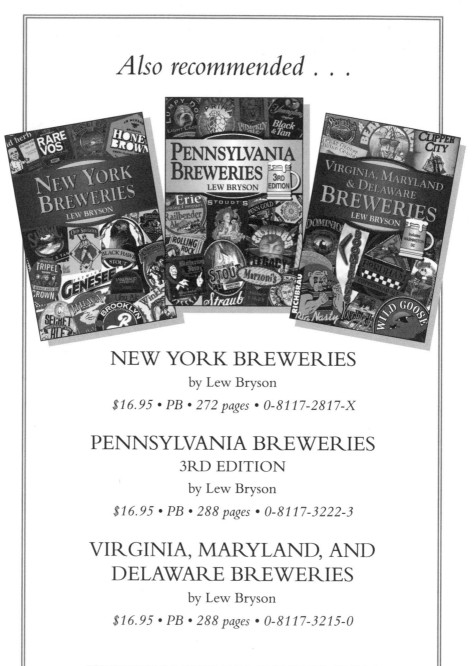